Architect-Designed Low-Rise
CONDOMINIUMS in Japan

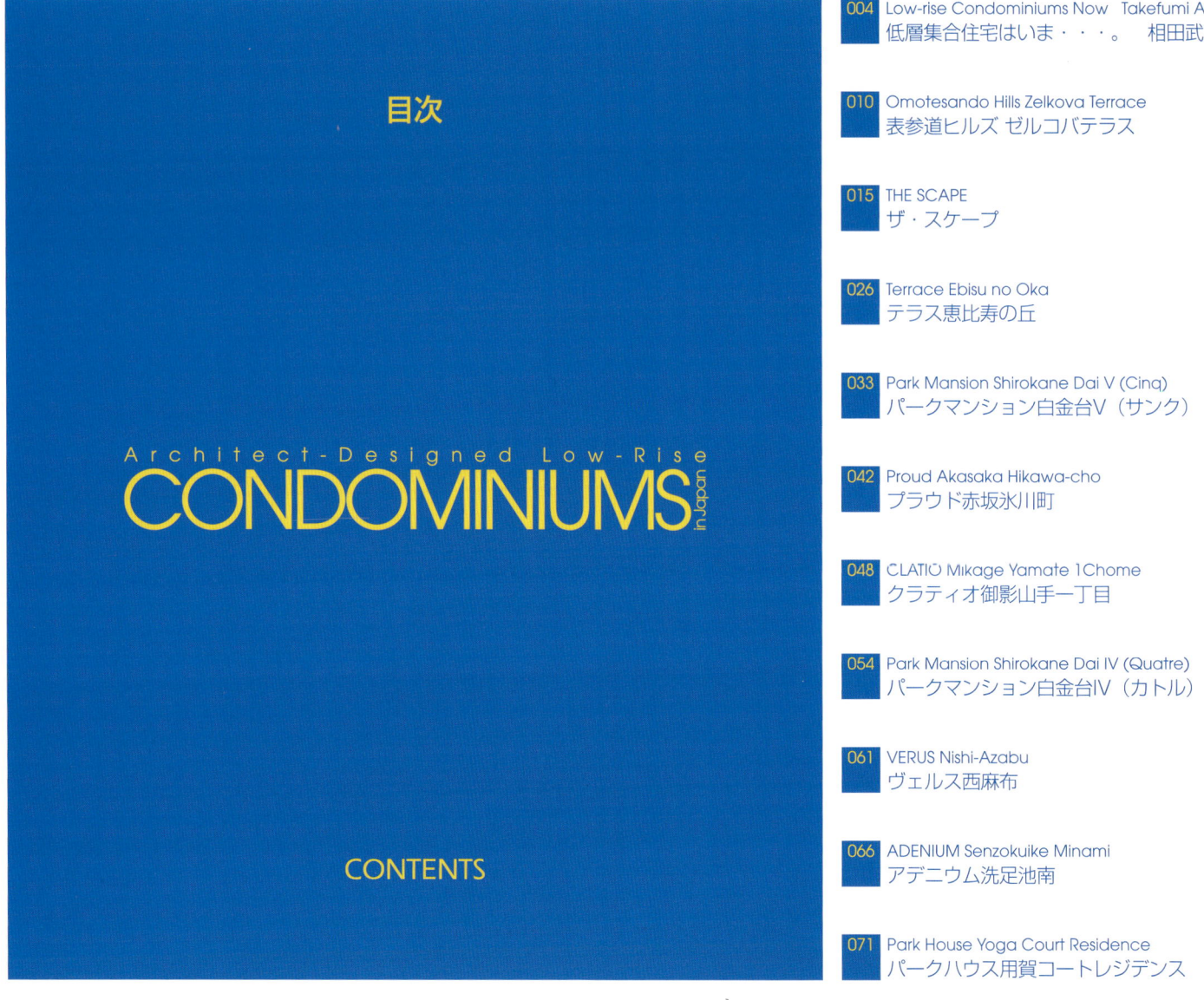

目次

Architect-Designed Low-Rise
CONDOMINIUMS in Japan

CONTENTS

004 Low-rise Condominiums Now　Takefumi Aida
低層集合住宅はいま・・・。　相田武文

010 Omotesando Hills Zelkova Terrace
表参道ヒルズ ゼルコバテラス

015 THE SCAPE
ザ・スケープ

026 Terrace Ebisu no Oka
テラス恵比寿の丘

033 Park Mansion Shirokane Dai V (Cinq)
パークマンション白金台Ⅴ（サンク）

042 Proud Akasaka Hikawa-cho
プラウド赤坂氷川町

048 CLATIO Mikage Yamate 1Chome
クラティオ御影山手一丁目

054 Park Mansion Shirokane Dai IV (Quatre)
パークマンション白金台Ⅳ（カトル）

061 VERUS Nishi-Azabu
ヴェルス西麻布

066 ADENIUM Senzokuike Minami
アデニウム洗足池南

071 Park House Yoga Court Residence
パークハウス用賀コートレジデンス

076	Promenade Ogikubo No.2,3,5	123	Scaletta	166	FLEG roppongi secondo
	プロムナード荻窪 2,3,5号棟		スカレッタ		FLEG六本木secondo
080	Chaleur Higashi Toyonaka B zone	128	SORGENTE	172	Wakohre Suma Passo
	シャレール東豊中B工区		ソルジェンテ向丘		ワコーレ須磨パッソ
082	Park House Daizawa Place	131	SILENZIO	175	Phoenix Building
	パークハウス代沢プレイス		シレンツィオ		フェニックス・ビルディング
084	ADENIUM Kichijoji	134	FLEG Hiroo 2nd Ave.	178	K court
	アデニウム吉祥寺		FLEG広尾2nd Ave.		Kコート
092	Izumigaoka Garden Hills JIOUZEN	140	I. flat	182	Proud Minami-Aoyama
	泉ヶ丘ガーデンヒルズJIOUZEN		I. flat		プラウド南青山
096	VERTIQUE Sumiyoshigawa	143	Minami-Gyotoku Quartetto	187	Maison de parc
	ヴェルティーク住吉川		南行徳の4奏住宅		パークメゾン
100	Proud Minami-Ogikubo	146	Sanctus Court Ashiya	190	BARONG
	プラウド南荻窪		サンクタスコート芦屋		バロン
106	Renai Seazon's Garden Nishinomiya Najio	154	PH-2	193	Syukugawa FLAT
	ルネ シーズンズ ガーデン 西宮名塩		PH-2		夙川FLAT
110	Navire Court Hourakucho	157	curva	196	Forest Plaza Omotesando
	ナビールコート豊楽町		curva		フォレストプラザ表参道
113	Asuta Shin-nagata Towers Court ALIVIO	160	Park Hills Oyake I	200	Biographies
	アスタ新長田タワーズコート アリビオ		パークヒルズ大宅 I		略歴
116	Brillia Daikanyama Prestige	163	Park Hills Oyake II	206	Afterword Fumio Shimizu
	Brillia代官山プレステージ		パークヒルズ大宅 II		あとがき 清水文夫

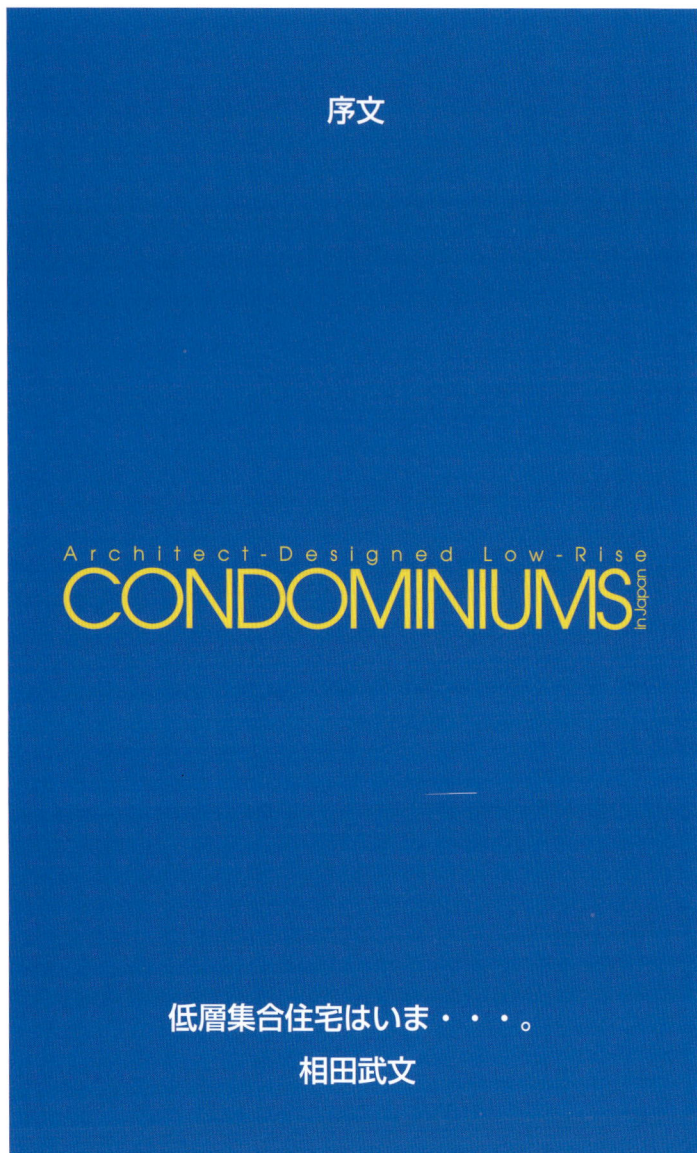

この本におさめられている低層集合住宅の特徴やそこから考えられることを述べれば以下のようになるだろう。

由緒ある場所を選定する
昔から住宅地として名高い場所は、デベロッツパーが開発する場合に有利なことは当然である。東京でいえば麻布など、関西では芦屋など住宅地として認知度が高いところは購買力が強い。この本の中でも多くの事例が見られ、グレードの高い良質な低層集合住宅ができる可能性が高い。

集合住宅のファサードがオフィスと見分けがつかない
最近の集合住宅の特徴のひとつに、オフィスのファサードと見分けがつかないものがある。つまり、集合住宅といえばバルコニーが突き出ており個々の住居単位が明確であった。ところが近年、都市がアノニマスな風情を漂わせる傾向が強まるにつれて、集合住宅にもその影響が出てきたように思える。内部機能の多様化、採光条件、洗濯物などのバルコニーからのあふれ出しなど種々考えられるが、いずれにせよ外観は無表情なつくり方をしながら、個々のインテリアに特徴をもたせるといった傾向が見られる。

ユニットの組み合わせが多様化してきた
低層集合住宅の特徴のひとつに接地性があげられるが、単なるユニットの積み重ねでない様々な工夫がなされてきた。一見すると３層の長屋に見えるものが、じつは３層で1住戸であったり、メゾネット形式とフラット形式の組み合わせだったり、多様なユニットの組み合わせが生まれてきた。多様化してきた住まい手のニーズにこたえるためにも、様々な工夫が今後なされるに違いない。

時代とともに変化する皮膚感覚

時代の変化とともに人間の皮膚感覚ともいえる感性も変わってきた。素材でいえば、打ち放しコンクリートがそのよい例だろう。ヨーロッパにおいて生まれた近代建築、その1920年代から今日に至るまで、打ち放しコンクリートを素材にした住宅や集合住宅はそれなりにつくられてきた。当初は、ル・コルビジェの作品に代表されるように、型枠材の木の肌が表出しているような粗野な感覚のものであった。

近年の打ち放しコンクリートはきめ細やかで、透明感さえ漂わせているようだ。当初は抵抗のあった一般の人たちも、今ではスタンダードな素材としてみるようになって来た。このことは素材にかぎらず色彩感覚などにもいえることで、時代の味ともいえるものが集合住宅には欠かせないものなのだろう。

やはり建築家が開拓してきた

近代建築が始まって今日に至るまで、人間が集合して住むための方策が、いろいろと試みられてきたことはいうまでもない。おそらく1970年代までは、建築家がその先導的な役割を果たしてきたように思える。しかしながら、わが国における経済の発展による個人の志向性の高まりは、かえって資本の論理に吸収され、むしろ全体的には没個性的な集合住宅が生まれてきたように思える。多くのデベロッパーにおいては、データにもとづいた管理体制、平面計画、資金回収などの日常業務が先行し、そこには建築家が入り込む余地がないように思える。建築家の側にも考えなくてはならない問題はあると思えるが、建築家にもう少し創造的な場を提供できる環境づくりも必要であろう。

いま一度ヴァイセンホーフ・ジードルンクを

ドイツのシュトゥットガルトにあるヴァイセンホーフ・ジードルンク（1927年竣工）をいま一度再考してみる必要がありそうだ。いうまでもなく、この低層集合住宅は、ミース・ファン・デル・ローエがオーガナイズし、ヨーロッパの著名な建築家10数人に設計を依頼したものである。いうならば、集合住宅の集合体ともいうべきものである。ここでは、種々の試みがなされた。今日では、それらの試みは技術的には止揚されているようだが、時代の気力ともいうべきものを背景にした先見性には学ぶべきものがある。持続可能な社会をどのように構築していくかといった今日的な問題に対して、低層集合住宅はどのようにこたえたらよいのだろうか。目先のニーズだけにとらわれることなく、社会全体の財産として定着するものを目指すべきであろう。この30年間、わずかな例を除いて集合住宅は進歩しなかったといってもよいだろう。いまこそ専門家が結集し、その中で建築家が先導的役割を果たすことができないのだろうか。ヴァイセンホーフ・ジードルンクができてから、はや80年も経ってしまった。今でもこの計画の先見性は生き続けているように思える。この本におさめられている低層集合住宅は、現代日本の様々な様相を示しており、時代の検証としての価値はあると思える。

相田武文　建築家／芝浦工業大学名誉教授

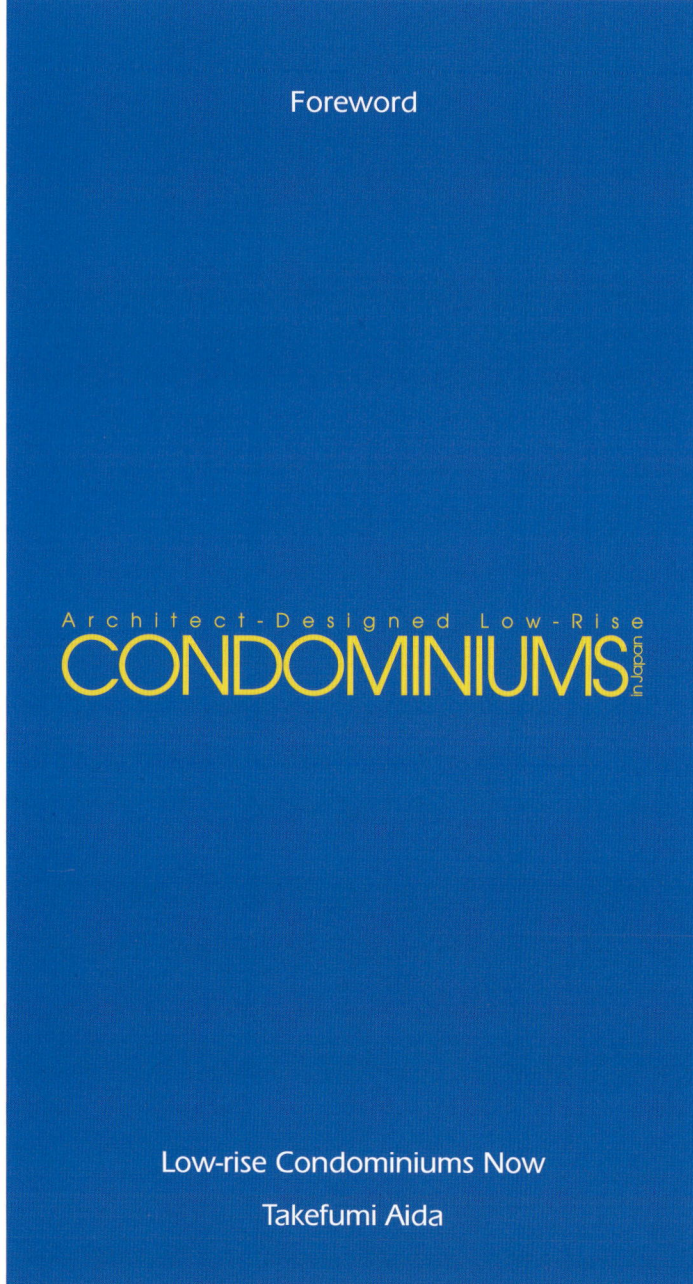

Foreword

Architect-Designed Low-Rise
CONDOMINIUMS in Japan

Low-rise Condominiums Now
Takefumi Aida

The characteristics of the low-rise condominiums described in this book and what we can infer from them may be summed up as follows:

Select a time-honored place
For developers, It is naturally advantageous to develop old residential areas because the demand for housing is strong in such highly recognized places as Azabu in Tokyo and Ashiya in Kansai. As many examples shown in this book, it is highly likely that this type of sites should be where high-grade low-rise condominiums with excellent quality will be built.

Indistinguishable facades of condominiums
One of the characteristics of recently developed condominiums is the fact that their facades are indistinguishable from those of offices. Once condominiums had projected balconies, and individual dwelling units were easy to identify. As cities have increases its anonymous atmosphere, however, it seems that this tendency has affected condominiums as well. Of course, there are diversified internal functions, different lighting conditions, disappearance of laundries from balconies and other variations, but, in any case, the exteriors are often designed anonymous while the interiors are individually characterized.

Diversified unit combinations
One of the characteristics of low-rise condominiums is closeness to ground, but various ideas have been applied to those buildings in order to avoid them from becoming simple accumulation of units. For example, a three-story tenement house at a first glance turns out to be a single residence or a combination of maisonnette- and flat-type units. To meet residents' needs that become more and more diversified, further elaboration will surely be provided for already diverse combinations of units in the future.

"Cutaneous sensation" that changes with the era
With change of the times, human sensitivities which may be compared to "cutaneous sensation" have also changed. A good example in terms of materials is exposed concrete. Throughout the era of modern architecture born in Europe since the 1920's, houses and condominiums using exposed concrete have more or less been built. At first, as represented by the works of Le Corbusier, wooden surfaces of the formworks were exposed, giving a sense of roughness.

On the other hand, recent exposed concrete works have become more sophisticated, even having an atmosphere of transparency. The general public who initially felt reluctant to the employment exposed concrete has come to regard it as a standard material now. The same goes with the sense of color, and it seems that the preference of the age is naturally be reflected upon condominiums.

Developed by architects anyway
It is needless to say that, from the beginning of the modern architecture till today, many measures for human beings to live together have been attempted and tested. Probably until the 1970's, architects had played the leading role in this aspect. In Japan, however, the increasing personal preferences based on the economic development seem to be absorbed in the harsh logic of capital, and in general, condominiums devoid of character have been created.

Many developers put priority to data-based management systems, layout plans, capital recovery, and other daily operations, and there seems to be little room for architects to intervene. Though there are surely issues on the side of architects, it is necessary to establish environments to provide them with opportunities to take advantage of their creativity.

Weissenhofsiedlung again
We must probably revisit Weissenhofsiedlung (completed in 1927) in Stuttgart, Germany. Needless to say, the low-rise condominiums were organized by Ludwig Mies van der Rohe who requested more than ten celebrated architects in Europe to contribute their designs. It is, as it were, a collection of condominiums. Many experiments were performed there. Today, these experiments are technologically sublated, but there are things to learn from their prescience like the spirit of the age.

To how to build a sustainable society and other challenges of today, how should low-rise condominiums respond? Instead of being prepossessed by needs at hand, we should try to build condominiums that can be inherited as social assets in the future. In the last three decades, condominiums have rarely made progress with only a few exceptions. It is high time that specialists combined their forces and that architects blazed a trail.

80 years have already passed since the completion of Weissenhofsiedlung, but its prescience seems to be still alive and relevant.

The low-rise condominiums covered in this book show many different aspects of modern Japan and are worthwhile for investigation to identify the era we are living in.

Takefumi Aida
Architect / professor emeritus, Shibaura Institute of Technology

企画
Executive Editor

大田　悟
Satoru Ohta

エディトリアル・ディレクター
Editorial Director

清水　文夫
Fumio Shimizu

装丁・本文デザイン
Cover & Book Design

丹治　竜一
Ryuichi Tanji

協力
Cooperation

内田　浩史
Hiroshi Uchida

鈴木　隆了
Ryuko Suzuki

Architect-Designed Low-Rise
CONDOMINIUMS in Japan

Omotesando Hills Zelkova Terrace
表参道ヒルズ ゼルコバテラス
Tadao Ando Architect & Associates / Mori Building joint design entity

日本を代表する国際的なファッション集積地として知られる街、＜表参道＞。その表参道に約250メートルの間口を持つ当施設は、地上6階、地下6階で構成された複合施設です。地下3階から地上3階の商業施設、38戸の住宅の他に、商業駐車場（約200台収容）も完備。商業施設の内部は、中央の吹き抜けとそれを囲むスロープにより、路面店感覚の店舗が6層にわたってつながる構造。地階まで自然光の入るアトリウムが、穏やかで新しい発見に溢れた空間を演出します。住宅は、東棟（青山側）と西棟（原宿側）の2棟で構成され、いずれも上部2層（一部3層）に配置。全戸の窓から見えるケヤキ並木が、四季の移り変わりを知らせます。また、24時間安全を守る管理体制や、商業施設との動線を完全に分離するなど、安全、安心、快適に暮らすことのできる空間となるよう配慮。屋上は可能な限り緑化し、計画地北側にひろがる住宅地の眺めは、緑豊かな潤いのある景観となります。

Omotesando is renowned as one of Japan's leading centers of fashion. Omotesando Hills, with approximately 250 meters of frontage on Omotesando, will from a multipurpose complex consisting of six floors above ground and six below: commercial facilities will be on the third-floor underground levels up to the third floor above ground; 38 apartment units on the upper levels; for parking, the bottom three floors will hold approx 200 vehicles for commercial facilities. A central atrium and enclosed slope will connect stores and restaurants. The atrium will allow natural light into the underground levels. The residential section of the complex will include an east wing (on the Aoyama side) and a west wing (on the Harajuku side), both in the uppermost levels of the building, with the zelkova trees making the changing seasons. Building management will ensure safety, security, and comfort. The apartments will be separated from visitor routes to the retail facilities. The rooftop will be planted with lush greenery, while those in the residential section will enjoy verdant vistas stretching north of the site.

| 1 | 2 | 3 |
| | 4 |

1
ケヤキ通り越しに東棟（青山側）外観を臨む
The facade of the eastern building (on the Aoyama side) beyond the street lined with zelkova.

2
商業施設のガラスのカーテンウォール
Glass curtain walls of the commercial building

3
鳥瞰図
Bird's-eye view

4
西棟（原宿側）のエントランスを臨む。表参道沿いに250mの商業施設の間口が連なる
Entrance of the western building (on the Harajuku side). The frontage of the commercial building expands for 250 meters along the Omotesando street.

間仕切りを少なくし、フリースペースを確保した1ROOM、1LDKのプラン。シンプルでありながら住宅としての機能性を兼ねた空間。緑豊かな窓からの眺めは都心での生活にやすらぎと潤いを与えます。

Open-plan 1ROOM, 1LDK layout with minimal partitioning into rooms. Simple yet practical living spaces. Views of verdant surroundings add tranquility and charm to the convenience of urban living.

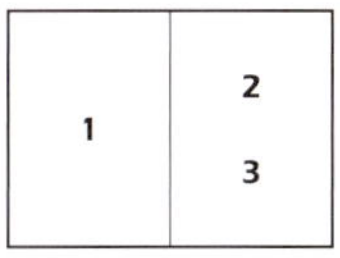

	2
1	---
	3

1
リビングダイニングルーム：窓からは四季の移り変わりを知らせるケヤキ並木が臨める
Living-dining: Zelkova trees in the window tell the changes of the seasons.

2
中間層免震構造による斜材がデザインのアクセントになっている住戸もある
In some of the units, the diagonal column going through the room as part of the mid-story seismic isolation structure serves as an accent on the design.

3
夜景：奥にベッドルームを配している
Night view: The bedroom is at the back.

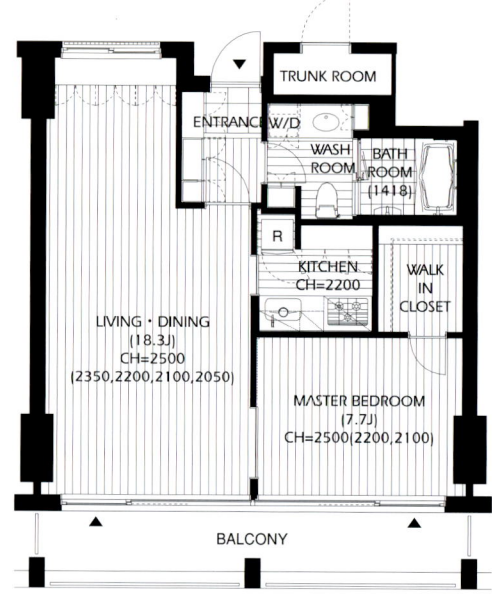

1
リビングダイニングルームからベッドルームを臨む。一面の窓から自然光をふんだんに取り込める
Bedroom seen from the living-dining room. Abundant natural light coming through a single window.

2
ベッドルームからリビングダイニングルームを臨む
Living-dining room seen from the bedroom.

Data

Title
Omotesando Hills Zelkova Terrace

Developer
Mori Building Co., Ltd.

Architect
Tadao Ando Architect & Associates
Mori Building joint design entity

Location
Shibuya-ku, Tokyo

Site area
6,051.36m²

Building area
5,030.76m²

Total floor area
34,061.72m²

Area
62.26m² (West side, Room-408)

Structure
SRC, RC+S in part

Completion
January, 2006

Materials
Exterior Wall :
  architectural concrete
  flouride resin painting
Public Floor :
  scrubbed finishing ballast
Interior Floor :
  stone, flooring

Photo
Koji Okumura

THE SCAPE
ザ・スケープ

Kengo Kuma (Kengo Kuma & Associates) / Santa Ohno (Kengo Kuma & Associates)
BALS Corporation / Katsumi Asaba (Asaba Design Co., Ltd.)

集合住宅の設計の順序を逆転してみた。通常、集合住宅は間取り（平面図）の設計からはじめる。それが決まった段階で、内装（壁、床、天井などの仕上げ）が決定され、その後に照明デザインが行われ、最後の最後に家具、小物などが決定されるという順序である。もっと正確にいえば、家具、小物は建築設計者のデザインの領分ではなく、建築物がほとんど完成した頃に、インテリアコーディネーターと呼ばれるような「プロ」がでてきて、すでに存在する建築のデザインと調子をあわせながら、適当にこなすというやり方が普通のやり方なのである。以前からこの順序に対して強い違和感があった。家具、小物こそ、人間の身体にもっとも近く、もっとも身近なアイテムであり、その部分こそがその空間を、そこでのアクティビティーを決定的に規定してしまうからである。その部分があとまわしにされ、しかも、マンションの「専門家」と称する人に適当に処理されてしまうのが、たまらないと感じていた。今回のTHE SCAPEではこの順序を逆転してみた。まず、家具、小物から決定するのである。クライアント（バルス）は家具、小物をビジネスとしていて、それらの小さい物達から空間全体を逆向きに構想することになれている。彼らと僕らが知恵を出しあい、まず、このスペースにはこの家具、この小物と決定し、そこから内装、間取りというように通常とは逆の方向で、デザインが進行していくのである。その際、重要なのは、その家具と置かれている「場所」である。常陸宮邸の大きな緑に面しては、このソファがいいな！このカーペットがいいな！といった感じで、場所がまず家具、小物へと投影をされるのである。隣りのマンションとの間には小窓しかあけられそうもないから、その小窓の前に置かれるダイニングテーブルはコレ！みたいな感じである。これを僕らは「官能性のデザイン」と呼んでみた。官能は間取りから刺激されたりはしない。物に直に反応するのである。たとえばソファの布地のザックっとした質感に太股が触れた時、官能のセンサーは、ピクッと起動するのである。このチャンネルこそ、近代建築がもっともネグレクトしてきた部分である。そのチャンネルを再起動させるような建築にしたかった。外部にはったガラスタイルもステンレスのルーバーもふくめて、すべてこのチャンネルを再起動させる仕掛けである。（隈研吾）

I've reversed the order of condominium design procedure. Normally, when we design a condominium, we start with a room plan (floor plan). When it is finalized, its interior design (wall, floor, ceiling and other finishes) is decided, followed by the lighting design. At the very last stage comes furniture, small articles, etc. To be more exact, furniture and small articles are not in the sphere of design by architects; when the building is almost completed, interior coordinators or other "professionals" appear and do their jobs at ease while just keeping harmony with the architectural design that already exist. I have felt a strong sense of discomfort about this order. Furniture and small articles are the closest to and the most familiar with human bodies, and they specify and determine the space and activities in it. I felt it unbearable that these elements receive a lower priority, and besides, are carelessly handled by those who name themselves to be "professionals" of condominiums. In planning the Scape, I have taken a reversed order, instead. First, I selected the furniture and small articles. The main line of business of the client (BALS) is sales of furniture and small articles, so the client is accustomed to reversely conceptualize a total space starting with these small items. We exchanged ideas with the client, assigned furniture and small articles for each space, and then decided the interior and floor plans. The designing process was progressed in a direction contrary to that of ordinary planning. When we take this approach, pieces of furniture and their "positions" are important. For example, when we looked at the large forest of the Hitachinomiya Palace, we exchanged opinions like "this sofa should be good!" or "that carpet perfectly fits"; in this way, the positions actually determined furniture and small articles to be selected. Only small windows could be provided on the wall facing the adjacent condominium, so it came to us, "this type of dining table must be set in front of the small window." We called this approach as "design of sensuality". No floor plan stimulates sensuality. Sensuality directly responds to things. For example, when your thigh touches a rough surface of the sofa, your sensuality sensor is immediately activated. This channel is the most neglected aspect in the modern architecture. I wanted to create a piece of architecture that would restart the channel. Everything including glass tiles attached to the exterior and stainless louvers is a mechanism to reactivate this channel. (Kengo Kuma)

Data

Title
 THE SCAPE

Design Supervision
 Kengo Kuma (Kengo Kuma & Associates)

Architect
 Santa Ohno (Kengo Kuma & Associates)

Produce
 BALS Corporation

Art Direction
 Katsumi Asaba (Asaba Design Co., Ltd.)

Location
 Shibuya-ku, Tokyo

Site area
 54.68m²

Building area
 331.79m²

Total floor area
 882.04m²

Structure
 RC+S

Completion
 March, 2005

Materials
 Exterior Wall :
  glass mosaic tile (BISAZZA), glass
  aluminum sash, stainless sash
 Public Floor :
  granite(oyster white), corrugate board

1	
2	4
3	

1
エントランスアプローチ：ガラスで仕切られた風除室を臨む

Entrance approach: Glass partitioned vestibule at the front

2
1階エントランスホールのラウンジ。大理石の床とカーテンが、冷たさと柔らかさを一体化させ、MODENATUREの家具と、パリのアートフラワーHERVE GAMBSで空間を引き締めている

Lounge in the 1st floor entrance hall. The marble floor and curtains integrate coolness and softness into one, and the furniture from Modenature and Parisian art flowers from Herve Gambs, giving a sense of firmness to the space.

3
エントランスホールからエレベーターホールを臨む

Elevator hall seen from the entrance hall

4
リビングルーム：天井の大きな穴は間接照明となっている

Living room: A large hole on the ceiling is for indirect illumination.

Italian Modern

イタリアンモダン

Kengo Kuma (Kengo Kuma & Associates)
Dam International Co.,Ltd. / BALS Corporation

THE SCAPE "ITALIAN MODERN" タイプはモダンデザインもさることながら、素材の良さを改めて感じ取れるような空間作りを心掛けている。それは例えるなら、LOLO PIANAやBARBA、BORRELLI、FRAY などのシャツと同じような上質さだ。現在、世界的に名の知れたデザイナーであるPIERO LISSONI、PATRICIA URQUIOLA、CARLO COLOMBOらのデザインでイタリアンソファメーカーの最高峰と謳われるLIVING DIVANI、MOROSOが製作したソファをメインにレイアウトしている。

In designing the "Italian Modern" type of the Scape, we focused on creating a space where one can feel the quality of materials afresh, not to mention the modern design itself. The high quality may be compared to shirts by Lolo Piana, Barba, Borrelli or Fray. The main features of the layout are sofas from Living Divani and Moroso famous for designs by internationally renowned designers including Piero Lissoni, Patricia Urquiola, and Carlo Colombo.

1	4	5
2		
3	6	

1
ダイニングから常陸宮邸の森を眺める
Woods of the Hitachinomiya Palace seen from the dining room

2
リビングから屋上緑化に囲まれたルーフテラスを臨む。ステンレスの手摺りを採用し、外との境界を曖昧にし、森の中で暮らしているような雰囲気を創り出している
Roof terrace surrounded by rooftop gardening. Stainless railings are employed for making the borders with the outside unclear, giving an atmosphere as if one were living in a forest.

3
ルーフテラス
Roof terrace

4
シックな雰囲気なサニタリールーム
Sanitary room with a chic atmosphere

5
Room 003：パウダールーム
Room 003: Powder room

6
明るく広々としたベッドルーム
Bright, extensive bedroom

Data

Title
  Italian Modern

Design Supervision
  Kengo Kuma (Kengo Kuma & Associates)

Interior Designer
  Dam International Co.,Ltd.

Coordinate
  BALS Corporation

Area
  156.88m² (Room011)

Materials
  Interior Wall :
    AEP, glass mosaic tile
  Interior Floor :
    600x600 ceramic tile, carpet, flooring
    glass mosaic tile

French Modern
フレンチモダン

Kengo Kuma (Kengo Kuma & Associates)
Dam International Co.,Ltd. / BALS Corporation

THE SCAPE "FRENCH MODERN" タイプはモダンを基調としながらも、決して冷たすぎない、かつ、フレンチエスプリを感じ取れる空間に仕上がっている。主な備品にはMODENATUREを多く採用。フランス人デザイナー、HENRY BECQが自らオーナーをつとめるMODENATUREの家具・照明は、木・革・クロームなどそれぞれの素材の質感を生かした、シンプルで美しいラインのデザインが特徴だ。また、空間全体の統一感にも配慮している。キッチンの面材は家具に合わせ、床材にはライムストーンを使用、塗り壁は色調を抑えるなど、一体化となることで、空間に安らぎと、そしてほどよい緊張感を生み出している。

The basic tone of the "French Modern" type room is modern yet not too cool, and the unit is finished with a sense of French spirit. Its furniture is mainly by Modenature, owned by the French designer, Henry Becq. The furnishings and illuminations by Modenature feature simple and beautiful lines in design, taking advantage of the texture of individual materials such as wood, leather and chrome. Consideration is also given to the integrity of the space in general. The facing material of the kitchen is same as that of the furniture, and limestone is selected for the floor. The plastered walls have a gentle tone. The integrity creates a sense of relaxation and provides adequate tension in the space.

	2
1	3
	4

1
リビング・ダイニングルーム
Living-dining room

2
リビングからダイニングを臨む。ライムストーンの床や色調を抑えた壁など、一体的な構成で空間に安らぎを醸しだしている
Dining area seen from the living space. This integrated configuration including limestone floors and gently toned walls gives a sense of comfort in the space.

3
Room 006：家具に合わせた面材を採用したキッチンなど、空間全体の統一感に配慮している
Room 006: Consideration is given to the consistency of the total space including the kitchen using facing materials that fit the furniture

4
什器で仕切られたベッドルーム
Bedroom partitioned by furniture

1	2	3

1
リビング・ダイニングと同じ構成で統一感をだしたパウダールーム
Powder room having a same configuration as that of the living-dining room

2
温かみを感じるバスルーム
Bathroom with a sense of warmth

3
自然素材を十分に感じられるリビング・ダイニング
Living-dining rooms to enjoy natural materials

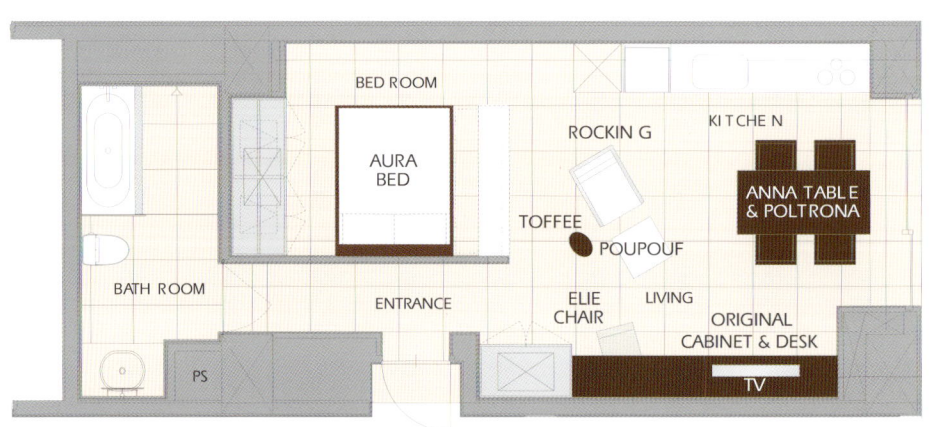

Data

Title
　French Modern
Design Supervision
　Kengo Kuma (Kengo Kuma & Associates)
Interior Designer
　Dam International Co.,Ltd.
Coordinate
　BALS Corporation
Area
　53.1m² (Room001)
Materials
　Interior Wall :
　　AEP, 600x600 limestone
　Interior Floor :
　　600x600 limestone

022

Morocco Primitive
モロッコプリミティブ

Kengo Kuma (Kengo Kuma & Associates)
Dam International Co.,Ltd. / BALS Corporation

THE SCAPE "MOROCCO PRIMITIVE" タイプは地中海沿岸で多感な文化を生み出してきたモロッコ文化を、現代風なインテリアに仕上げた空間。インテリアエレメントとしては、天然素材を多く取り入れ、たとえば家具・床材にはオーク材、チーク材の無垢材を使用したもので、素材感を十分に感じられ、贅沢に構成されている。部屋の印象を大きく変えるソファには、素朴ながらも存在感のあるGERVASONI、ソファマーケットにおいて最高峰と謳われるLIVING DIVANI、MOROSOをコーディネートしている。各部屋で、それぞれ違った魅力を堪能できる。

The "Morocco Primitive" type room of the Scape is a space where the sensitive Moroccan culture grown along the Mediterranean coast is imported and finished as a modern interior design. Many natural materials are used as interior elements. For example, furniture and floor are made of solid natural oak and teak wood, appealing their presence in this luxurious configuration. Sofas that give a strong impact on the impression of the individual rooms are from Gervasoni that is simple yet with a presence, Living Divani regarded as number one in the sofa market, and Morso. One can enjoy different types of attraction in each room.

1	4	5
2	6	
3		

1
リビング・ダイニング：奥にガラスで仕切られたバスルームを臨む
Living-dining: Glass-partitioned bathroom at the back

2
落ち着いた雰囲気のベッドルーム。リズミカルにニッチを配している
Bedroom with a comfortable atmosphere. Sundries are arranged to give rhythms.

3
ステンレスと木調が美しいキッチン
Kitchen with beautiful stainless and wooden texture

4
モザイクタイルを施したパウダーカウンター
Countertop arranged with mosaic tiles in the bathroom

5
サニタリースペース
Sanitary space

6
床と壁を風合いのある粘板岩でしつらえたバスルーム
Bathroom whose floor and wall are finished with clay stone having a unique feel

Data

Title
  Morocco Primitive

Design Supervision
  Kengo Kuma (Kengo Kuma & Associates)

Interior Designer
  Dam International Co.,Ltd.

Coordinate
  BALS Corporation

Area
  69.2m² (Room002)

Materials
  Interior Wall :
    interior thin painting
    400x400 cray stone
  Interior Floor :
    flooring, 400x400 cray stone

025

Terrace Ebisu no Oka
テラス恵比寿の丘
TOYOTA HOUSING CORPORATION / Nomura Real Estate Development Co., Ltd.
Studio P.E.R / Takenaka Corporation

街の喧噪から逃れて心を落ち着ける場所。恵比寿の丘の上は静けさの中にあった。ノイズのかわりに聞こえてくる風に揺れる葉の音。プライベートは静けさのなかに存在してこそ、深い幸福感に満たされる。都心居住に欠かせないプライバシー性、デザイン性を満たしながら、陽光や風を採り入れるための創意工夫を凝らして、都心では得難い開放感を実現している。丘の上という地形を活かした住まいは、西から南方向に豊かな緑を見下ろし、その先に街のパノラマが広がる。低層でありながらタワーマンションにも匹敵する遙かなる眺望を楽しめる。緑に包まれた低層５階建ての住棟は、穏やかな空気感の中にも堂々とした風格を感じさせる。ラウンドした飾り壁が訪れる人々の視線を受け止め、大きなキャノピーの張り出したエントランスへと導く。外壁の素材を巧みに貼り分けた外観は、モダンなのに落ち着きがあり、重厚感がありながらもスタイリッシュな仕上がりだ。エクステリアが硬質な素材で構成されているのにくらべ、エントランス内は木肌のぬくもりを感じさせる優しい空間となっている。直線を主体とした構成で、内と外の融合、人の手によるモダンな意匠と自然の調和を演出している。「都心を愉しみ、都心にくつろぐ私邸」をテーマに、そこに生まれる住まいの新たな価値。この上質が、これからの都心居住の基準となる。

A place of comfort, away from the hustle and bustle of the big city. At the top of the hill of Ebisu is silence. Rustling leaves stirred by the wind, no harsh noises. A deep sense of happiness can be achieved only in private silence. The design realizes a sense of openness rarely available at the heart of the city while satisfying strict privacy and sophisticated design requirements indispensable in the city life and offering well-thought-out and original devices to utilize natural light and wind. The building taking advantage of the topographic feature of a hilltop offers a grand view of rich green to the west and south and a panorama of the city beyond. Though the building is low-rise, its command of view is comparable to that of a residential apartment tower. The five-story low-rise residential building surrounded by green gives a sense of dignity in a comfortable atmosphere. Rounded decoration walls attract the eyes of the visitors and guide them to the entrance with an overhanging large canopy. The facade having carefully arranged exterior wall materials is modern yet well-balanced and finished with depth and style. Compared with the exterior made of "hard" materials, the interior of the entrance is designed as a "soft" space with a comfortable wooden texture. In the straight-line-based configuration, the exterior and interior are integrated, producing a sense of harmony between modern artificial design and nature. On the theme of "a private residence to enjoy and feel at ease in the heart of the city," a new value of residence is created. This high level of quality will be the standard of urban living.

	2	3
1	4	
	5	

1
南西側の既存緑地から外観を望む。遙かなる眺望に恵まれた、丘の上にある邸宅
Facade seen from the existing green space in the southwest. The condominium on the hill commands a far and wide view.

2
穏やかな空気感の中にも堂々とした風格を感じさせるエントランス
Entrance with a sense of dignity in a comfortable atmosphere

3
エントランス夕景
Entrance at dusk

4
ヒルサイドエントランス：2つのエントランスを持ち、出入りのしやすさに配慮している
Hillside entrance : Two entrances are provided for improved accessibility

5
敷地配置図
Site plan

027

1
2
3

1
自然光と緑の眺めを楽しみながら、くつろげるラウンジ
Lounge to take a relax while enjoying natural light and the green of plants

2
野外の緑を望む天井の高いヒルサイドエントランスホール
High ceiling hillside entrance hall with a view of the green trees outside

3
ホテルのような居住空間でくつろげるゲストスイート
Guest suit room offering a hotel-like living space

Data
Title
  Terrace Ebisu no Oka
Developer
  TOYOTA HOUSING CORPORATION
  Nomura Real Estate Development Co.,Ltd.
Design Supervision
  Studio P.E.R
Architect
  Takenaka Corporation
Location
  Naka-meguro, Meguro-ku, Tokyo
Site area
  4,441.85m²
Building area
  2,537.83m²
Total floor area
  11,808.42m²
Structure
  RC
Completion
  July, 2006
Materials
  Exterior Wall :
    tile, water-repellent painting on architectural concrete
  Public Wall :
    granite, 227x60 tile, natural stone
  Public Floor :
    stone-finish tile, natural stone

140-I type
140-I タイプ
Forward Style

木目調の温かみのある重厚なドアを開けると、イタリア製のタイルを敷き詰めたフロアが、柔らかな質感とともに迎えてくれる。ジャパニーズ・モダンを感じる上質な空間。暮らしのメインとなるリビング・ダイニングはのびやかな空間で、大きな窓から陽光が差し込む。床面のカーペットと調和しながら、その周りを彩るタイルは部屋に洒落たアクセントをもたらし、美意識を心地よく目覚めさせる。広さや設えだけでなく、イメージを刺激する雰囲気を誇りたくなる。人はここで、開放感を楽しみながら、やすらぎに包まれる。

When one opens a substantial wood grain door giving a sense of warmth, the floor covered with Italian tiles welcome one with its soft texture. The space inspires one of the modern Japanese style. The living-dining room as the center of living is a comfortable space with sunlight coming from a large window. The tiles around and matching the carpet place a sophisticated accent on the room, awakens one's sense of beauty. One feels pride in not only the size and facilities but also the atmosphere to stimulate one's inspiration. One can enjoy a sense of freedom and peace of mind.

1	2	4
		5
	3	6

1
ジャパニーズ・モダンを感じるエントランス。奥にプライベートルームを臨む
Entrance suggesting a sense of modern Japanesque. Beyond is a private room.

2
居室へとつづく廊下では、落ち着いた雰囲気のなかに柔らかなダウンライトの灯が落ちる
The corridor leading to the living room is illuminated by downlight, producing a quiet atmosphere.

3
リビング：多くのダウンライトや間接照明がつくる優しい光のリズム、ウッドのアクセントが効いたシックな雰囲気
Living room : Many downlights and indirect illumination creates soft rhythms of light in a chic atmosphere accentuated by the wood finish.

4
リビングからダイニング・キッチンを臨む。自然光をふんだんに取り込む壁一面の窓の外には、ガーデニングも存分に楽しめるほど広いバルコニーが付随している
Dining-kitchen seen from the living room. Outside the wall-sized window to let natural light come through is a balcony large enough for gardening.

5
贅沢なくつろぎに満ちているプライベートルーム
Private room for the time of relaxation

6
キッチン：カウンタートップに天然石を使用したアイランドカウンターは、重厚感がありながら洗練された存在
Kitchen : The island kitchen counter has a natural stone top, giving a sense of both depth and sophistication.

1	
2	3

1
ダウンライトが柔らかな光を落とし、住まう人をリラクゼーションの時へと誘ってくれるベッドルーム
Master bedroom where a downlight gives a soft light, leading the residents to time of relaxation

2
上質な美観と耐久性のある天然石のカウンタートップを使用したパウダールーム
Powder room using natural stone counter top with a quality outlook and durability

3
強化ガラスを使用したホテルライクな扉が印象的なバスルーム
Bathroom with an impressive hotel-like door, using tempered glass

Data

Title
140-I type

Designer
Forward Style

Area
140.14m²

Materials
Interior Wall :
vinyl cloth
Interior Floor :
stone-finish tile, carpet

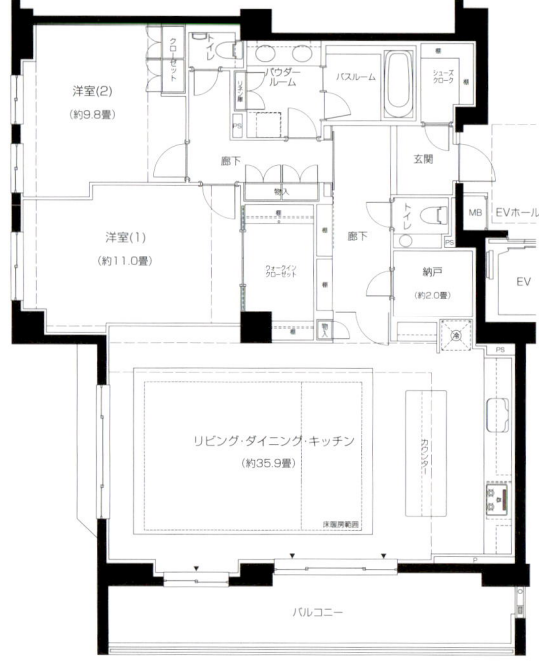

Park Mansion Shirokane Dai V (Cinq)
パークマンション白金台V（サンク）

Mitsui Fudosan Co., Ltd. / ZECS Co., Ltd.
Ryoichi Misawa / Tokyu Construction

通りから入った静けさの中に建つその住まいは、緑あふれる自然教育園の近くという上質な環境にある。さらに、贅を尽くした共用スペースや地下駐車場の設置など、スタイルだけではなく、日々の快適性も充実。白金台、その場所に建つ邸宅は、私生活を愛する、すべての大人が見る夢にあふれている。モダンな雰囲気のなか、ディテールに施された職人の手による装飾やルーフを形どるアールの曲線が、全体に与える優美な印象。そして、自然石を多用した低層部、タイルの質感と緑青色の屋根をもった中層部は住まいとしての温かさと上質感に満ちている。アールデコの様式美をエッセンスとしながら、洗練と暮らし心地を追求した、白金台という街に似合う住まい。

Set back from the street, the condominium in the tranquility enjoys a quality environment near a park for nature study filled with green. The building offers not only the style but also daily comfortability including a luxurious common space and underground parking lot. Standing in a posh residential district of Shiroganedai, this quality condominium is full of dreams hoped by every adult who loves his or her privacy. In the modern atmosphere, details decorated by craftsmen and art deco curves of the roof give an elegant impression. While the lower stories abundantly employ natural stone, the middle stories have greenish blue roofs and tiled facades; the condominium shows a sense of warmth and quality as a community. The design is based on the stylistic beauty of the art deco but pursues sophistication and comfortability of life in the special town of Shiroganedai.

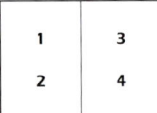

1
陽を受けて襟を正したくなるような佇まいを見せる正面玄関。アールデコの工芸品を彷彿させる扉を入ると、背の高い窓越しに大広間が見える

Front entrance that makes one unconsciously feel like straighten oneself up in the sunlight. Beyond the doors reminding one of an art deco craftwork, the large hall can be seen through high windows.

2
サロン：自然石を積み上げた壁と水磨きの壁が向かい合うその空間は、手づくりによる温かみと、ずっと以前からそこにあるような風格を湛えている。繊細な装飾を施された一枚のガラスと静かにくすぶる暖炉が、ここに佇む人を静かな安らぎへと誘う

Salon : The space where the wall of piled natural stone and the wall of honed finish are facing with each other is full of warmth of hand-made works and dignity as if it had a long history and tradition. The single delicately decorated glass and the warming fireplace guides residents to tranquility and comfort.

3
ヴェスティビュール：アールデコの芸術品が置かれた贅沢なスペース

Vestibule : Luxurious space decorated with art deco art pieces

4
上質なホスピタリティを感じるコンシェルジュカウンター

Concierge counter suggesting quality hospitality service

035

1	
2	3

1
コリドー：陽射しの下に緑の表情が揺らぎ、その向こうには流れ落ちる滝や噴水の水がきらめく
Corridor: Green trees shining under the sun, and beyond, the water of the running fall and the spring sparkling

2
自然との一体感が楽しめるプライベートガーデン
Private garden to feel to become one with the nature

3
リビングダイニング：透明感に溢れ、凛とした空気感がある。工芸的な色調の格子扉。時間をかけて生み出されたアートが優美な表情を創り出す。
Living-dining : The room has a sense of transparency with a sharp atmosphere. Lattice doors with a handicraft-like texture. Arts to which a lot of time is put add elegant expressions.

Data

Title
  Park Mansion Shirokane Dai V (Cinq)

Developer
  Mitsui Fudosan Co., Ltd.
  ZECS Co., Ltd.

Design Supervision
  Ryoichi Misawa

Architect
  Tokyu Construction

Location
  Minato-ku, Tokyo

Site area
  2,559.04m²

Building area
  1,686.50m²

Total floor area
  9,662.11m²

Structure
  RC

Completion
  March, 2006

Materials
  Exterior Wall :
    natural stone, tile
  Public Wall :
    natural stone, plastering finish
    sliced veneer
  Public Floor :
    natural stone, flooring

Misawa Taste (220-Htype)
三沢 テイスト
Ryoichi Misawa

一歩足を踏み入れれば、凛とした空気感を感じる。ラリックの調度品が似合うその空間は、上質とともに暮らす歓びを教えてくれる。眠っていた美意識が、ゆっくりと、心地よく目覚めだす。アートのある日常、それは人生を豊かにする。

A step inside, and one feels an awe-inspiring air of the condominium. The space suitable for furnishings designed by Lalique lets one feel a pleasure of leading a quality life. One's dormant sense of beauty is slowly and comfortably inspired. An ordinary life with artworks makes one's days richer.

1

コンサバトリー：上質な空間へのプロローグには、アンティークなテラコッタの焼きムラを忠実に再現したイタリア産タイルを丁寧に敷き詰めた。

Conservatory : As an approach to the quality space, the floor is carefully covered with Italian tiles that reproduce the color and texture of antique terracotta that has been fired unevenly.

2

リビングルームからダイニングルームを臨む
Dining room seen from the living room

3

ルーフ・バルコニー：燦々と降り注ぐ陽光や緑の色を愉しむ。自然と調和し、爽やかな風合いを発揮するスペイン産のタイルを敷き詰めている。

Balcony with a roof : Place to enjoy blazing sunlight and the color of green. The floor is covered with Spanish tiles that have refreshing texture characteristics.

4

手づくりの温かさを感じる贅にあふれた空間
Luxurious space with a hand-made touch

5

ルーフバルコニー
Balcony with a roof

1	3	
2	4	5

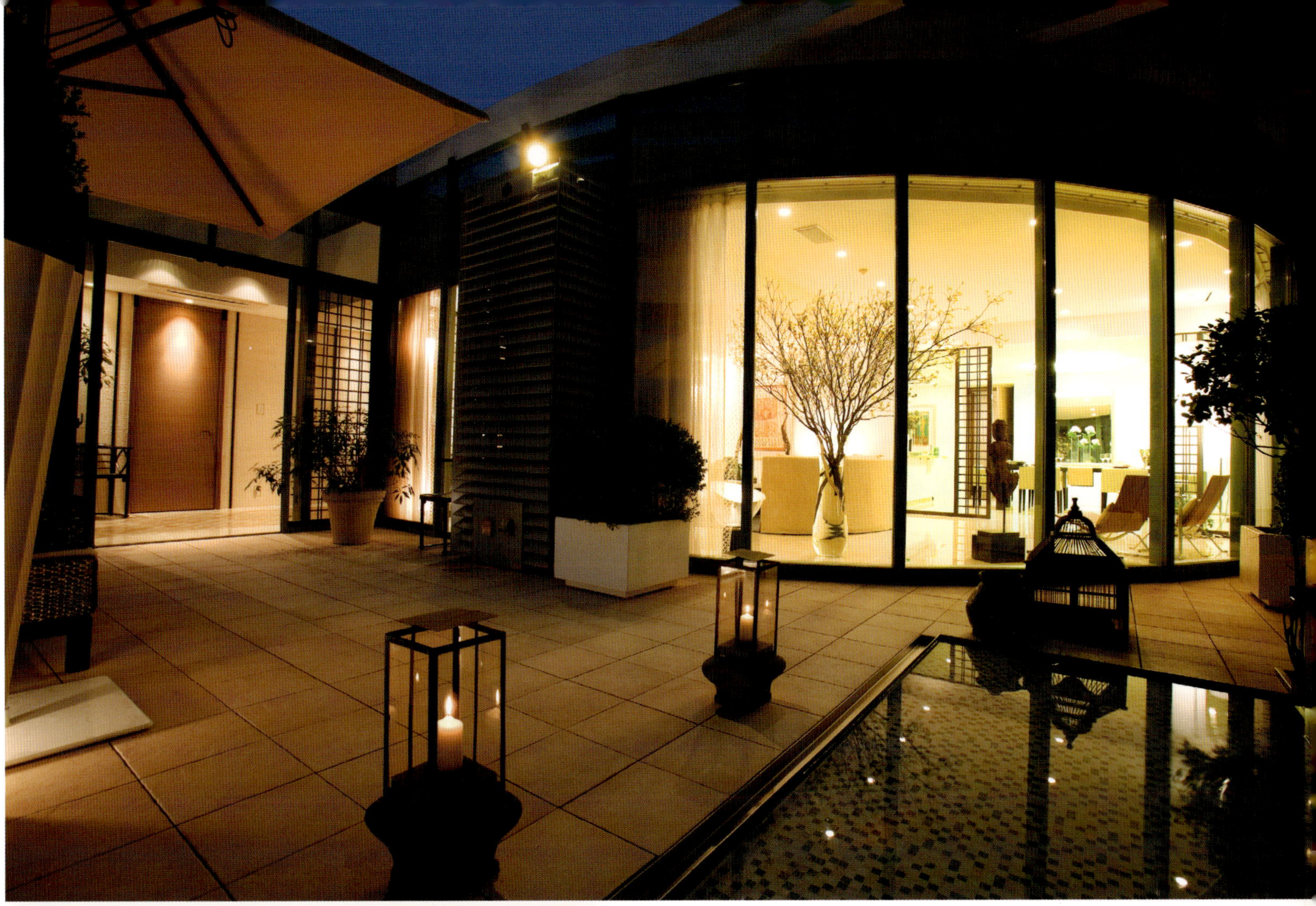

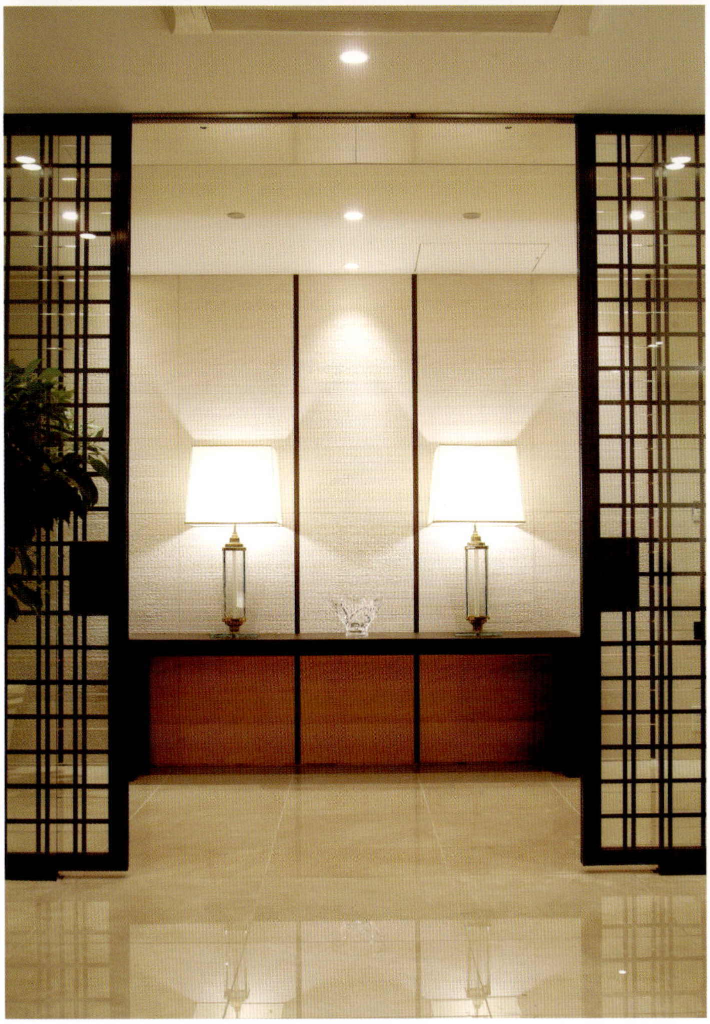

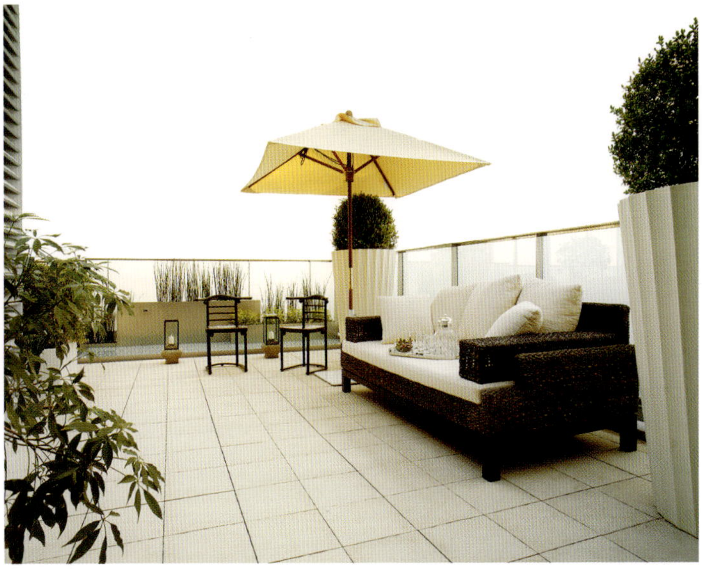

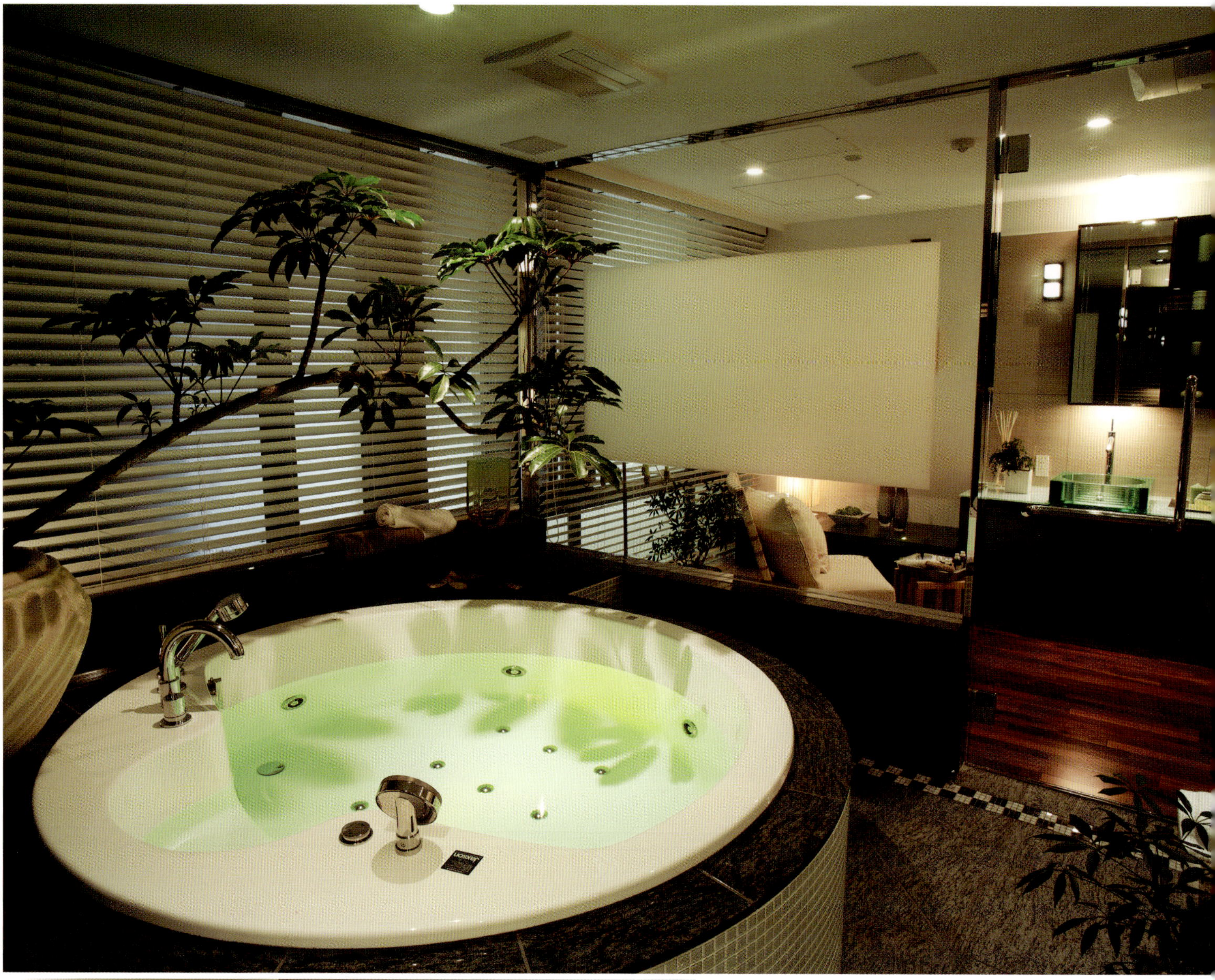

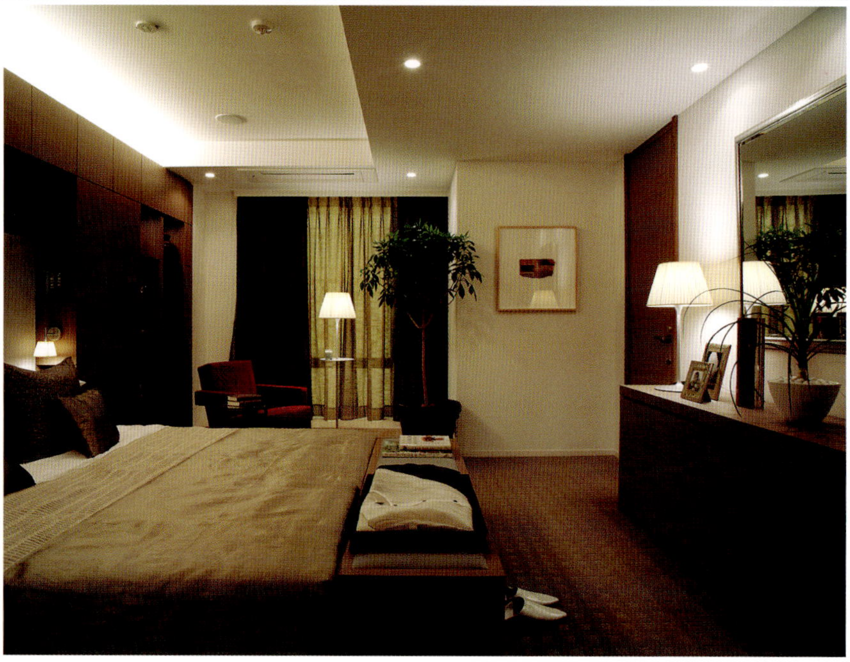

1	3	
2	4	5

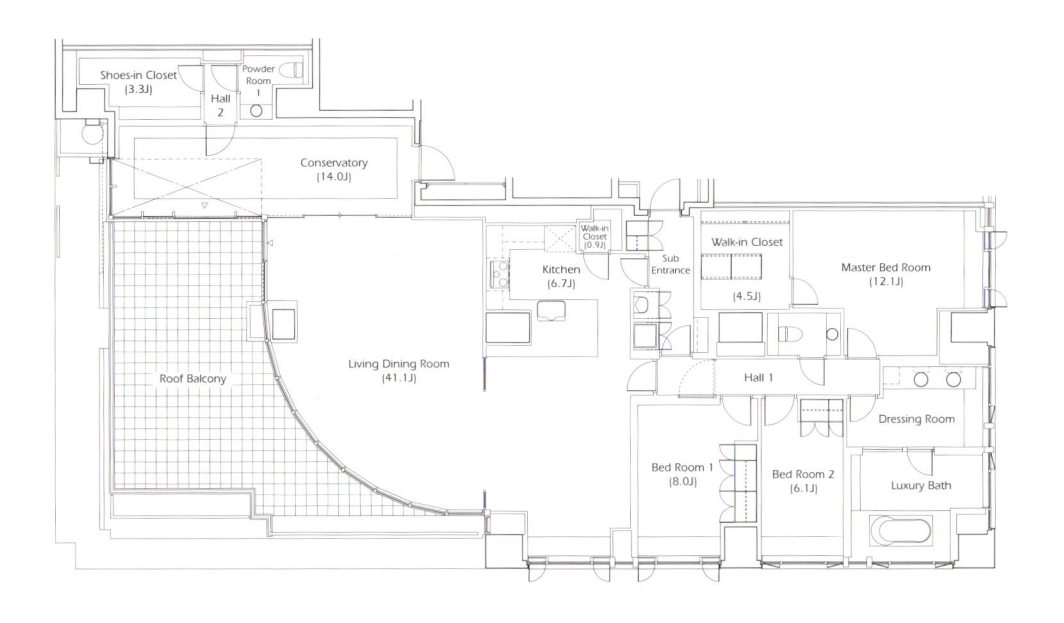

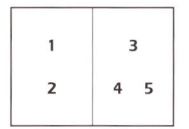

1
ラグジュアリーバス：フィジカル・メンタルともにリラクゼーションという贅を。家具のような美しさと陶器のようななめらかさと共に温かみをそなえたjaxson社のラグジュアリーバス。
Luxury bath : Offering a luxury both physical and mental. The Jaxson luxury bath has a beauty of furniture, smoothness of china, and a sense of warmth.

2
マスターベッドルーム：上質なカーペットや櫛を引いたようなピックルド仕上げの建具を採用して手の温もりを演出している。
Master bedroom : Employment of a quality carpet and pickled finish furnishings gives a sense of warmth of hands.

3
ドレッシングルーム：床材にチークの王様と称され、木材そのものが優雅な色艶を有するミャンマー産のチークの無垢材を使用。
Dressing room : To highlight the beauty of the room, glass sinks and other devices reveal their presences with a sense of transparency suitable for this space.

4
シャワールーム
Shower room

5
ウォーク・イン・クロゼット
Walk-in closet

Data

Title
  Misawa Taste (220-Htype)
Designer / Architect
  Ryoichi Misawa
Area
  217.35m²
Materials
  Interior Wall :
    painting
  Interior Floor :
    natural stone, carpet, flooring
    ceramic tile

041

Proud Akasaka Hikawa-cho
プラウド赤坂氷川町
Nomura Real Estate Development Co., Ltd. / KAJIMA Corporation

静けさ、品格、歴史。そして都心の中心に在ることさえ忘れてしまうような、漂う時間と空気感。三百年の杜に鬱蒼とつつまれた御屋敷街。今この場所は世界が着目するインターナショナル・タウンが開発されようという歴史の転換期。御屋敷街としての伝統に新しい価値を携えて、この地は都心の聖域たる表情をさらに深める。「普遍」と「本質」を志向しながらも、けっして色褪せることのない建築美。邸宅を構成するエレメントは、国籍を問わず「本物」の輝きをもつものだけに限られる。御影石の擁壁が連なる基壇部。天然石の柱、ガラス、力強いラインと面によるファサード。空と溶け合うガラス素材による、上層部。その安定感に満ちたフォルムは、低層宅ならではの威風堂々たる表情を街並みに醸し出す。ここにあるのは、邸宅が本来持つべき、このうえなく「豊かな」姿といえる。異なる表情を見せて連なる大理石が、微妙な対称を描いて、静かからさらなる静へ、極めて私的な時へと誘うように広がるエントランスアプローチ。自然石による壁と床は、柔らかな光を受けて美しいマテリアルの質感を伝えてくる。深みある黒檀調の自然木の風合いが、凛とした触感で、心を満たす。その全てが、端正なラインで構成される静的な空間が、この場所に流れる悠々の時と協調していく。

Silence, dignity, history. And then relaxing time and atmosphere makes one forget that one is at the heart of the city. A fashionable district surrounded by 300-year-old forests. With the international redevelopment project in progress, the area is at a turning point of its history. New values are added to its tradition as a quality residential block, and the neighborhood further increases its expression as a sanctuary. While "universality" and "essence" of architecture are pursued, the building shows never-fading beauty only found with constructions that are "genuine", regardless of their nationalities. The podium is covered with granite retaining walls. The facade is constituted by native rock columns, glass, and strong lines and surfaces. Upper stories use glass materials that match with the color of the sky. The stable form of the building appeals its majestic expression only found with low-rise architectural works in the townscape. The building represents the "rich" presence that is the essence of mansions. The entrance approach has a series of marble blocks with different faces creating delicate symmetries and guides residents and guests into a stronger sense of silence and privacy. The native rock walls and floors reveal a sense of quality, reflecting soft lighting. Touching the ebony-like texture of natural wood makes one feel a sense of luxury and dignity. Every detail of this quiet space created by sophisticated lines achieves harmony with a slow passage of time.

	2
1	3
	4
	5

1
威風堂々とした外観。界隈には静かな空気と上質な気品に満ちている
Facade with an impressive appearance. The neighborhood has a quiet atmosphere and distinguished elegance.

2
自然石をふんだんに使用した凛としたエントランスホール
Entrance hall with a sense of dignity, abundantly using natural stone

3
エントランスホール：レセプションフロアへの階段を臨む
Entrance hall : The stairway to the reception floor at the back

4
レセプションフロア：素材の持つ凛とした質感やあたたかく灯るライティング、ホールから下階へ連なるガラスの手摺り。そこに流れている時間そのものの豊かさを五感で感じる空間
Reception floor : Textures of the materials, warm lighting, and glass guardrails running from the hall to the downstairs. The space enables one to feel its richness through five senses.

5
パーティールーム
Party room

Data

Title
　Proud Akasaka Hikawa-cho
Developer
　Nomura Real Estate Development Co.,Ltd.
Architect
　KAJIMA Corporation
Location
　Akasaka, Minato-ku, Tokyo
Site area
　947.84m²
Building area
　568.62m²
Total floor area
　3,541.67m²
Structure
　RC
Completion
　March, 2007
Materials
　Exterior Wall :
　　227x60 tile, granite, concrete
　Public Wall :
　　natural stone, wooden panel
　Public Floor :
　　natural stone, flooring

B-type
B - タイプ
Forward Style

こだわり抜いた素材の数々は高級感を誇るためのものではない。ライティングは単に照度を与えるためのものではない。壁面にもたらされる優しい灯りは、素材そのものが持つ豊かさを、五感を通じてゆっくりと深く、伝えていく。静的なその空気感は、例えるなら国際的なミュージアムを思わせる。明から暗へ。空間は多様に広がり、繊細なひとつひとつのエレメントは、限りない豊かさを伝えてくる。水平と垂直のラインが美しく交錯する空間設計に、五感は豊穣な時を得て満たされていく。

Thoroughly careful selections of materials are not to boast a sense of high quality. Lighting is not just for giving illuminations. Through a soft and gentle light that reaches the surface of the wall, one slowly feels the richness of the materials through the five senses. The silent atmosphere is like that of an internationally renowned museum. Light and shade. The space has different faces, and individual delicate elements show their limitless quality. The spatial design of beautifully combined vertical and horizontal lines fills one's heart with time of richness and luxury.

	2	3
1		4
		5

1
リビングルーム：自然石や表情に富んだ紫檀調のフローリングなど、本物だからこそ五感を深く満たしていく端正かつフレームレスな空間
Living room: This decent, frameless space using genuine materials such as natural stone and rosewood flooring appeals to one's five senses.

2
玄関より自然石貼りの静謐な空間が広がる廊下
Silent corridor covered with natural stone tiles extends from the entrance.

3
ダイニングよりガラスのパーティションで仕切られたキッチンを臨む
Glass-partitioned kitchen seen from the dining room

4
ダイニング・キッチンを臨む
A view of the dining kitchen

5
リビングの続きにしつらえた洋室
Western style room arranged as an extension of the living room

045

1	2	
	3	5
	4	

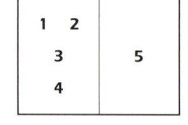

1
大理石の貼りのゆとりある玄関の表情
Comfortable marble floored entrance

2
廊下からリビング・ダイニングを臨む
Living-dining room seen from the corridor

3
御影石カウンターにツインボウルをしつらえた
パウダーカウンター
Granite powder counter with twin sinks

4
御影石でコーディネイトした、機能美とクオリ
ティの限りを尽くしたキッチン
Kitchen with full functional beauty and quality coordinated with granite

5
主寝室：英国産天然ウールカーペットの触感や、自然光の移ろいに、色合いまでを微かに変えていく塗装仕上げの壁。深い安らぎを醸すマテリアルだけを求めた個室空間
Master bedroom : Paint-finished walls that delicately change their faces by the texture of English natural wool carpet and natural light. Private space only using materials that are filled with serenity.

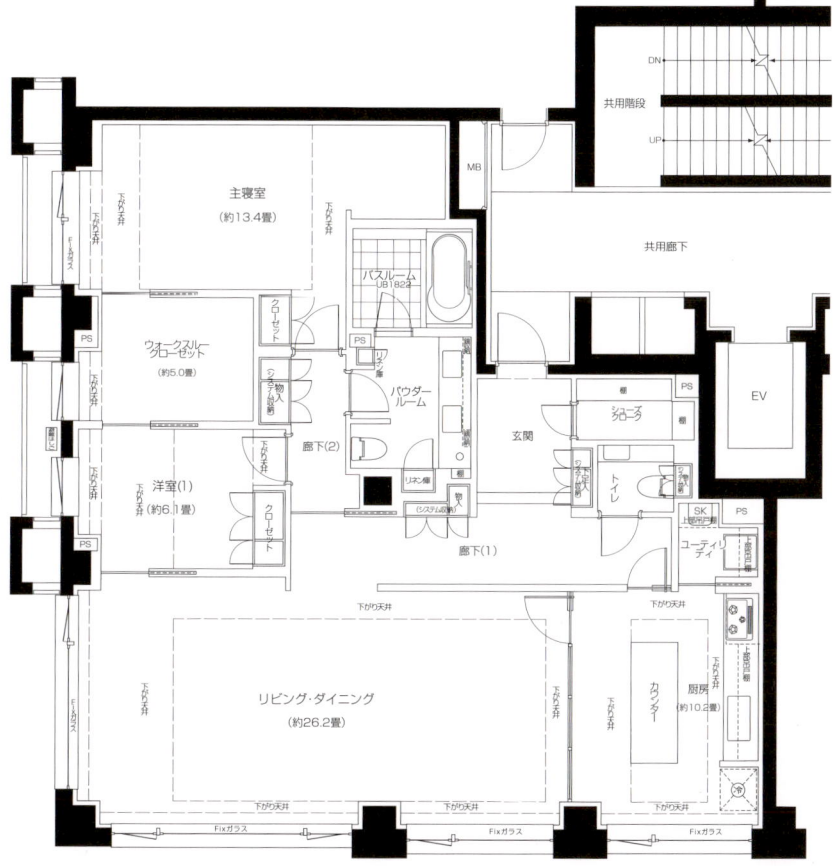

Data

Title
B-type

Designer
Forward Style

Area
140.92m²

Materials
Interior Wall :
marble, painting
Interior Floor :
marble, flooring

CLATIO Mikage Yamate 1 Chome
クラティオ御影山手一丁目

ORIX Real Estate Corporation
Ken Asai Architectural Research Inc.

豊かな緑と深田池の水景、風雅な環境に抱かれた悠然の地。現地に佇んで南を望めば、素晴らしい眺望が広がる。まさに、人々が羨望した風光明媚がここにある。緑濃き背景に抱かれて建つ、洗練された凛とした佇まい。それは饒舌な豪華さが豊かさと信じられた時代とは一線を画す、新たな豊かさと美しさへの、優雅なるプレゼンテーション。それは"御影山手一丁目"という類希なる地と、卓越したアーキテクト達との邂逅から生まれた、それぞれに個性際立つ、二十五篇の暮らしの珠玉集。そこに暮らす人々のさまざまな時間を深い包容力で受け止め、ともに年齢を重ね、豊饒な時間を育んでいくような上質な空間の設計力。これは熟成の思想と先進の技術とが生み出した、ひとつの結論。色褪せることなく、ひときわ輝きを増す住まいへと磨かれていくだろう。

The site is located in rich green woods and enjoys the waterscape of the Fukadaike Pond and elegant surroundings. When one is on site and looks at the south, a wonderful view is before one's eyes. A scenic beauty everyone wants is there. With the green mountains at background, the building stands sophisticated and awe-inspiring. It is a graceful presentation of a new sense of richness and beauty, clearly distinguished from that of the days when splendid luxuriance was believed to mean richness. The 25 apartments, each of which offers opportunities of leading a unique lifestyle, are results of the meeting between a one-of-a-kind residential area of Mikage Yamate 1-Chome and excellent architects. The power of this quality space design enables the condominium to support the fruitful years of the different lifestyles of the residents and to get older with them. This is a conclusion given by a mature philosophy and cutting-edge technology. The apartments will become true residences with joyful moments.

	2
1	3
	4

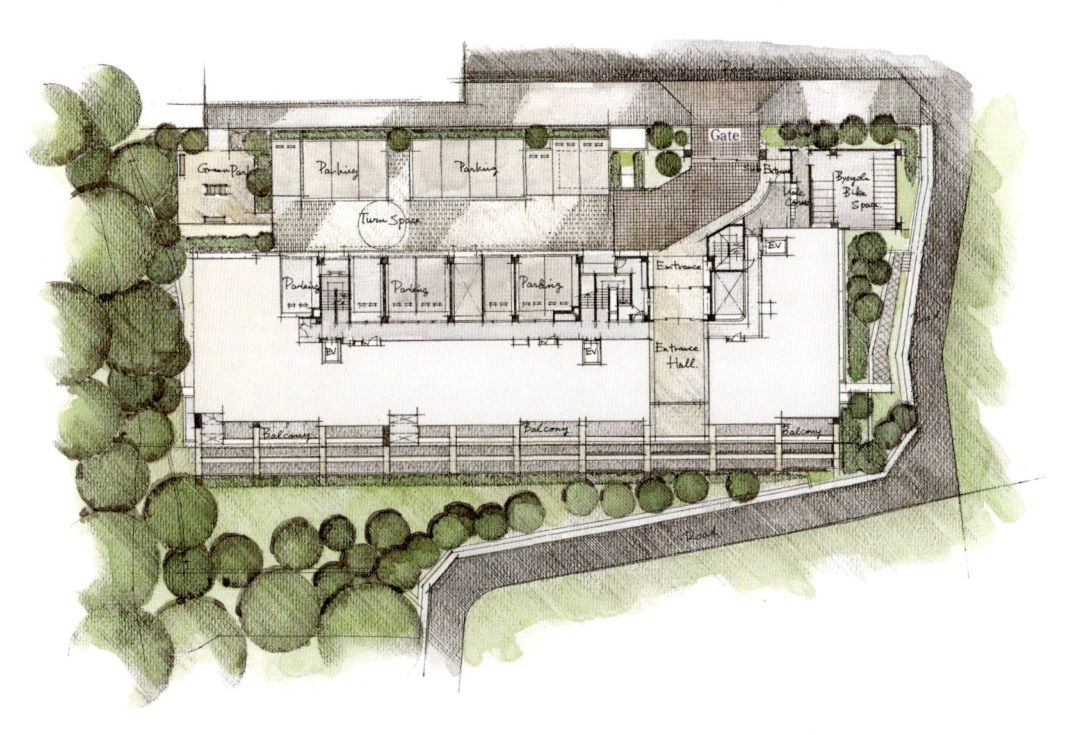

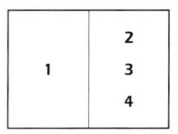

1
美しい自然景観の中に建つ凛とした佇まい
Awe-inspiring appearance in the beautiful scenery of nature

2
御影の真の姿を、人生の本質を映し出す威風堂々としたエントランス。重厚な趣のゲートが迎えるアプローチは、御影石とインターロッキングで舗装された優雅な設え。
Commanding entrance that reflects the true shape of Mikage and the essence of life. The approach with the profound gate at the back is elegantly paved with granite and interlocking blocks.

3
敷地配置図
Site Plan

4
高級ホテルを彷彿させる車寄せが住まわれる人を優しく迎えるメインエントランス
The main entrance where the marquee inspiring a high-grade hotel welcomes residents.

Data

Title
  CLATIO Mikage Yamate 1Chome

Developer
  ORIX Real Estate Corporation

Design Supervision / Architect
  Ken Asai Architectural Research Inc.

Location
  Higasi-Nada-ku, Kobe city, Hyogo

Site area
  2,828.51m²

Building area
  1,129.09m²

Total floor area
  4,289.57m²

Structure
  RC

Completion
  March, 2006

Materials
  Exterior Wall :
    natural stone, 227x60 tile
    sprayed coating
  Public Wall :
    natural stone
    wooden sliced veneer panel
  Public Floor :
    natural stone, tile carpet

049

P-type
P - タイプ
Shinichi Eto

玄関を一歩中に入れば、そこは広々としたゆとりとくつろぎの住まい。リビングからキッチン、ダイニングへとつながる大空間。パノラマに広がる美しい夜景とクラシックの旋律に包まれる贅沢。綴られるストーリーの豊かさと優雅さは、まぎれもない邸宅の実感を与える。人を迎え、出会いを慈しみ、時間を愉しむ、迎賓の思想がここにある。

A step into the entrance, and one is in a wide, comfortable and relaxing residence. A large space leading from the living room to the kitchen and dining space. Luxurious time at hand with a panoramic nightscape and classical background music. The richness and elegance of the experience gives one an impression of living in a mansion with the philosophy of welcoming guest, enjoying a meeting, and having a good time.

| 1 | 2 |
| | 3 |

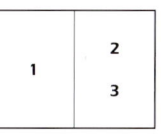

1
美意識、ゆとり、機能性の上質なコラボレイト。その先を見つめたキッチンは、クオリティ優先の空間から家族の交流を拡げるセカンドリビングとなる
Quality collaboration of the sense of beauty, comfortability and functionality

2
迎賓の思想が活きた高級感ある玄関
Quality entrance based on the philosophy of welcoming guests

3
ホールからリビングルームを臨む
Living room seen from the hall

1	3	5
2	4	

1
リビングルーム：奥にベッドルームの扉を臨む
Living room : The door to the bedroom at the back

2
相応しい贅と品格を惜し気もなくしつらえたダイニング・キッチン
Dining-kitchen unsparingly provided with luxury and dignity

3
大きな窓から景色を愉しむくつろぎのビューバス。ホテルライクなしつらえのなかでのグルーミング。快適であること、清潔であることはもちろん、ステイタスですらあるスペースのゆとりとクオリティが感じられる
Relaxing bath with a command of view. Hair making in a hotel-like facility. The comfortable space of quality gives a sense of status as well as comfort and cleanliness.

4
サニタリールーム
Sanitary room

5
しつらえや家具のひとつひとつに、こだわりを極めたプライベート空間。ライティングの紡ぎ出す陰影にまで妥協なくこだわりを尽くした、その寛ぎには、豊潤な香りすら漂う
Private space with attention paid to every detail of apparatus and furniture. The sense of comfort created by uncompromised consideration given to shades by lighting even has hints of abundance.

Data

Title
P-type

Coordinate
Shinichi Eto

Area
141.80m²

Materials
Interior Wall :
vinyl cloth
Interior Floor :
natural stone, flooring

Park Mansion Shirokane Dai IV (Quatre)
パークマンション白金台IV（カトル）
Mitsui Fudosan Co., Ltd. / Ryoichi Misawa
Tokyu Construction

パリのメゾンを思わせる瀟洒な館。プラチナ通りの洗練された雰囲気のなか、都心であることを忘れさせる静けさと華やかなプライベート空間をもった、私邸と呼ぶにふさわしい贅にあふれた邸宅。白金台の空気を存分に愉しみながら、ここから大人の幸せがはじまる。アールデコ様式のフレーミングを施された扉を開けば、そこは神聖な美しさをも感じさせる吹抜の広間。細部までをていねいに、職人によりつくり込まれた空間は射し込む光さえやさしい。サロンにはアールデコ傑作を数多くてがけた、ラリックとホフマンの作品が置かれ、贅沢な雰囲気をもたらしている。旧朝香宮邸に対するオマージュともなるアートのある暮らし。白金台の上質な空気が、ここでも満喫できる。

This posh building reminds one of a grand maison in Paris. In the sophisticated neighborhood of the Platinum Street, the condominium offers the silence and gallant private spaces that make one forget its location at the heart of the city; it is comparable to the name of a private residence. While enjoying a atmosphere of Shiroganedai, one can step on a path to a mature happiness. When the door framed in the art-deco style, one finds oneself in an open-ceiling lobby inspiring holy beauty. The space carefully built by craftsmen to its details makes even streaming sunlight softer. The salon is decorated with the works of Lalique and Hoffmann who created many art-deco masterpieces, creating a luxurious atmosphere. It is a life with artworks as an homage to the old Asakanomiya residence. One can sense the high-class air of Shiroganedai here, too.

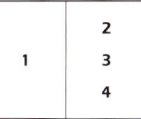

	2
1	3
	4

1

大きな木陰に隠されるように、静かに佇むガラスの扉。アールデコ様式のフレーミングを施され、風格さえ湛えている

Silently standing glass door in the shade of a tree. Framed in the art deco style, it gives an elegant impression.

2

神聖な美しさをも感じさせる吹抜の広間。細部までを丁寧に、職人の手によりつくり込まれた空間は、射し込む光さえやさしく感じられる

Open-ceiling lobby inspiring holy beauty. The space carefully built by craftsmen to its details makes even streaming sunlight softer.

3

ワインの貯蔵庫

Wine cellar

4

サロンにはアールデコの傑作を数多くてがけた、ラリックとホフマンの作品が置かれ、贅沢な雰囲気をもたらしている。旧朝香宮邸に対するオマージュともなるアートのある暮らし。白金台の上質な空気が、ここでも満喫できる

The salon is decorated with the works of Lalique and Hoffmann who created many art-deco masterpieces, creating a luxurious atmosphere. It is a life with artworks as homage to the old Asakanomiya residence. One can sense the high-class air of Shiroganedai here, too.

Data

Title
  Park Mansion Shirokane Dai IV (Quatre)
Developer
  Mitsui Fudosan Co., Ltd.
Design Supervision
  Ryoichi Misawa
Architect
  Tokyu Construction
Location
  Minato-ku, Tokyo
Site area
  923.61m²
Building area
  600.38m²
Total floor area
  2,844.00m²
Structure
  RC
Completion
  February, 2006
Materials
  Exterior Wall :
    natural stone, 195x45 tile
  Public Wall :
    natural stone, plastering finish
  Public Floor :
    natural stone

Jerome & Erwan Taste (160-Atype)
ジェローム＆エルワン テイスト
Jerome Clynckemaillie & Erwan Le Bourdonnec

気品という贅を尽くした質の高い寛ぎの空間。人そして光と風を導く場所として優しい演出をしている。それぞれの空間には美しさを際立たせるため、上質で耐久性が高い素材で仕上げられ、その空間にふさわしい存在感を与えている。手間と時間を惜しみなくかけることで、住まいは体温を持つ。そして職人の手仕事による温もりは、人の心を気持ちよく揺り動かす。

This is a quality, relaxing space with luxury of dignity. It is designed as a comfortable place to welcome people as well as light and wind. Each space is finished with high quality, durable materials highlighting its beauty and making their presence ideal for the space. By sparing time and efforts generously, each residence comes to have its own "body temperature". And the warmth of the workmanship pleasantly moves the hearts of the people.

1

リビングダイニング：フローリングには「キング・オブ・フォレスト」と呼ばれるホワイトオークの無垢材を採用。強硬、高耐久、さらには不浸透性をもちあわせている。

Living-dining: Flooring employs natural wood of white oak, also called as the "King of the Forest". The wood is strong, highly durable, and impermeable.

1
感性を刺激するスタディールーム。建具には褐色から黒の独特の縞柄で、重厚な木材の素材感をいかんなく主張するゼブラウッドを使用。時間を掛けて、乾燥させ、自然な光沢で美しく仕上げられている。
Study room stimulating one's sensitivity. Furnishings are made of Zebrawood which is distinctive for its zebra like light and dark stripes, emphasizing the deep texture of wood. Dried for a long time, they are beautifully finished with a natural luster.

2
ダイニングからリビングを臨む
Living space seen from the dining

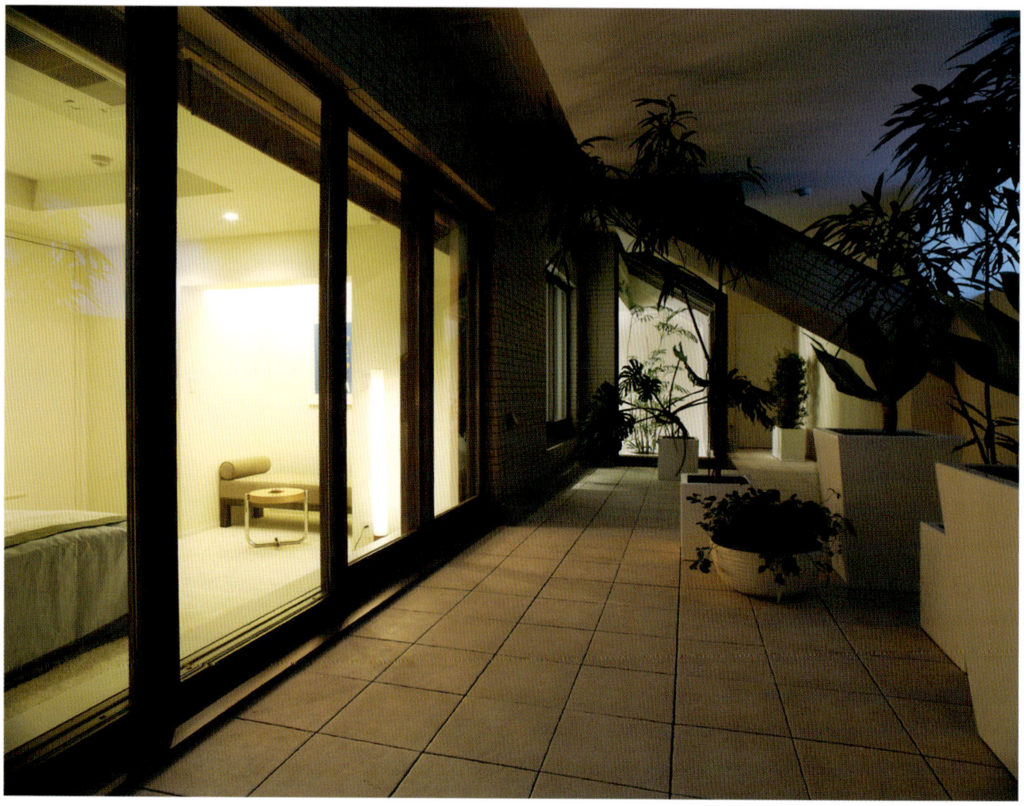

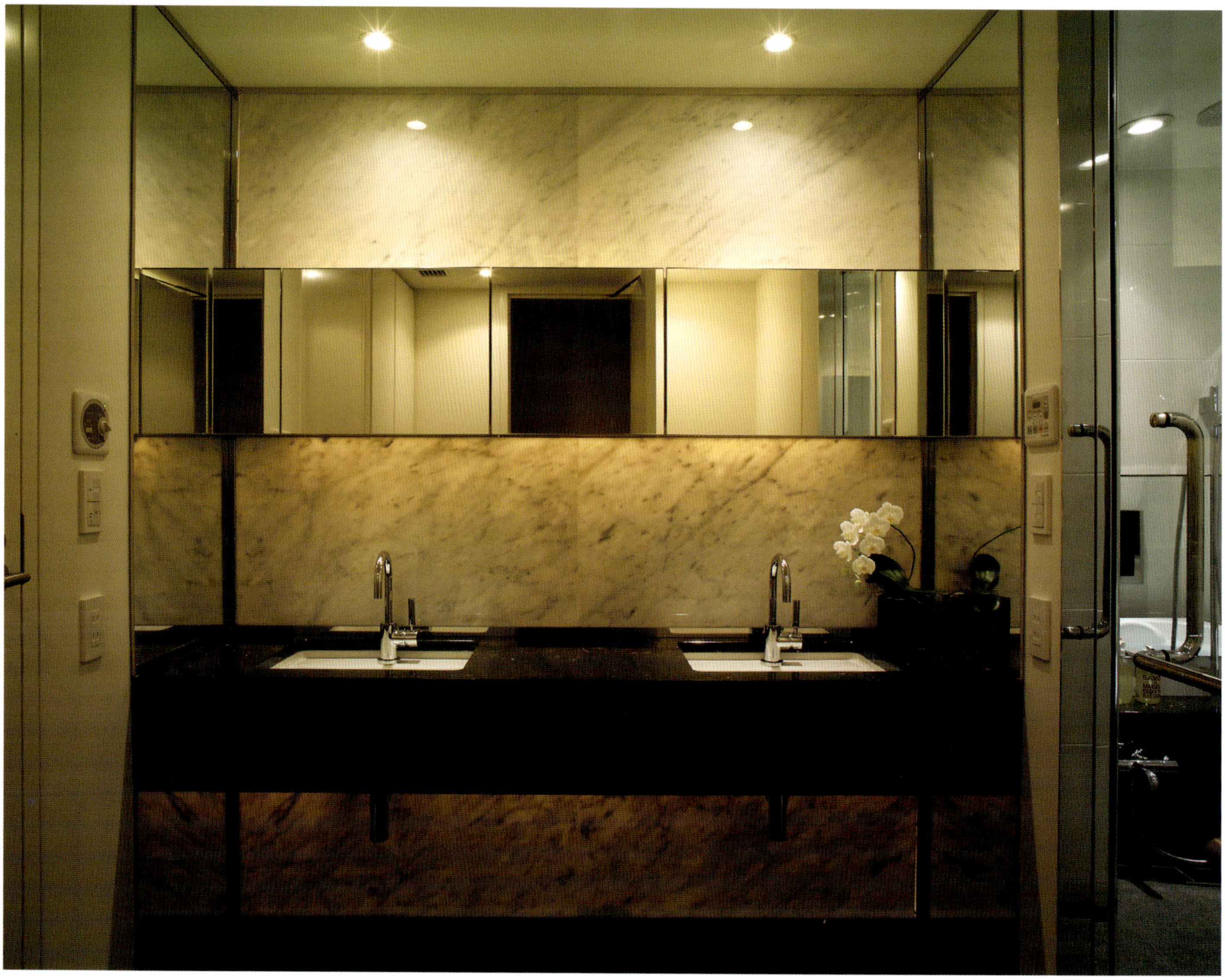

1	3
2	4

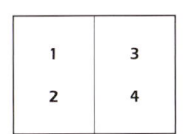

1
スペイン産のタイルを敷き詰めた、広々とした
バルコニー
Extensive balcony covered by Spanish tiles

2
イタリア産の大理石を使用し上質な空間に仕上げたドレッシングルーム。選び抜かれた透明度の高い大理石の裏側から光を幻想的に映し出し、この空間にふさわしい存在感と透明感を与えている。
Dressing room finished as an elegant space using Italian marble. A fantastic light from behind the selected, highly lucid marble is reflected, giving a sense of presence and transparency.

3
バスルーム：漆黒の夜空に散りばめられた星をイメージさせる天然石「スターギャラクシー」。同一素材という統一感の中に、異なる手法の仕上げを施し空間にリズムを与えている。
Bathroom: Star Galaxy is a natural stone that reminds one of stars jewelling the black night sky. In the consistent use of the same material, different styles of finishes accentuate the space.

4
上質な日々をしっかり受け止めるマスターベッドルーム。カーペットには耐久性の高いドイツ製の素材を採用。
Master bedroom to support high quality days. The carpet uses highly durable materials from Germany.

1

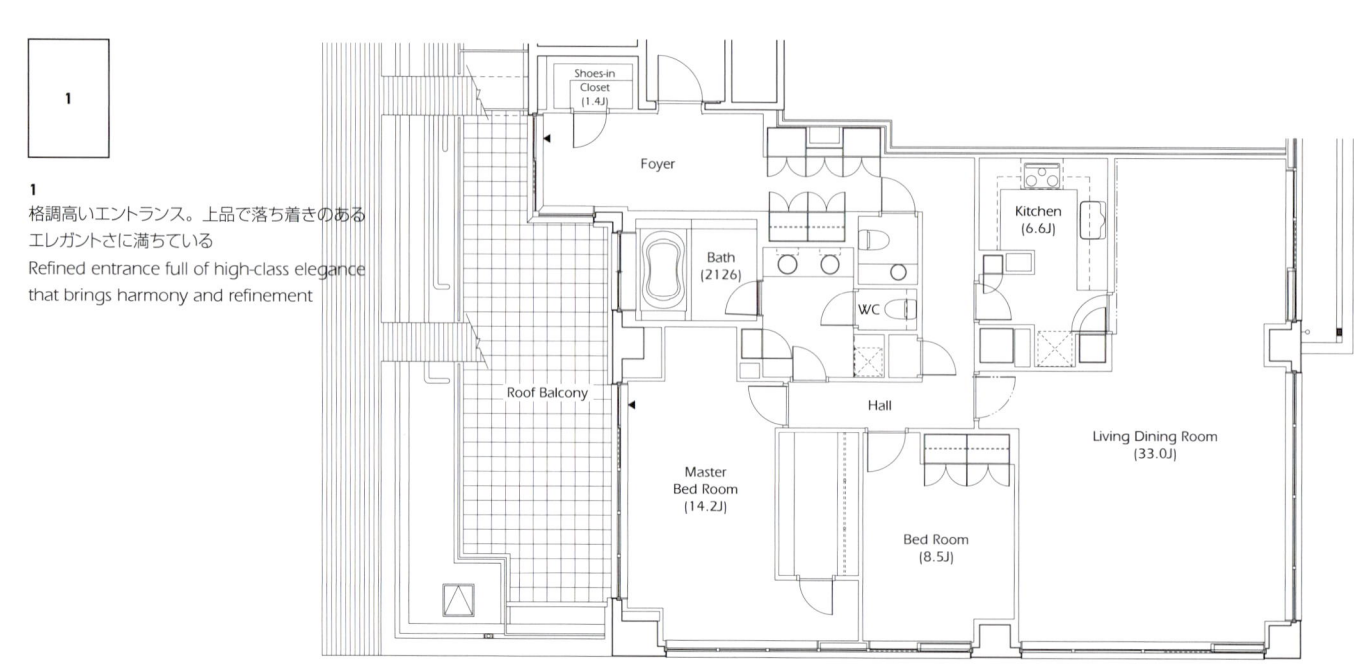

格調高いエントランス。上品で落ち着きのある
エレガントさに満ちている
Refined entrance full of high-class elegance
that brings harmony and refinement

Data

Title
  Jerome & Erwan Taste (160-Atype)
Designer / Architect
  Jerome Clynckemaillie
  & Erwan Le Bourdonnec
Area
  160.61m²
Materials
  Interior Wall :
    painting
  Interior Floor :
    natural stone, carpet, flooring

VERUS Nishi-Azabu
ヴェルス西麻布
ORIX Real Estate Corporation / Kenichi Yokobori

西麻布4丁目。その街は、つねに都市の躍動を享受しながら、この上ない邸宅地として穏やかな空気に包まれている。美意識を満たす住空間。その住まいは、自分らしくスタイリッシュ＆ラグジュアリーなライフスタイルを描く。華美な装飾を排除すること、シンプルな上質さに徹すること、すべてを本物の寛ぎのために統一すること。アートの領域にまで完成度を高めた、このインテリアが、美しい音楽の調べのように、住まう方をやすらぎで包んでくれる。時代の最先端を感じながら、上質な都市生活を愉しめる。住まいの顔となるエントランスには、素材そのもののクオリティにおいて比類のない、無垢の天然大理石や御影石を配している。ずっしりとした重厚感の中に、緊張感のある構成を見せる空間は、いっさいの虚飾をはねつけるソリッドな美に満ちている。また外壁はディティールの質感にまでこだわったショットブラストタイルを用い、さらに目地材を骨材の入ったモルタルで仕上げることにより、素材の持ち味を活かした印象深い雰囲気を醸し出す。ここから予感されるもの、それは美しさとやすらぎがみごとに調和した、西麻布ならではのライフスタイル。

Nishi-Azabu 4-chome. Having always enjoyed the energy of the city, the town still remains in a comfortable atmosphere as one of the finest residential area. The condominium offers a living space to satisfy one's sense of beauty where one can obtain and enjoy a stylish and luxurious lifestyle best suitable for one's taste. Elimination of gorgeous decoration, thoroughly simple yet high quality, and fully consistent design for true relaxation all contributed to the perfection of the building in the domain of art. The interior based on such philosophy embraces residents with the peace of mind as if it were a melody of beautiful music. One can enjoy first-rate city life at the forefront of the age. The entrance to represent the residence employs solid natural marble and granite of the finest quality. The massive space with a sense of tension is full of solid beauty getting rid of all ostentation. Shot blasting is used for the exterior walls to give a texture to details, and by finishing with mortar containing aggregate as jointing, given is an impressive atmosphere taking advantage of the characteristics of the materials. From the design, one anticipates a Nishi-Azabu-like lifestyle where beauty and comfort are perfectly in harmony.

1
美しく気品あふれるエントランス
Beautiful and elegant entrance

1	2	5
	3	
	4	6

1
エントランス：質感にこだわった外壁やフロストガラスが美しい印象を醸し出す
Entrance: The exterior wall emphasizing the texture and frosted glass gives an impression of beauty.

2
洗練と独創のファサードデザイン。そこに息づく生活の美学を感じる
Facade design with sophistication and originality, letting one feel a beautiful life in there

3
壁や床に無垢の天然大理石を配し、ずっしりとした重厚感の中に、緊張感のある構成を見せるエントランス
Massive entrance with a sense of tension, employing solid natural marble and granite

4
落ち着いた雰囲気を感じさせるエントランスホール
Entrance hall with a chic atmosphere

5
ダイニングルームからリビングを臨む
Living room seen from the dining room.

6
リビングからダイニング・キッチンを臨む
Dining-kitchen seen from the Living room.

063

1
安らぎを演出する調光設備など、隅々にまで永住のクオリティが息づくリビングダイニング
Living-dining space with lighting for a sense of comfort and other quality designs ideal for permanent residence

2
自然素材をあしらった温かみのある廊下
Corridor using natural materials with a sense of warmth

3
華美な装飾を排除し、シンプルな上質さに徹したゆとり溢れるダイニング
Dining space with thoroughly simple yet high quality, getting rid of all ostentation

4
書斎
Study room

5
主寝室：心地よい安らぎを育む広々としたプライベートルーム
Master bedroom: Extensive private room to ensure comfort and relaxation

6
美しく使い勝手のよいステンレス製カウンターと温もりのあるウォールナット面材を使用した快適さと機能美を追求したシステムキッチン
Beautiful and easy-to-use stainless counter and built-in kitchen with walnut facing materials giving a sense of warmth in pursuit of comfort and functional beauty

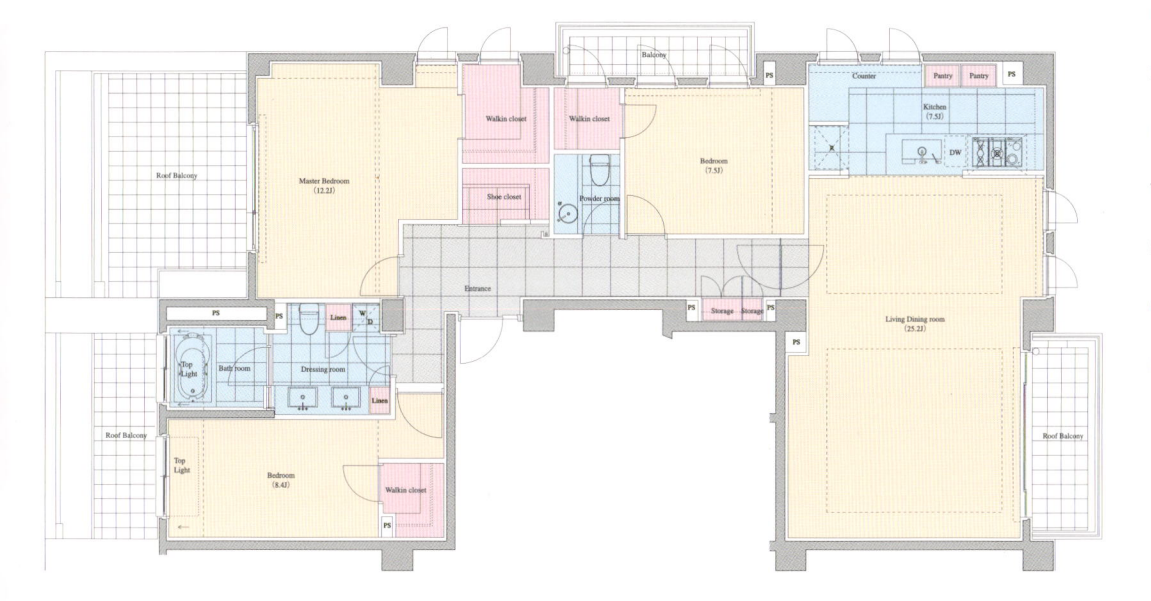

Data

Title
 VERUS Nishi-Azabu

Developer
 ORIX Real Estate Corporation

Architect
 Kenichi Yokobori

Location
 Nishi-Azabu, Minato-ku, Tokyo

Site area
 548.33m²

Building area
 378.38m²

Total floor area
 1,843.44m²

Structure
 RC

Completion
 June, 2004

Materials
 Exterior Wall :
  shot blasting tile, joly pate
 Public Wall :
  limestone
 Public Floor :
  terrazzo tile, limestone
 Interior Wall :
  cloth, carpet
 Interior Floor :
  marble

065

ADENIUM Senzokuike Minami
アデニウム洗足池南

Joint Corporation Co.,Ltd.
Hiromi Shirasawa (Architectural Creator's Group)

洗足池の淑やか風景、四季の美しさ、歴史の中に育まれてきた価値を受け継ぎ、新たに生まれた「離宮」という和邸宅思想。静穏な邸宅街を背景にひときわ上品な表情を纏い、この住宅は存在する。ゆったりとした水平ラインが印象的な伸びやかなフォルム。それを支える重厚感漂う石積の壁面が落ち着いた色調で外観を彩る。その姿は、集合邸宅の域を超えた屋敷の風格を伝える。穏やかな温もりを湛えると同時に、誇り高き暮らしを象徴する重厚な門の表情。素材の妙趣が織り成す格調高い門構えは、邸宅美を追求した意匠発想。また、住まう人を持て成すに相応しい迎賓の構えは、門の内に広がる特別な時間を沸騰させるとともに、威厳とステイタスを主張している。エントランスへ足を踏み入れると、穏やかな光が射し込む優美な空間が出迎える。大谷石など自然素材があしらわれ、温もりを醸し出す静謐な時の中へ心は導かれていく。雪見窓から垣間見える中庭の植栽など、さりげない心配りに彩られた空間のなかで、心は解きほどかれて、自分時間へと気持ちが切り替わっていく。古雅な空間で情趣を心に灯しながら私邸へ向かうやすらぎの動線となっている。

Inheriting the gentle landscape of Senzokuike, beauty of the four seasons, and values cultivated through the history, the new design concept of "rikyu" (detached palace) Japanese-style residence has been developed. With a quiet residential area as its background, this condominium is present with a very elegant facade. Its clean form features impressive extensive horizontal lines, supported by massive stone masonry walls with an unobtrusive texture. The presence of the building is more like a mansion rather than a condominium. The presence of the massive gate giving a sense of soothing warmth symbolizes a life that one can be proud of. The refined style of the gate created by tastefully using different materials is based on the design concept to pursue the residential beauty. Its atmosphere suitable for welcoming the residents remind them of special time and space they can enjoy behind the gate that reveals a sense of dignity and status. One step inside the entrance, one is welcomed by a graceful space illuminated by the soft sunshine. Oya tuff stone and other natural materials are employed to guide one to the quiet moments with a sense of warmth. In the space with an unobtrusive attention to details represented by planting seen through the window enabling one to see the snow, one feels relaxed and achieves peace of mind to enjoy private time. It is the passage toward one's private residence to gradually unfold one's sentiment in this antique and elegant space.

1	2
	3
	4

1

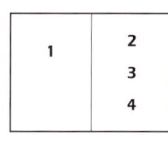

古都の庭園のようなエントランス前の中庭：和の趣が漂う木調の格子戸を抜けると静謐なヴェールに包まれる

Inner garden in front of the entrance, reminding one of a garden in a historical city: Through the wooden lattice door, one will find oneself in a veil of silence.

2

迎賓の雅門：邸宅としての品格を意識し、一つひとつの素材感と水平ラインが際立つ美しいフォルム

Graceful gate to welcome guests: Beautifully formed, highlighting the texture of materials and horizontal lines in consideration of dignity as residence

3

エントランスホール：壁面に贅沢にあしらわれた大谷石、木目が美しい天井、和を意識した朱のアクセントが相まって、落ち着きと温もりを醸す

Entrance hall: Oya tuff stone abundantly used on the wall, ceiling with a beautiful wood-grain texture, and the use of red as accents all contribute to a sense of comfort and warmth.

4

中庭の植栽が垣間見える雪見窓

Glass window to enable one to see the snow in winter (yukimimado) through which one can see the planting in the inner garden

Data

Title
  ADENIUM Senzokuike Minami

Developer
  Joint Corporation Co.,Ltd.

Architect
  Hiromi Shirasawa
    (Architectural Creator's Group)

Location
  Ota-ku, Tokyo

Site area
  1,219.89m²

Building area
  837.86m²

Total floor area
  3,826.92m²

Structure
  RC

Completion
  March, 2006

Materials
  Exterior Wall : sandstone, 45x90 tile
  Public Wall : Oya tuff stone, 45x90 tile
    sprayed coating
  Public Floor : ceramic tile

Kmg-type

Kmg-type
Einan Takeshita (MITSUI Designtec Co., Ltd.)

共用部からの静かな趣を引き継ぐ玄関ホールは、柔らかな光を綾なす照明により落ち着きのある空間に演出。リビング・ダイニングはシンプルな空間を基調に和室との一体感を高めるなど安らぎを深めるための工夫がなされている。上質でモダンな設えの中に、和の風情がほのかに薫る優雅な私邸宅空間。

The entrance hall succeeding the serene atmosphere of the common use area is produced as a comfortable space by employing soft illuminations. The living-dining room is a simply designed space having a sense of integrity with the Japanese style room to promote deeper relaxation. This is an elegant private residential space with a delicate Japanesque taste in the context of quality and modern design.

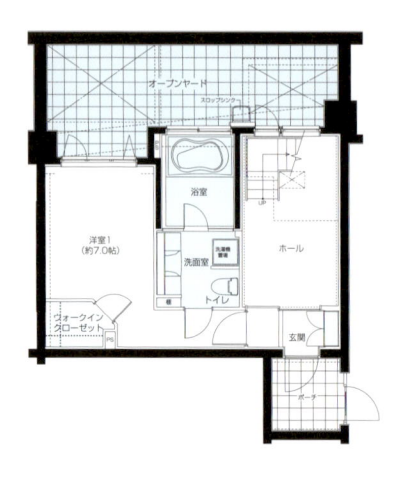

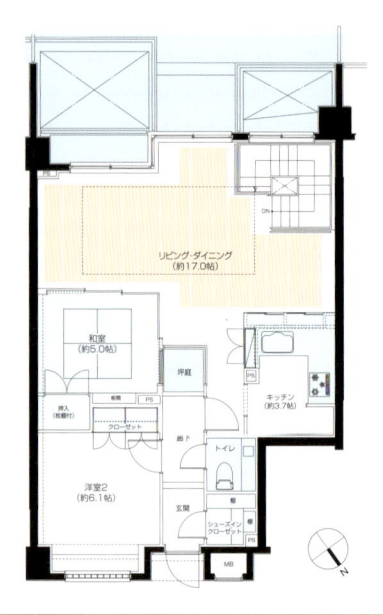

	2	3
1	4	
	5	6

1
和室との一体感を高めたリビング・ダイニングルーム
Living-dining room with a sense of integrity with the Japanese style room

2
玄関から坪庭を臨む
Spot garden seen from the entrance

3
プライベートギャラリー
Private gallery

4
伸びやかなリビング・ダイニング：大きな窓から降り注ぐ陽光と開放感に恵まれた空間
Spacious living-dining: Rich in sunshine through large windows and a sense of openness

5
スタイリッシュな中に趣を漂わせるモダンな和室
Stylish yet tasteful modern Japanese-style room

6
厳選された機能とクオリティのあるキッチン
Kitchen having selected functions and quality

1
穏やかにやすらぎを慈しみ、贅沢な時間を過ごせるベッドルーム
Bedroom to give a peace of mind and offer luxurious time to spend

2
ベッドルームからバルコニーを臨む
Balcony seen from the bedroom

3
プライベートルーム
Private room

Data
Title
 Kmg-type
Designer
 Einan Takeshita
 (MITSUI Designtec Co., Ltd.)
Area
 110.15m²
Materials
 Interior Wall : vinyl cloth
 Interior Floor : flooring, carpet

Park House Yoga Court Residence

パークハウス用賀コートレジデンス

Mitsubishi Estate Co., Ltd.
Hiroo Nanjo (Atelier Nanjo Inc.) / DAIHO Co., Ltd.

表通りから一歩奥まった角地という恵まれた立地条件。周辺は交通量が少なく、閑静な住環境が保たれている。都市の喧噪を忘れる穏やかな住環境に調和する建築造形。清楚な雰囲気のなかにも、「個」の集合体をイメージさせるモダンな外観デザイン。凹凸を付けた精妙な建築を施すことで、「パークハウス用賀コートレジデンス」ならではの斬新なプロポーションを構築している。その斬新なフォルムをよりモダンな建築へと高めていくために、建物のテクスチャーにこだわっている。エントランスウォールには表情豊かな割肌に黒雲母が点在する粘板岩を、ボーダータイルには重量感のある風合いを持つ割肌タイルを、外壁にはスタイリッシュな印象を与える質感豊かなホワイトタイルを採用し、シャープな印象を醸すガラス素材も多用。これらの上質な素材と外観デザインの融合により、歳月とともに味わいを深めていく低層住宅がつくりだされた。

The site is conveniently located on the corner a street back from the main street. There is not so much traffic in the neighborhood, which contributes to the quiet living environment. The form of the building is in harmony with the comfortable residential area where one can forget about the hustle and bustle of the city. The modern exterior design suggests that the building is a collection of "individual" units in this neat atmosphere. The carefully designed irregular form contributes to realization of the brand-new design with proportion unique to the "Park House Yoga Court Residence". In order to enhance a sense of modernity of the unique form, we also paid special attention to the texture of the building. The entrance wall employs clay stone dotted with biotite on its impressive chopped face; chopped face tiles with a massive texture are used as border tiles; white tiles with a texture giving a stylish image covers the exterior walls; in addition, glass materials to give a well-defined impression are used in various positions. The result of the integration of these quality materials and designs is this low-rise condominium that increases its charm with a passage of time.

1

1
エントランスアプローチ：洗練された街並みに調和する斬新な外観
Entrance approach: A radical exterior in harmony with the sophisticated townscape

1	3
2	4

1
独創的な空間設計により光が射し込むよう工夫された玄関ホール
Entrance hall to let natural light in, thanks to original spatial design

2
リビング・ダイニングの広がりを際立たせる大型出窓カウンター
Large counter tops and bay windows to highlight the expansion of the living-dining space

3
ナチュラルな素材感を持つウォールナットをフローリングに用いた、モダンなリビング・ダイニング
Modern living-dining room having flooring of walnut with a natural texture

4
ダイニングからリビングを臨む。二つの大きな窓は光庭から招く自然光を採り込み、開放的な雰囲気を演出する
Living space seen from the dining area. Two large windows take in the natural light, producing an open atmosphere.

073

従来の箱型の間取りではなく、光庭を取り囲むように空間をレイアウトしたL字型の間取りを採用。これは、ワイドフローンテージがあるからこそ実現できたユニット形状。L字型の間取りが居住空間に「採光性」「開放性」「プライバシー」の快適性能のクオリティをもたらした。心地よい住まいであるために必要な条件を十分に満たしてくれる、集合住宅の新しいカタチです。

Instead of the conventional box-type layout, we adopted the L-shaped one to surround the light court. This became possible thanks to the wide frontage of the building. The L-shaped layout brought a high level of quality comfort of "daylighting", "openness", and "privacy". The design presents a new shape of condominium to satisfy every requirement for comfortable living.

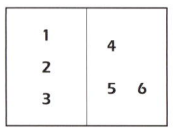

1	4	
2		
3	5	6

1
アウトドアリビングとしても使えるタイル敷きのテラス
Tiled terrace that can be used as outside living room

2
フレキシブルに活用できるコンサバトリー
Conservatory for flexible use

3
コンサバトリーに面していて、空間連続性に配慮した洋室
Western-style room next to the conservatory with consideration given to the continuity of the spaces

4
シンプルなデザインを貫いたベッドルーム
Bedroom with a consistently simple design

5
パウダールーム
Powder room

6
清潔な印象と使いやすさを重視したキッチン
Kitchen with a clean and neat impression and emphasis on usability

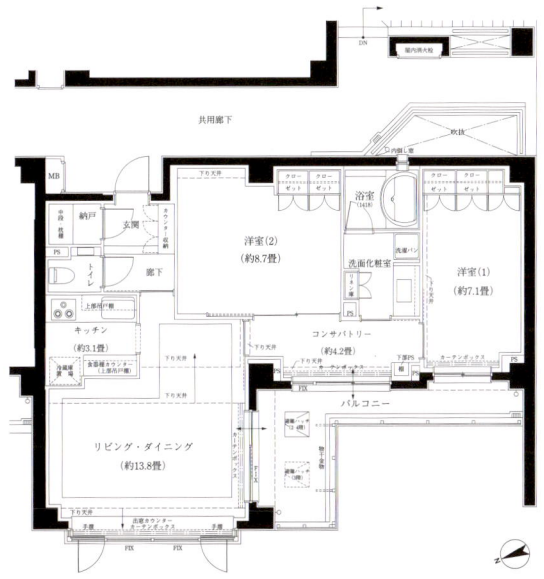

Data

Title
  Park House Yoga Court Residence
Developer
  Mitsubishi Estate Co., Ltd.
Design Supervision
  Hiroo Nanjo (Atelier Nanjo Inc.)
Architect
  DAIHO Co., Ltd.
Location
  Yoga, Setagaya-ku, Tokyo
Site area
  1,755.02m^2
Building area
  840.55m^2
Total floor area
  2,684.21m^2
Structure
  RC
Completion
  February, 2006
Materials
  Exterior Wall :
    ceramic 45x90tile, boder tile
    sprayed coating
  Public Wall :
    clay stone, boder tile
  Public Floor :
    granite
  Interior Wall :
    vinyl cloth
  Interior Floor :
    marble, flooring

Promenade Ogikubo No.2,3,5
プロムナード荻窪 2,3,5号棟
Urban Renaissance Agency Tokyo Office
Takao Endo Architect Office

古い街の中に新しい街をつくるということは、周辺の街と新しい街の要素の関係性を計ることだと考えています。具体的に、この街を構成する要素は福祉施設、商業施設、民間が事業主体の分譲、賃貸集合住宅、立体駐車場、そして、都市再生機構の賃貸集合住宅とその中に計画された保育園と学童クラブ等です。それらの中、特に都市再生機構の集合住宅では高層の集合住宅と、戸建住宅的な3戸の賃貸住宅が計画されています。この戸建的な住宅は、大きなスケールの建物が多い中で、少し様相の異なるヒューマンなスケールを持った建物になっていますが、街並にスケールの変化を与え、調子を変え、街に対して閉じながら開く3軒の連続住宅として計画しました。この5号棟の街に対する表情は、波型の亜鉛合金板とプロフィリットを用い、全体をグレーにまとめ、意図的に対立調和の手法を用い、街にストレスを与え、異化された空間によって全体を引き締める役割を担っています。道路から各住戸の玄関へのアプローチは、プランの違いなどから個別性のある計画になっています。この計画では内側に中庭を設け、吹抜けやトップライトを多用し、プロフィリットの活用もあり、明るい空間の中に意外性があり、かつ住まいの安全が守られる開放的な住戸が生まれています。3住戸のプランは全部異なり、屋上庭園も各自の好みによって使い方に工夫が出来る計画になっています。

Creating a new town in an old town means balancing the relationship between the elements of the surrounding town and those of the new town. To be concrete, after implementing this project, the town comprises of welfare facilities, commercial facilities, condominiums for sales and rent built by private sector, multi-story car parks, and planned condominiums for rent with a day nursery/children's club built by the Urban Renaissance Agency. The condominiums by the Agency were to include a high-rise residential building and three townhouse-like residential buildings for rent. These human-scaled, independent-house-like residences are slightly different from other large-scale buildings and give variations of scales and rhythms to the townscape; they were planned as a series of three residential buildings that are both open and closed to the town. The design expression of this 5th building has a role to give a stress on the townscape and create a tense atmosphere with the differentiated space by employing waved zinc alloy boards and Profilit structural glass, using the basic color of gray, and intentionally applying the method of contrasting harmony. The approaches from the road to the entrances of the individual units are not identical because their plans are different. In this project, inner gardens are provided, and open ceilings and top light as well as Profilit glass are fully used, so the dwelling units are safe and secure yet have an approachable feel and give a sense of unpredictability in the well-lit spaces. All the three units have different plans, and the rooftop gardens can be customized depending on the residents' tastes.

1
立体駐車場の屋上が緑に囲まれた子供達の遊び場になっている
The rooftops of the multi-story car parks are children's playgrounds surrounded by the green.

2
防災公園に向かって延びる南プロムナードに既存の緑と松かさをイメージしたオブジェのある風景
A view of the southern promenade extended to the disaster prevention park, having the existing trees and an art object suggesting a pineal

3
プロフィリットガラスによって歩道を歩く人々の視線を遮りながら、採光や街の様子を何となく楽しめる計画になっている
In the plan, lighting and a view of the town can casually be enjoyed while the lines of sights of passers-by are shut off by the Profilit glass.

4
亜鉛合金板とプロフィリットガラスの幅の違いは、内部の空間の場所毎の性格の違いを表している
Different widths between the zinc alloy boards and Profilit structural glass represent those of the characteristics of the individual inner spaces.

1	2	3
	4	

| 1 | 2 | 5 |
| 3 | 4 | |

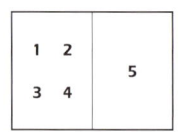

1
高層棟の1階玄関ロビーのコーナー
Corner of the entrance lobby on the first floor of one of the high-rise residential buildings

2
3戸連続の長屋（5号棟）の中住戸リビングの吹抜け
Open ceiling of the living room in the central unit of the three town houses (No. 5)

3
バーベキューを楽しんだり、花や緑も育てられる中住戸屋上空間
Rooftop space where one can enjoy barbecuing and gardening to grow plants and flowers

4
7m上からトップライトの光が降り注ぐ便所
Bathroom well lit by the top light at seven meters high

5
高層棟和室集会所から庭を臨む
A view of the garden seen from the Japanese-style assembly room of the high-rise building

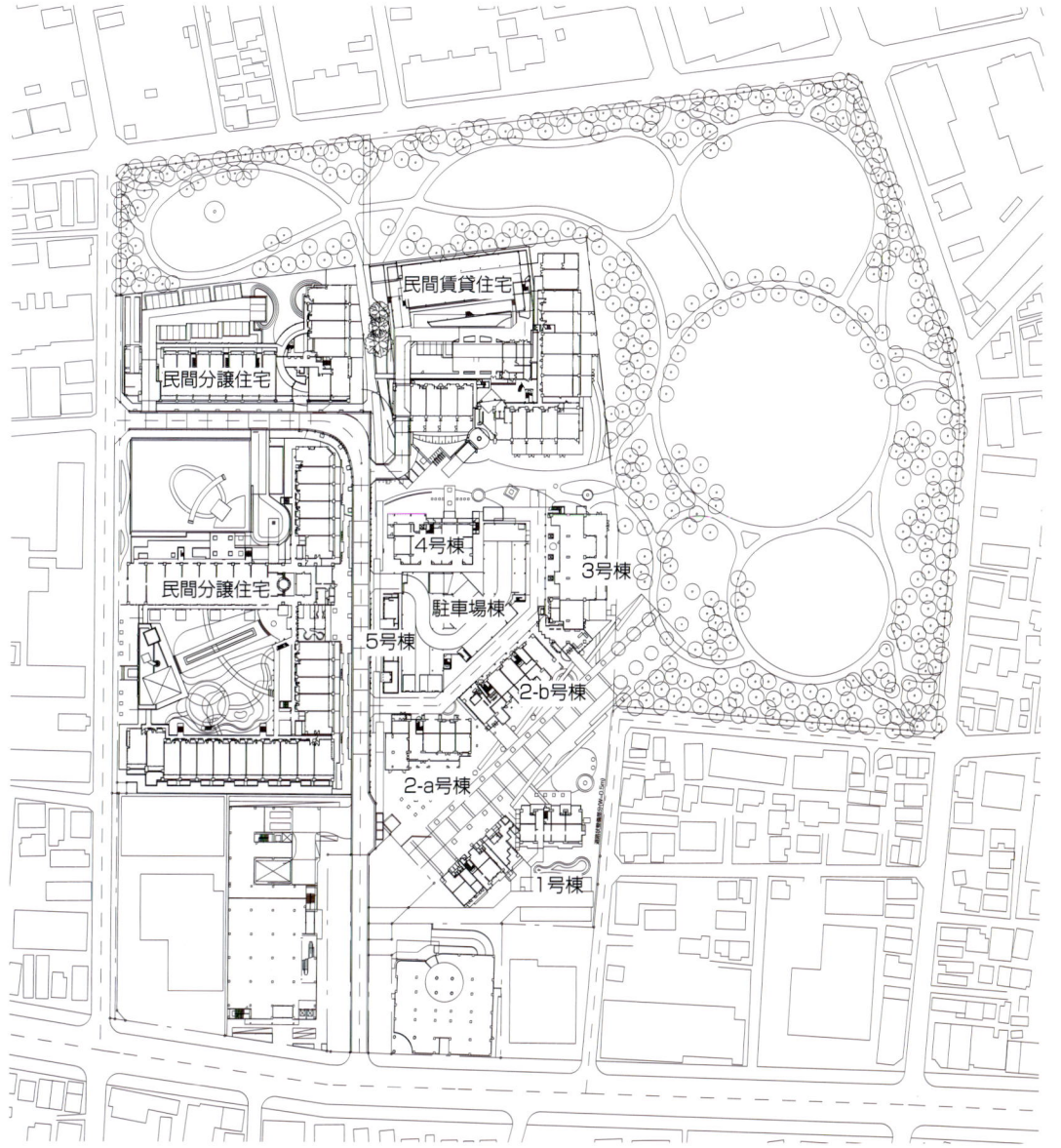

Data

Title
  Promenade Ogikubo No.2,3,5

Architect
  Urban Renaissance Agency Tokyo Office
  Takao Endo Architect Office

Location
  Suginami-ku, Tokyo

Site area
  15428.30m²

Building area
  5,609.01m²
  No.2 : 1,236.81m²
  No.3 : 949.48m²,
  No.5 : 168.94m²

Total floor area
  34,223.53m²
  No.2 : 10,881.13m²
  No.3 : 6,782.2m²
  No.5 : 283.53m²

Area
  No.2 : 46.33-93.79m²
  No.3 : 44.79-98.70m²
  No.5 : 91.64-98.89m²

Structure
  No.2 : reinforced concrete wall-frame
  No.3 : reinforced concrete frame
  No.5 : reinforced concrete wall
      construction

Completion
  August, 2005

Materials
  Exterior Wall :
    zinc alloy corrugated sheet, red wood
    multi-layer wall emulsion coating for
    glossy textured finish
  Public Wall :
    rust stone (dabbed finish, J&P finish)
  Public Floor :
    rust stone (dabbed finish, J&P finish)
  Interior Wall :
    vinyl cloth
  Interior Floor :
    multi-layer flooring

Photo
  Seiichi Ohsawa (Shinkenchiku-sha)

Chaleur Higashi Toyonaka B zone
シャレール東豊中B工区
Urban Renaissance Agency KANSAI Office / Takao Endo Architect Office

東豊中第一団地は建設されてからすでに40年以上経過し、住戸の広さや設備の社会的劣化や、エレベーターのない中層住棟と高齢者の居住等、種々の問題を解決すべく、建替が行われている団地である。この街の骨格は団地の北側を走る道路に面し、この団地の建設後に生まれた商業施設群や、幼稚園等との連続一体性を考慮しようと考えている「交流軸」と、旧千里丘陵の一部を形成していたドングリ山、きのこ山等、この団地の自然の緑を豊かに残している南北に延びる「自然軸」と、計画地のほぼ中央に東西に配置された芝生の緑と、その両サイドで1人1棟ずつの住棟設計を担当し、建築家のアイデンティティーの連鎖によって街並を形成しようと考えている「景観軸」によって、全体の骨格が形成されている。本計画は、これら3つの軸によって構成された、計画地の一番北側に面するBゾーンであるが、このゾーンは特に北側道路に面するこの場所に、5階建の既設棟よりもはるかに大きく育ったメタセコイヤの片側並木もあり、高低差のある敷地的条件も加え、この団地の北西の玄関を形成する住棟群として計画が進められた。この団地全体の計画手法は、多数の建築家によるコラボレーションから生まれる多様さと、先述の3つの軸と、敷地の高低差と、メタセコイヤの緑等によって、新しい団地の個性を形成し、外側の一般市街地とも共生する計画を目指している。

More than 40 years have passed since the 1st Higashi Toyonaka Housing Complex was completed. Rebuilding is now underway in order to address many challenges of the existing buildings including small units, outdated facilities, medium-rise buildings without elevator, and lack of designs for elderly citizens. The framework of this residential block comprises of the "exchange axis" to establish continuity and integrity with the kindergarten, commercial facilities built after the completion of the original complex and facing the road running to the north of the complex, etc.; the "nature axis" running from north to south of the area including Mt. Donguriyama and Mt. Kinokoyama which were once part of the old Senri Hills covered with rich green; and the "landscape axis" intended to form a landscape taking advantage of the eastern and western green lawns near the center of the site and the residential buildings to be constructed on the sides of these lawns. All the buildings were designed by different architects, and the combination of their unique styles also contributes to the landscape formation. This project is for the Zone B facing the north end of the site constituted by the above-described three axes. In consideration of the existing single row of Metasequoia trees which are higher than the 5-story existing buildings and difference in elevation, the new condominiums are planned to serve as the northern entrance of the complex. The goal of the planning method applied to the complex in general is establishment of diversity thanks to collaboration by many architects, characterization of the renewed housing complex taking advantage of the said three axes, elevation difference and green of Metasequoia trees, and formation of harmony with the urban districts surrounding the site.

	2	3	4
1		5	

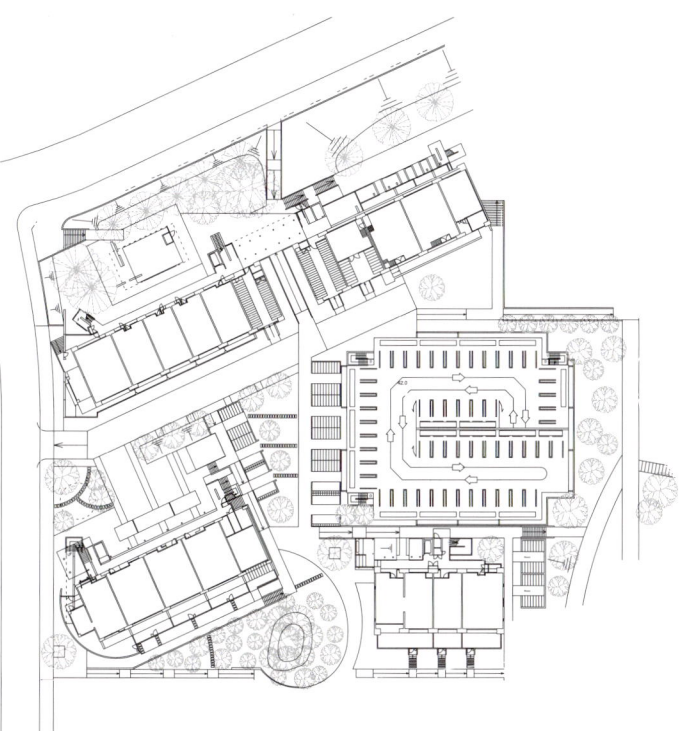

1
既存メタセコイヤの春夏秋冬の葉の色の変化と調和することを意図して、デザインされた道路沿いの住棟

Roadside residential buildings whose design was intended to match the changing colors of the existing Metasequoia trees through four seasons

2
身障者や高齢者用住戸の玄関の見える風景

A view with the entrances of the units for physically challenged persons and senior residents

3
2つの住棟の間に生まれたこの住宅地のサブエントランス風景

Sub-entrance to the site between two residential buildings

4
北側道路の歩道からサブの集会所等にアプローチするルート

Route to approach the sub-assembly facility from the northern road

5
既存の緑に囲まれたサブエントランスを北側道路沿いから臨む

Sub-entrance surrounded by the exiting green trees seen from the northern roadside

Data

Title
Chaleur Higashi Toyonaka B zone

Developer
Urban Renaissance Agency KANSAI Office
Takao Endo Architect Office

Location
Toyonaka city, Osaka

Site area
12,146.43m² (B zone)

Building area
3,954.31m² (B zone)

Total floor area
16,369.62m² (B zone)

Area
37.42-112.84m²

Structure
RC

Completion
October, 2004

Materials
Exterior Wall :
  mastic on concrete placing
  sprayed coating on architectural
  concrete, ceramic tile in part
Interior Wall :
  vinyl cloth
Interior Floor :
  flooring

Photo
Yoshiharu Matsumura

Park House Daizawa Place
パークハウス代沢プレイス

Mitsubishi Estate Co., Ltd.
Hiroo Nanjo (Atelier Nanjo Inc.) / Norihide Imagawa

代沢は、欅の大樹がそこかしこで緑陰を描く落ち着きのある住宅地でありながら、下北沢、三宿、三軒茶屋などを生活圏にする街。建物と外構のデザインにあたっては、この土地の持つ伝統と先進という異なる要素をいかに住まいとして昇華できるかが考えられている。街並みの調和という命題には、この地の歴史と共に年輪を重ねてきた既存樹を、建物の顔であるエントランスアプローチに保存することで具現化。さらに味わいのある庭石を選び、空間をより潤い高く演出している。現代の建物としての美しさという命題には、TWFS工法（厚肉床壁構造）の良さを最大限に活かしたシャープなデザインを外観に施し応えている。また、この二つの主題が相反することなく、ひとつの建物としての存在感と心地よさを創出するための意匠、配慮を随所に施している。柱がなく梁も最小限に留めた躯体は、住空間に広がりを与え、豊かな陽光を取り込むと共に、建物のフォルムもすっきりとさせている。空へと続くかのような真っ直ぐなラインを描く住戸間の壁面には、特注のタイルを用いることでシャープさの中にも温かみも加味。さらに、ガラスを用いたバルコニーを基軸に水平ラインを側面にも連続させ、より明るい住空間と建物の落ち着きを創出している。街並みをさらに美しく描く外観の佇まいと、心地よさに包まれた私空間の融合。新しい時代の代沢が求めた住まいの姿がここにある。

Daizawa is a quiet residential area where large, old zelkova trees give shades here and there, but its livelihood zone includes cool areas like Shimokitazawa, Mishuku, and Sangenzyaya. In designing the building and its exterior, due consideration has been given to how contrasting factors of tradition and advancedness can be integrated into a single condominium. To solve the proposition of matching the building with the atmosphere of the neighborhood, the existing trees that have been grown with the history of the area are preserved at the entrance approach serving as the face of the building. Further, garden stones with a rustic charm are selected to give a sense of richness to the space. As for the challenge of creating the beauty as a modern piece of architecture, well-defined designs are applied to the exterior, fully taking advantage of the TWFS (Thick Wall and Floor Structure) construction method. Wherever appropriate, designs and considerations are given to emphasize a sense of the presence of the building and a feeling of comfort without making these two themes contradictory. The structure without columns and with the minimum number of beams gives a sense of expansion in the living spaces, admits rich sunlight, and makes the form of the building cleanly styled. The exterior walls between the dwelling units that draw straight lines toward the sky use custom-made tiles to add a sense of warmth to the sharp-looking exterior. Further, based on the balconies using glass, horizontal lines are extended to the sides of the building, realizing better-lit living spaces and an impression matching the neighborhood. The exterior to beautify the townscape is integrated with the private spaces of comfort. This is the ideal shape of residence in Daizawa in the new age.

	2
1	3
	4

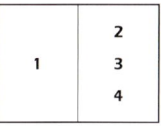

1
シャープさに温かみと伸びやかさを融合し誇れるデザインに昇華した外観
Sharp-looking exterior integrated with a sense of warmth and expansion, resulting in a design one can be proud of

2
大樹を保存したエントランスアプローチ
Entrance approach with the large trees preserved

3
優しい景観と明るい住空間に配慮した西側の外構デザイン
The exterior design on the west side of the building, giving consideration to unobtrusive appearance and well-lit residential spaces

4
美しさに味わいを秘めて未来へと時を紡ぐエントランス
Entrance with a beauty and a style looking toward the future

Data

Title
  Park House Daizawa Place
Developer
  Mitsubishi Estate Co., Ltd.
Design Supervision
  Hiroo Nanjo (Atelier Nanjo Inc.)
Structural Design
  Norihide Imagawa
Location
  Setagaya-ku, Tokyo
Site area
  3,243.99m²
Building area
  1,554.86m²
Total floor area
  7,744.23m²
Structure
  RC
Completion
  February, 2007
Materials
  Exterior Wall :
    ceramic tile, stoneware tile
    sprayed coating in part
  Public Wall :
    stone, DI-NOC sheet
  Public Floor :
    450x450 ceramic tile
  Interior Wall :
    vinyl cloth

ADENIUM Kichijoji

アデニウム吉祥寺

Joint Corporation Co., Ltd. / Masaki Nakane (Media For Space Inc.)
Masahiro Mino (Penta-Ocean Construction Co., Ltd.)

アジアン・アイデンティティ。それがこの「アデニウム吉祥寺」のコンセプトとなっている。アジアンリゾートにあふれる水や緑や装飾、そしてオリエンタルな空気感によって、アジア古来の原風景を吉祥寺に再現する。あるがままの自然の森を再現した生命感あふれるアジアンガーデンや数々の施設によって癒しを提供する"住まいの楽園"。生命感やスピリチュアルな雰囲気いっぱいの自然を切り撮った"楽園"。この二つの楽園コンセプトが共鳴することによって、より深い癒しの生活を愉しめる。外観ファサードは周辺地域と調和した落ち着いた色調・デザインとし、一歩敷地内に踏み込むと、アジアのリゾートホテルのような上質で落ち着いた空間が広がる。そして趣ある設えによってエキゾチックな雰囲気を創り出すと同時に、どこかノスタルジーを感じさせるような空間を創造している。また、自然素材での造形にこだわった中庭を配置し、豊かな自然の中に建物が共存共栄するイメージを打ち出している。有機的デザインを基調に、道と植栽のエッジがボーダレスになるよう潅木をかぶせたり、道を意図的に迂回させたり、幅をランダムにするなど、アジア的な自然の癒し空間を創出している。豊かな緑と陰影、そして澄んだ水が流れ、香しい風がそよぐ上質なる別世界。そこに一歩足を踏み入れるとONからOFFへ瞬時にスイッチが切り替わる、まさしく「大人の隠れ家」的な癒しの住まい。

An Asian identity. It is the concept of Adenium Kichijoji. The Asian landscape dear to one's heart is reproduced in the land of Kichijoji by taking advantage of water, green and decor arrangements suggesting Asian resorts and an oriental atmosphere. The condominium is a "residence as paradise" offering a sense of healing with a lively Asian garden with natural woods and many other unique facilities. It also is a "paradise" adopted from nature full of a sense of being alive and spirituality. These two "paradise" concepts are coordinated to enable a life with profound healing effects. The exterior facade has an unobtrusive texture and design, and one step into the site, one will find a quality space with a sense of comfort, suggesting that of an Asian resort hotel. The furnishings give an exotic flavor in the space having a touch of nostalgia. The inner garden focused on natural materials is provided to give an impression that the building coexists with the rich nature. Based on the organic design, an Asian healing space abundant with nature is created by, for example, shrubs making the borders between passages and planting ambiguous, intentionally curving approaches, and paths with different widths. It is like in a different world rich in green and light and shade, with clear water running and a gentle breeze blowing. Once inside, one immediately feels as if one were on vacation, off business. It is a residence that heals, a hideaway for adults.

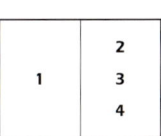

	2
1	3
	4

1
風情ある四阿とそのまわりに広がる「憩いの広場」
Arbor with a refined elegance, and the "plaza of relaxation" around it

2
エントランス：穏やかな表情の石積みが導く、上質で洗練された楽園生活への入口。夜は柔らかな光が灯り、優美な佇まいで住まう人を迎える
Entrance: Soft stone blocks and masonry leading to the doorway to the high quality, sophisticated life in paradise. Lit by soothing light at night, it welcomes residents with its elegant appearance.

3
オープンコリドー：光の柱が導く、セミオープンの回廊。水辺越しの緑とせせらぎの水音、頬を撫でる微風が深い安らぎを演出する
Open corridor: Semi-open corridor led by columns of light. The green beyond the waterside, a murmur of running water, and a breeze touching one's face bring a profound sense of comfort.

4
敷地配置図
Site Plan

1	3
2	4
	5

1
エントランスホール：オープンコリドーを臨み、吹抜が高々と広がる開放的な空間。独特のシャンデリアがエキゾチックな雰囲気を醸し出す
Entrance hall: Facing the open corridor, this open space has a high open ceiling. Uniquely shaped chandeliers give an exotic atmosphere.

2
ガーデンラウンジ：アジアンガーデンを臨みながら語らいのひとときが持てる2層吹抜の開放的な空間
Garden lounge: Open space with a two-story open ceiling, enabling one to have a time of enjoying conversation looking at the Asian garden

3
ガーデンラウンジからオープンコリドーを臨む
Open corridor from the garden lounge

4
自然の清流を思わせる爽やかな「緑のせせらぎ」：木々の間をぬい迎賓の庭へと続く水の流れや、水面にきらめく光やせせらぐ音で癒しの空気をつくる
Stream in green reminding one of a clear limpid stream: An atmosphere of comfort created by water running among the trees and leading up to the garden to welcome guests and sparkling light on the water and its murmur

5
ゲストルーム：リゾートホテルをイメージしたホスピタリティあふれる空間。大切なお客様を心地よくもてなし、癒しの空気で包み込む
Guestroom: Space full of hospitality based on an image of a resort hotel, serving important guests with a sense of comfort and relaxation.

Data

Title
 ADENIUM Kichijoji

Developer
 Joint Corporation Co., Ltd.

Design / Design Supervision
 Masaki Nakane (Media For Space Inc.)

Architect
 Masahiro Mino
  (Penta-Ocean Construction Co., Ltd.)

Location
 Mitaka city, Tokyo

Site area
 9,566.34m²

Building area
 3,873.09m²

Total floor area
 21,668.69m²

Structure
 RC+S

Completion
 March, 2007

Materials
 Exterior Wall :
  stone, spray painting, 45x90 tile
  boder tile
 Public Wall :
  stone, spray painting, 45x90 tile
 Public Floor :
  stone

Comfortable Monsoon-type

コンフォータブル・モンスーン・タイプ

Masaki Nakane (Media For Space Inc.)

繊細なる美意識、気品が漂う美空間。自然に家族が集まり、温かなひと時がはじまる団欒のスペース。自分だけの自由を愉しむ個の領域。それを両立させつつ、「住まい」というひとつの空間として総合し、生活のあらゆるシーンに上質な寛ぎと豊かさを満たす。

The condominium offers a delicate sense of beauty and a space of elegant beauty. It is a space to settle in the pleasures of a happy home. The private area to enjoy one's freedom for oneself. These factors are integrated to form a "residence", filling every scene of life with quality relaxation and richness.

	2	3
1	4	
	5	

1
落ち着いた色使いや素材で仕上げたリビング・ダイニングルーム
Living-dining room finished with well-matched colors and materials

2
上質な美しさのある廊下
Corridor with quality beauty

3
気品漂うパウダールーム
Elegant powder room

4
開放感のある癒しのベッドルーム
Bedroom with a sense of openness and healing

5
書斎
Study room

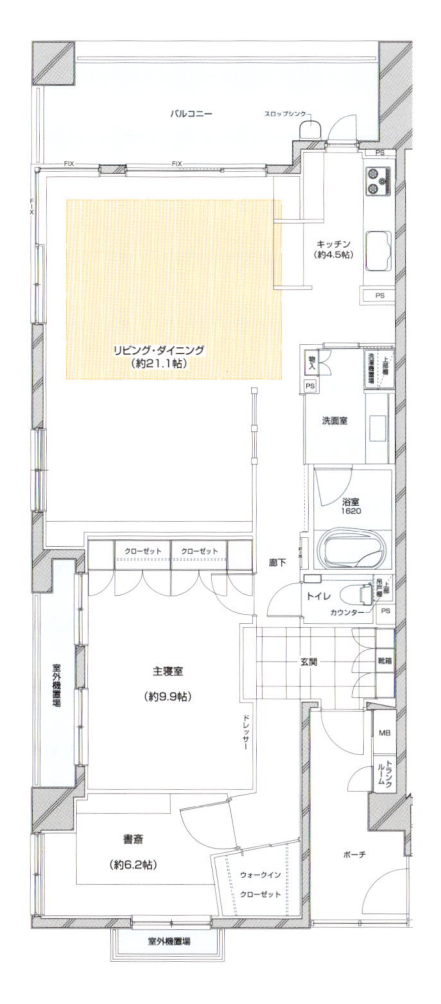

Data

Title
　Comfortable Monsoon-type

Designer
　Masaki Nakane (Media For Space Inc.)

Area
　102.07m²

Materials
　Interior Wall :
　　vinyl cloth
　Interior Floor :
　　flooring

Lohas Clear-type
ロハス・クリア・タイプ
Einan Takeshita (MITSUI Designtec Co., Ltd.)

寛ぎと食のシーンを広々とゆとりある空間に一体化し、家族の絆を強く紡ぐ巧みな空間構成。また語らいを愉しみながら料理の腕を揮うこまやかな配慮など、平穏という贅に満ちた上質で優美なる私空間。

The carefully designed, extensive space integrates the scenes of comfort and dining, strengthening the family ties. This selected private space of elegance is full of luxury named tranquility including delicate consideration to enable one to show cooking ability while chatting.

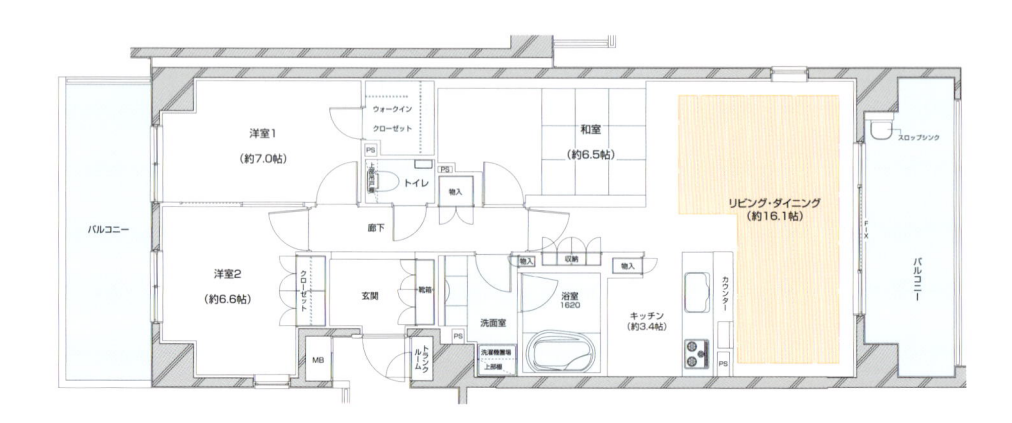

1
自然素材をあしらった柔らかで暖かみのある空間
Soft and warm space using natural materials

2
モダンな和室：隣の部屋とのパーティションにもなっている造作棚を臨む
Modern Japanese room: Furnished shelves also serving as a partition from an adjacent room

3
ダイニングからリビング、和室を臨む
Living and Japanese style rooms seen from the dining space

4
リビングルーム
Living room

5
広々としたバルコニー
Extensive balcony

Data

Title
  Lohas Clear-type

Designer
  Einan Takeshita
    (MITSUI Designtec Co., Ltd.)

Area
  87.74m²

Materials
  Interior Wall :
    vinyl cloth
  Interior Floor :
    flooring

Izumigaoka Garden Hills JIOUZEN
泉ヶ丘ガーデンヒルズJIOUZEN

Matsumoto Komuten Co.,Ltd.
M.I.B Co., Ltd. / Takushi Kodama (Archiwerk)

多くの人が、金沢に愛着を感ずるのは、ほどよく、めりはりの利いた春夏秋冬があるからだろう。いま都市に暮らす人にとって必要な条件は、鮮やかな自然と、洗練された都市のリズム。この二つに着目したとき、あらためて住みやすさを教えてくれる街がある。旧鶴来街道沿いの由緒ある金沢の住宅街。泉ヶ丘一丁目界隈は今でも金沢らしい佇まいを残す数少ない立地。そんな風格のある土地を背景に佇む品格ある住宅。日本の集合住宅は、欧米諸国の住宅の追従ではじまった。ところが、昨今になって、日本の住宅環境を逆に、欧米がマネるケースが出ている。最初に実行したのは個人主義のフランス人で、彼らはそれを「TATAMIZE」と表現した。日本人の情緒豊かな生活様式こそ緊張したいまの時代に、絶対不可欠と判断したのだろう。「TATAMIZE」とは、ぬくもりとゆとりを機能性でレイアウトした究極のプライベートルーム。上質で居心地のいい空間に仕上がったリビング・ダイニングやぬくもりとゆとりにあふれたベッドルームなど快適なマンションライフを堪能できる。やはり豊かさの本質は、凝った作りよりも、もてなす心や気配りの作りにあるのだろう。

Many people feel attached to Kanazawa probably because the town has moderate yet varied four seasons. Modern urban residents require both vivid nature and sophisticated rhythms of cities. When we focus on these two elements, we come to notice an area that shows us what comfort ability of living is: residential neighborhood along the old Tsurugi street in Kanazawa. This neighborhood in Izumigaoka 1-chome is one of the few areas where the historical townscape of Kanazawa still remains. The condominium with a sense of dignity is built with such a land of elegance and splendor. Condominiums in Japan started by following the Western style ones. But in recent years, the Western architects has started to imitate the Japanese residential styles. The first was a people of individualism, Frenchmen, and they called it "TATAMIZE". It appears that they thought it necessary to adopt Japanese atmosphere should be indispensable for the modern age of tension. "TATAMIZE" is the ultimate private room having a functional layout with warmth and comfort, enabling one to enjoy a pleasant condominium life, thanks to a living-dining room finished as a quality, relaxing space and an extensive bedroom. The essence of richness should lie in our heart of welcome and delicate consideration rather than the elaborate design.

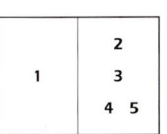

1
東北面外観
Exterior on the northeastern side

2
品格のあるエントランスアプローチ
Entrance approach with a sense of dignity

3
エントランスホールから連なる、広々としたラウンジ
Entrance hall leading to this extensive lounge

4
風情ある竹林の中庭
Inner garden in the bamboo forest with a refined elegance

5
フロストガラスの手摺りを配し、さり気なく視界に配慮した南側外観
Southern exterior employing frosted glass railings with nonchalant consideration for the view

1
ホスピタリティー（心からのもてなし）が感じられるリビング・ダイニング
Living-dining room with warmth and hospitality

2
ダイニング・キッチン
Dining kitchen

3
TATAMIZE：世間の雑音を追い出し、プライバシーに守られた空間
TATAMIZE: Purely private space to escape the hustles and bustles of the world

4
洗面室・バスルーム
Toilet room and bathroom

5
デザインと機能を重視した使い勝手の良いキッチン
Easy-to-use kitchen putting priority to design and functionality

6
ぬくもりとゆとりにあふれた寝室
Bedroom with warmth and comfort

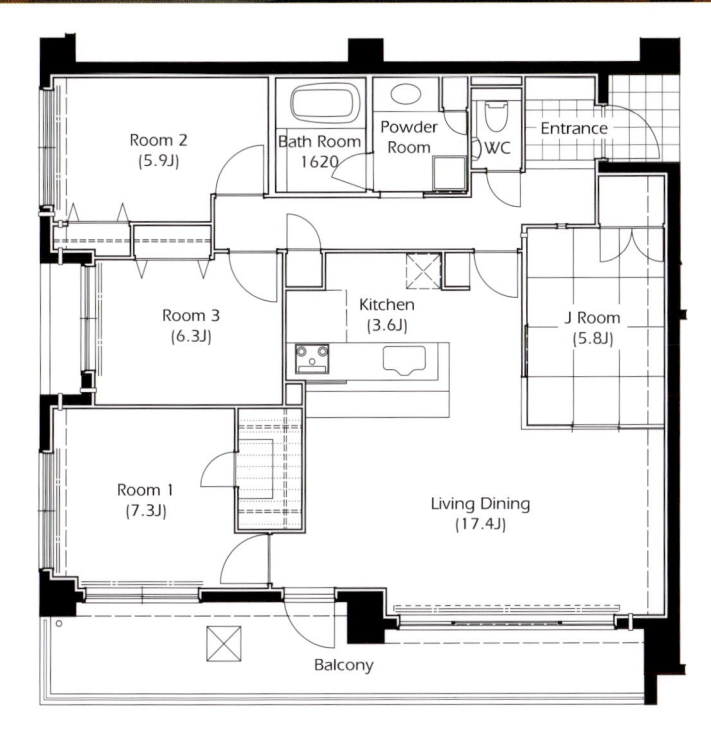

Data

Title
Izumigaoka Garden Hills JIOUZEN

Developer
Matsumoto Komuten Co.,Ltd.
M.I.B Co., Ltd.

Architect
Takushi Kodama (Archiwerk)

Basic planning
Masaru Kimura (Artstation Co.,Ltd.)

Design Supervision
Youkou Umesawa

Location
Kanazawa city, Ishikawa

Site area
1540.05m²

Building area
1083.55m²

Total floor area
2935.49m²

Structure
RC

Completion
March, 2005

Materials
Exterior Wall :
227x60 tile, plasterer finish
Public Wall :
plasterer finish
Public Floor :
300x300 ceramic tile
Interior Wall :
vinyl cloth
Interior Floor :
ceramic tile, flooring

VERTIQUE Sumiyoshigawa
ヴェルティーク住吉川
Jun Setomoto

この敷地は、さまざまな時代を映しながら邸宅街の景観をかたちづくってきた六甲山から流れてくる、住吉川の清流沿いに位置する。灘中、灘高のグラウンドの南側でもある。敷地内の松並木の瑞々しい緑を生かすことから、この２つのアールをもつフォルムが必然的に生まれた。景観に対して、やわらかさを与え、かつ、お屋敷文化の住環境を受け継いだ、神戸スタイルの高級なデザインコードを提案することができた。閑静な風景と調和させるため、美術館（当事務所設計の世良美術館等）をイメージするような素材、色彩を使用した。このコンセプトが中庭の豊かなコミュニケーションが期待できるフィールド空間の芸術化につながった。パーゴラのある大きなデッキ空間、大きな水盤、自然広場などの周辺にオブジェアートを配し、回遊できる芸術広場として計画された、文化発信型の広場である。中庭の下は地下駐車場となっており、車と人の動線とを別の入口にし、かつ利便性を確保している。通りに面してはエントランス部の外にベンチコーナーを設置したり、ティールームのようなギャラリーホールを外から楽しめるように計画した。アート・光・風・川の音・木々・花の香、こんな五感を刺激する小さな魅力が人と人とをつなげ街を活性化することにつながればと考えている。

The site is located along a limpid stream of Sumiyoshi River running from Mount Rokko that has served as part of the landscape of this prime location and witnessed its history. It is also in the south of the ground of Nada Junior and Senior High School. The form with two curved exterior walls is a natural result when we attempted to preserve a row of fresh green pine trees on the site. The design provides the context of the given landscape with a sense of softness and inherits the essence of the living environment in the Japanese mansion culture. We could propose a high quality design code in a Kobe style. In order to make the building in harmony with the quiet scenery, employed are materials and colors that remind one of a museum (like Sera Art Gallery we designed). Thanks to this concept, the field space of the inner garden expected to be a place for rich communications became a work of art. Artistic objects are installed in and around the large deck space with a pergola, large fountain and nature plaza, and the inner garden is planned to be an art plaza for cultural transmission where one can enjoy promenading. The underground parking lot is under the plaza, but human and car traffic has different entrances with due consideration given to convenience. As to the side facing the street, an area with a bench outside the entrance is provided, and the tearoom-like gallery hall can be seen from the outside. Such small objects of attraction including works of art, light, wind, sound of running water, trees, and scent of flowers are expected to establish links among people and vitalize the town.

	2
1	3
	4

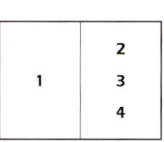

1
駐車場の上を利用した豊かな芸術空間の中庭
Inner garden as a rich art space, taking advantage of the roof of the parking lot

2
パーゴラを設けた水盤の前の開放的なデッキスペース
Open deck space before a fountain with a pergola

3
美術館をイメージさせるやわらかな曲線美の風貌
Softly curved contours that remind one of a museum

4
開放的な演出の中にアートを感じるエントランスホール
Entrance hall with a sense of art in an open atmosphere

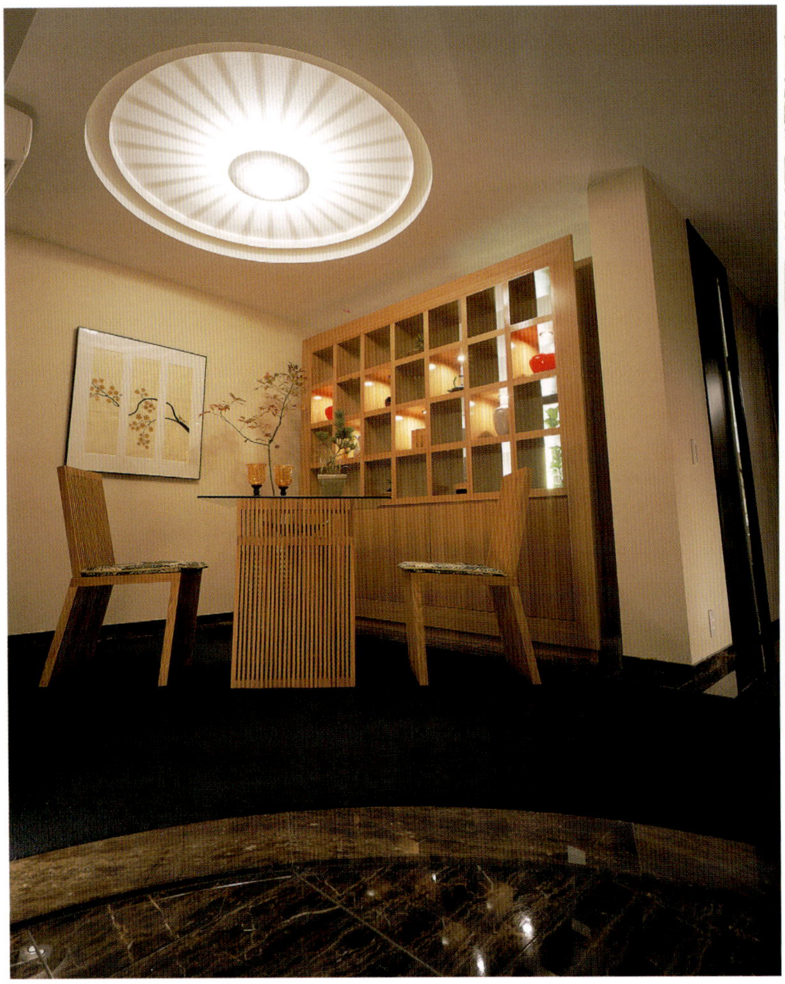

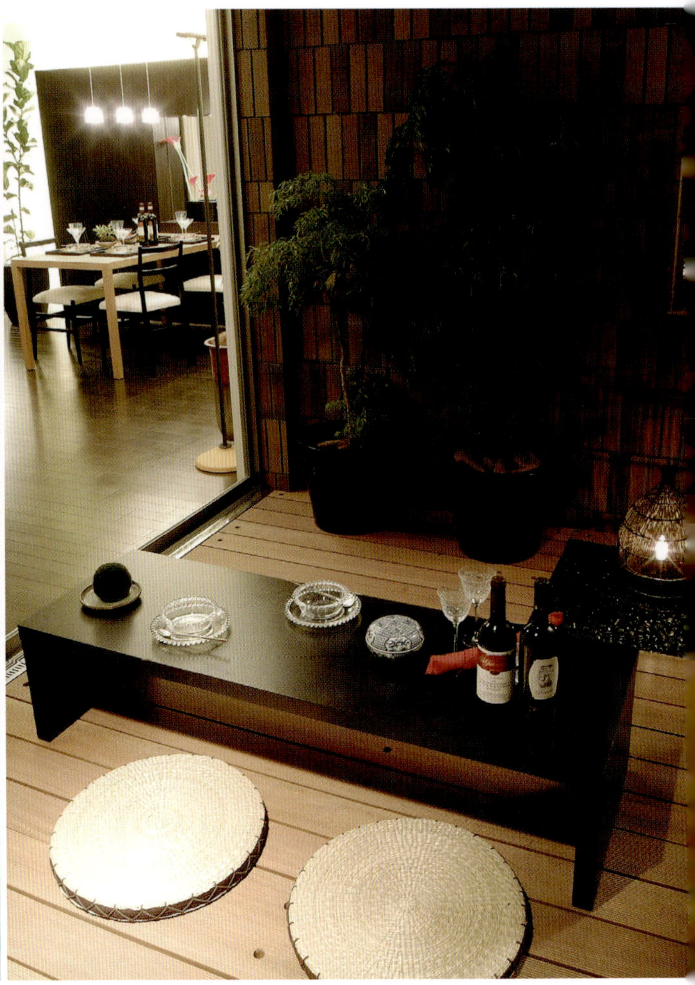

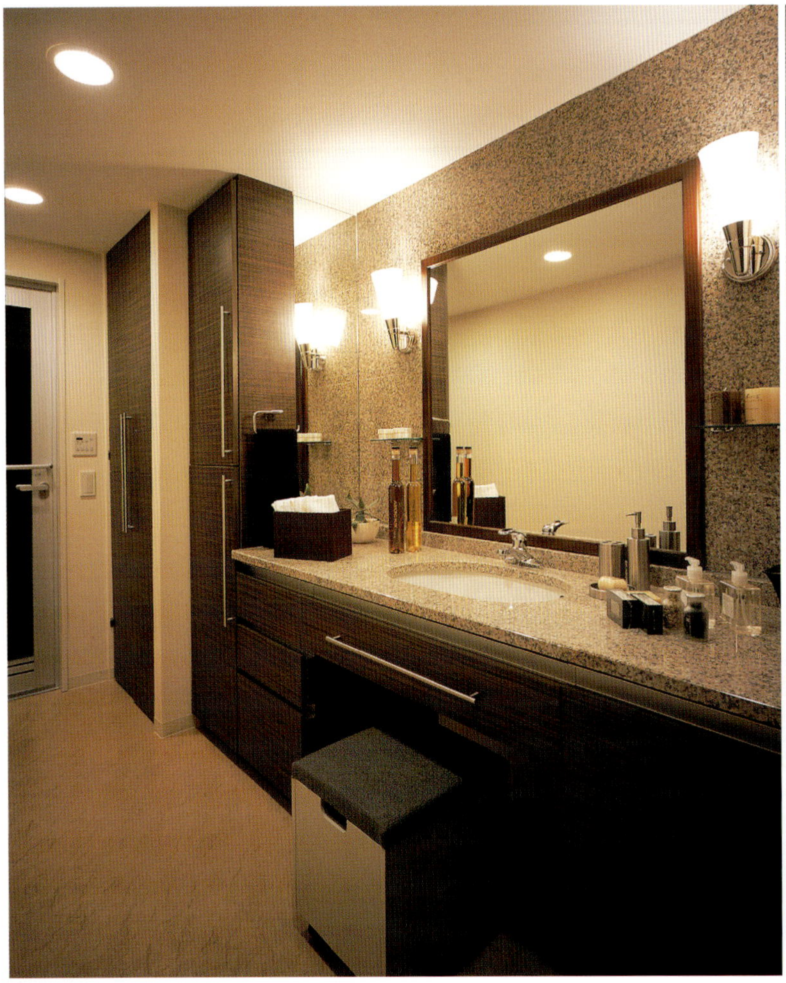

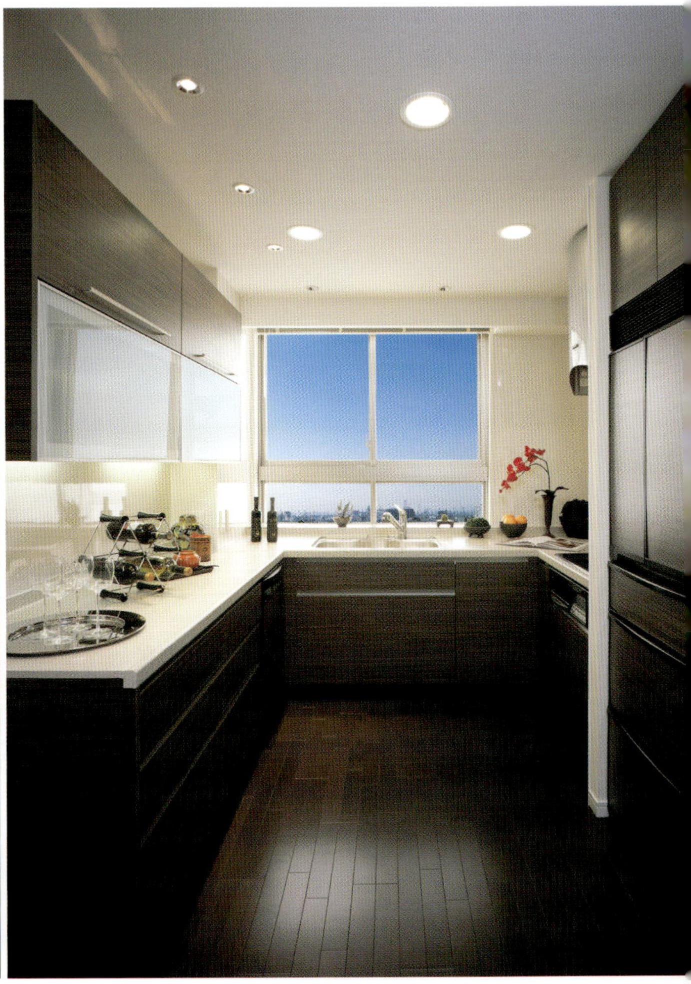

1	2	5
3	4	6

1
玄関ホールのしつらえ
Entrance hall furnishings

2
ゆとりのバルコニー
Extensive balcony

3
ホテルのパウダールームのような化粧室
Dressing room like a powder room of a high grade hotel

4
景色を楽しむビューキッチン
Kitchen with a view to enjoy

5
人が集い、語らうリビング・ダイニング
Living-dining where people gather and chat

6
玄関ホール
Entrance hall

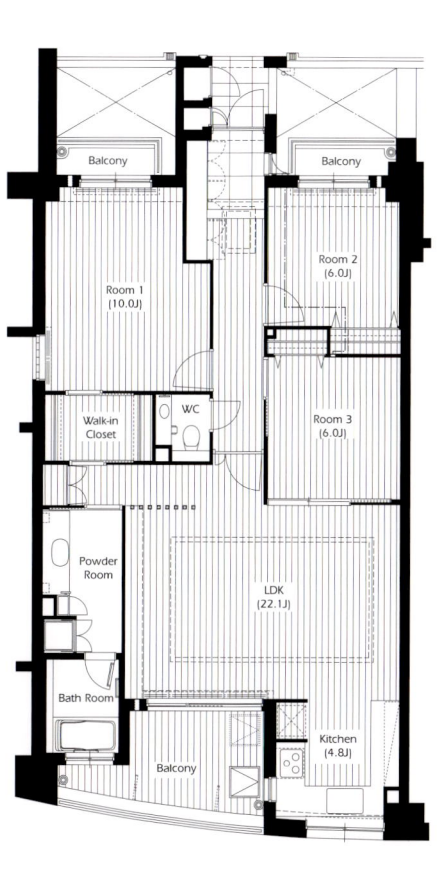

Data

Title
  VERTIQUE Sumiyoshigawa

Developer
  Wadakohsan Corporation

Architect
  Jun Setomoto

Location
  HigashiNada-ku, Kobe city, Hyogo

Site area
  2,092.28m²

Building area
  836.67m²

Total floor area
  4,444.09m²

Structure
  RC

Completion
  October, 2004

Materials
  Exterior Wall :
    227x60 tile, butt end tile, 45x90tile
    sprayed coating, architectural concrete
  Public Wall :
    227x60 tile, 25x25 mosaic
    mild plaster trowel finish
  Public Floor :
    300x300 tile, granite
  Interior Wall :
    cloth
  Interior Floor :
    marble, flooring

Photo
  Takashi Ehara (Ehara Photo Office)

Proud Minami-Ogikubo

プラウド南荻窪

Nomura Real Estate Development Co., Ltd.
Atelier G&B Co. / Obayashi Corporation

喧噪から一歩奥まった杉並の静地、南荻窪二丁目。交通量の少ない道路に三方向が面していて、低層住宅街の低邸宅として恵まれた正形の敷地条件が、開放感とプライバシー性をもたらす。4300㎡超の広い敷地があったからこそ可能になった、アトリウムガーデン（中庭）を中心とした、南面住戸の比率を高めるコの字型の配棟計画。二つの棟に間隔をつくり、中庭に面する住戸に豊かな通風と採光をもたらす。すべての空間に貫かれているコンセプトはオーセンティック&モダン。シャープな直線美を際立たせることにより外観の統一感を守りながら品格を主張しつつ、素材やテイストを部分的に変えることで表情に深みを創出している。さらに縦格子とスリット状のデザインされた細長い窓は落ち着いた街並みと響き合い、リズムとスケールを生み出している。内と外をやさしく繋ぐガラス素材の手摺り壁。駐車車両の目隠しとしては主に櫛引の意匠壁を採用。景観美を追求した外周の植栽。すべてが街並みと調和するための意匠となっている。素材のひとつひとつにこだわり、触れたときやふと目にとまったとき、自然の豊かさや温もりを身近に感じる事ができるように、本物が持つ手触りや風合いにこだわり、吟味している。「プラウド南荻窪」は街の顔となる邸宅のあるべき姿を静かに主張している。

Set back from the hustle and bustle of the city, Minami-Ogikubo 2-chome is a silent area in Suginami ward. The lot faces three streets with a little traffic, and this rich site condition for low-rise building gives a sense of openness and privacy at the same time. The project became possible thanks to the presence of a wide expansion of the site of more than 4,300m². A U-shaped building planning is adopted to surround the atrium (inner) garden in order to increase the number of units facing south. A wide space between the two buildings provides abundant ventilation and natural light for the dwelling units facing the inner garden. The keywords of the concept common for all the spaces are "authentic and modern". By highlighting the sharp linear beauty, while maintaining the integrity of appearances and emphasizing a sense of dignity, diversity of details through careful selection of materials and textures contributes to give a meaningful expression to the building. Slender windows designed with vertical grilles and slits make harmony with the quiet neighborhood, giving a sense of rhythm and scale. Glass balustrade wall connects the inside and outside of the building. As a screen for cars in the parking lot, designed walls of scratch finish are mainly employed. Planting to surround the lot pursues the scenic beauty. Everything is part of the design to harmonize with the townscape. Careful attention is paid to each and every material. Its selection is based on the genuine touch and texture so that when one touches or sees it, one could enjoy richness or warmth of nature close at hand. Proud Minami-Ogikubo tacitly shows the shape of residence to represent the town.

	2
1	3
	4

1
エントランスホール、または住戸から鑑賞するための中庭、アトリウムガーデン。幾何学的な植栽とアートを配した美術館のスカルプチャーガーデン（彫刻的な庭）を思わせる
Atrium garden or the inner garden to appreciate from the entrance hall or dwelling units, reminding one of a sculpture garden at a museum where geometric planting and artworks

2
外観の統一感を守りながら、ガラスの素材を生かしたシャープな直線美を際立たせる外観
Exterior maintaining the exterior integrity and highlighting the sharp linear beauty by taking advantage of glass materials

3
エントランス側外観：縦格子とスリット状の窓をリズミカルに配置したファサードデザイン
Exterior of the entrance side: Facade design features vertical grilles and slit-like windows giving a sense of rhythm

4
車寄せを設けたエレガントなエントランス。建物の庇と共調するデザイン性の高いキャノピーを設けている
Elegant entrance with a porch. A carefully designed canopy fitting the eaves of the building is also provided.

1	4
2	5
3	

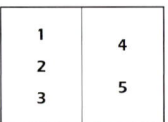

1
ガラス越しにやわらかな光がふりそそぐ開放感あふれるエントランスホール。床や意匠壁には、外観やエントランスアプローチと同じ素材を使用し、内と外との連続性を感じさせる一体感を演出
Entrance hall with a sense of spaciousness, lit by soft natural light through the glass. The floor and designed walls employ same materials as those of the exterior and entrance approach so that a sense of continuity between the interior and exterior should be created.

2
敷地配置図
Site plan

3
アトリウムガーデンを望む憩いの場として利用できるエントランスラウンジ。両サイドをガラス壁とした半野外的な開放感あふれる空間
Entrance lounge that can be used as a place for relaxation, with a view of the atrium garden. Glass walls on the sides give a sense of openness.

4
扁平ラーメン構造と約2.3メートルのハイサッシがもたらした明るく伸びやかなリビング・ダイニングルーム
Well-lit and extensive living-dining room, thanks to low profile rigid framed structure and about 2.3m-high windows

5
ダイニングからリビングを臨む
Living area seen from the dining section

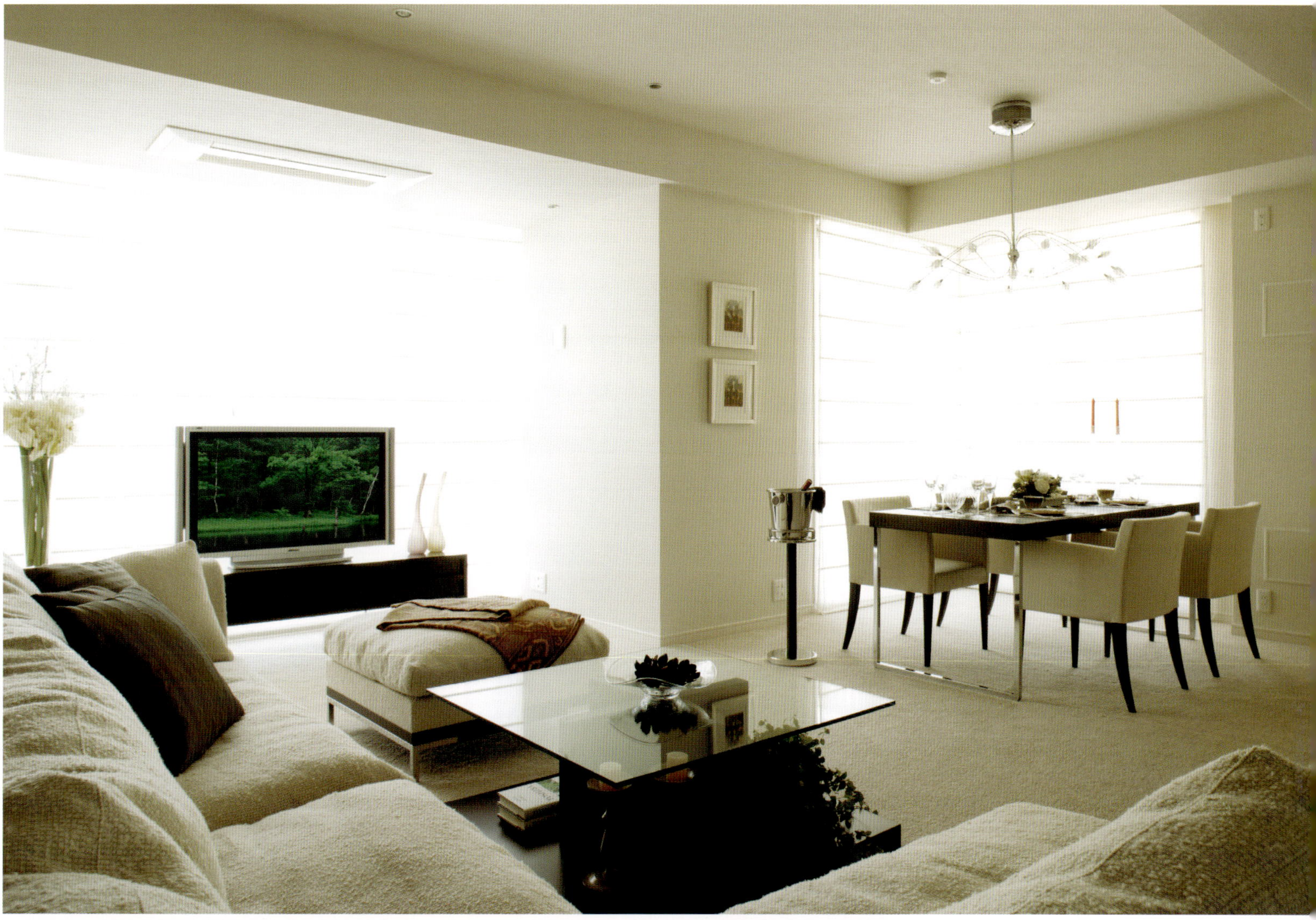

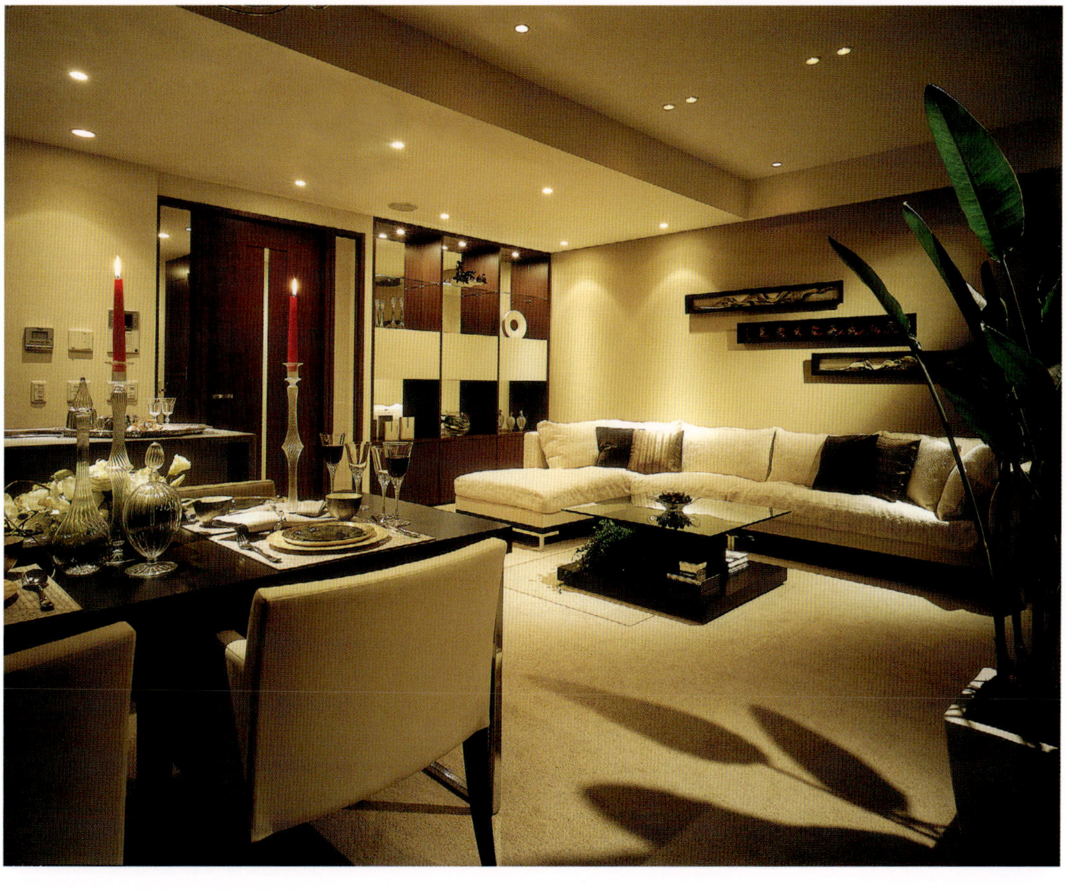

1	4	5	
2		6	
3	7	8	

1
キッチンワークを楽しくするデザインと収納力を高めたシステムキッチン
Designed for enjoyable kitchen work and having a built-in kitchen with a high storage capability

2
広々としたプライベートテラス
Spacious private terrace

3
上質な空間のためのこだわりを随所に配慮して深く、やわらかく、やさしい時間が過ごせるマスターベッドルーム
Master bedroom to spend profound, soft and gentle time, thanks to details for a quality space

4
エントランスホール
Entrance hall

5
書斎スペースが付随した洋室
Western-style room with a study space

6
ひとりの世界が楽しめるDENスペース
Den space to enjoy time of privacy

7
マスターベッドルームからDENを臨む。奥にウォークインクロゼットを配している
Den space seen from the master bedroom. A walk-in closet is at the back.

8
快適で使いやすいパウダールーム
Comfortable and easy-to-use powder room

Custom made plan

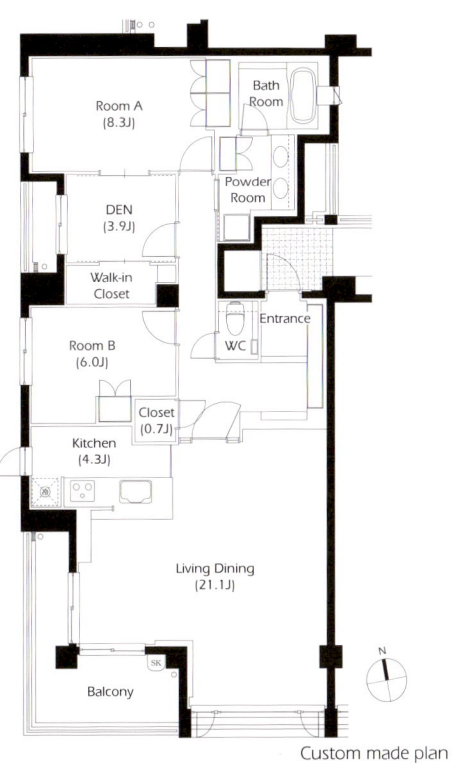

Data

Title
 Proud Minami-Ogikubo

Developer
 Nomura Real Estate Development Co.,Ltd

Basic plan / Exterior / Public
Inner Garden
 Atelier G&B Co.

Architect / Design
 Obayashi Corporation

Location
 Minami-Ogikubo, Suginami-ku, Tokyo

Site area
 4,379.224m²

Building area
 2,321.90m²

Total floor area
 6,991.20m²

Structure
 RC+S

Completion
 August, 2006

Materials
 Exterior Wall :
  boder tile 22x145, 45x225
  decorated wall coating,
  multi-layer wall coating,
  sprayed coating
 Public Wall :
  boder tile 45x225, 300x600 tile
  painting
 Public Floor :
  300x600 tile
 Interior Wall :
  vinyl cloth
 Interior Floor :
  marble, flooring, carpet

Renai Seazon's Garden Nishinomiya Najio
ルネ シーズンズ ガーデン 西宮名塩
Takao Endo Architect Office

昭和50年代に数多く計画されたいわゆる「タウンハウス」は、その後地価の高騰等によって成立条件を失い、再度このような計画が生まれるとは考えてもいなかった。しかし、再びタウンハウスが日の目を見る機会がやってきたかに思われるが、多分昨今の土地に対する状況は長く続いてゆくものとも思えない。このような状況の中で生まれたのがこの計画である。そもそも名塩ニュータウン自身は、いわゆる「都心居住」の住宅とは考え方を異にしており、低密度の集合住宅と豊かな自然に育まれ、ゆったりとした時間の流れる、郊外型の住宅地の典型のような団地である。しかし、JR西宮名塩駅からわずか30分程度で、大阪駅に到れる利便性も高く、やはりこのような自然の豊かさと利便性が高いからこそ成立したプロジェクトだとも言えるだろう。具体的な計画では、フラット盤の上に5階建のフラットタイプの住戸を配置し、斜面の肩の部分と斜面に、準接地型及び接地型の住棟を配置し、ヒューマンスケールを持った子育てステージの家族の住宅として、活用されればと考えながら計画された住宅である。又、敷地南端にはクラインガルテンも用意され、長い時間の中で自然と生活環境が馴染み、人と人の関係も育つことを望みながら計画されたプロジェクトである。

The so-called "townhouses", many of which were planned in Showa 50's (1975-1984), lost their plausibility due to soaring land prices and other reasons, so we didn't think that such projects would be planned again. In recent years, however, it seems that townhouse projects have finally got unexpected opportunities to see the light of day again though such favorable land price conditions don't seem to last long. This project was planned with such background. The Najio New Town is not based on the concept of "living in the heart of the city"; with low-density condominiums and rich nature, it is rather a typical suburban residential area where time seems to be running slow. Still it takes only 30 minutes from JR Nishinomiya Najio station to Osaka station; this combination of nature and convenience contributed to realizing this project. In the concrete planning, 5-story buildings of flat type apartments are laid out on the hilltop while residential buildings with ground contact or semi-ground contact are on the edges of the slope or on the slope. The human-scale dwelling units are designed primarily for families on the child-rearing stage. At the southern end of the site is even a kleingarten. The project expects to achieve harmony between nature and living environments over time and build relationship among people, too.

	2
1	3
	4 5

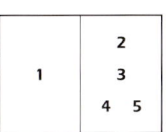

1
敷地の最下段に配置されたタウンハウスのサブエントランスの見える風景
A view of the sub-entrance of the town house positioned at the lowest level of the site

2
3列配置の中間に配置された連続接地型住棟と準接地型住棟
Connected apartments with direct ground access and residential buildings with semi-direct ground access in the middle of the residential buildings plotted in three rows

3
3列配置の一番北側に配置されたフラットタイプがある住棟と中庭の風景
Residential building having flat-type units and plotted the north side in the three rows and a view of inner garden

4
この住宅地の中心軸を構成する階段と、3列住棟がオーバーレイする風景
Stairway serving as the central axis of this residential block and a view of three residential buildings overlapped

5
フラットタイプ住棟のジョイント部分
Joint sections between the flat-type residential buildings

1
段違いメゾネットタイプのリビングから階段と中廊下を臨む

Stairway and central corridor of the maisonnette-type unit with different levels seen from the living room

2
ハイサッシュのあるリビングから宝塚、大阪方面の風景を臨む

A view toward Takaraduka and Osaka from the living room with full-height saches

3
フラットタイプ1階のリビングと専用庭の関係を表す

Relationship between the living room and the exclusive garden on the first floor of the flat-type unit

4
ラウンジから中庭越しに準接地住棟の見える風景

Residential buildings with semi-direct ground access beyond the inner garden seen from the lounge

Data

Title
Renai Seazon's Garden Nishinomiya Najio

Architect
Takao Endo Architect Office

Location
Nishinomiya city, Hyogo

Site area
22,565.75m²

Building area
5,548.14m²

Total floor area
15,665.56m²

Area
76.84 - 117.54m²

Structure
RC

Completion
February, 2006

Materials
Exterior Wall :
  sprayed coating, 45x90tile in part
Public Wall :
  tile, vinyl cloth
Public Floor :
  tile, flooring
Interior Wall :
  vinyl cloth
Interior Floor :
  flooring

Photo
Yoshiharu Matsumura

Navire Court Hourakucho

ナビールコート豊楽町

Teruyuki Morisaki

この計画は、「個(トリプルメゾネット)」の16軒連繋住戸である。テーマは『個と集合』

敷地は元、竹藪であった。周辺環境との調和を図り低層住宅(3層)とし、外壁後退(4m以上)を可能な限り設け緑豊かな自然環境を復元させている。各住戸内は、自由度の高い居住空間を得る為に、断熱性能を兼ね備えた打込み型枠(脱型の要がないので環境にも優しい)で、外断熱を行い室内インテリアにコンクリート打放し仕上げも可能となる様計画した。又、光や風の感受装置として中庭を設け、この部分にも緑を挿入させている。戸建感覚の為の必要な庭や駐車(2台)のスペースは、無論確保されている。

In this project, 16 residences are built as linked "individual houses (triple maisonnettes)". The theme of the project is "individuality and assembly". The site was once a bamboo thicket. In order to make harmony with the neighborhood, the building is designed low rise (three stories), setbacks (more than four meters) are provided wherever plausible, and a green-rich natural environment is restored. In order to make the space inside each residence flexible, external insulation is provided by cast-in mold having heat insulation property (environment-friendly because no form removal is required) so that exposed concrete finish should be possible for interior. As an mechanism to enable residents to feel light and wind, an inner court decorated with green is provided. As a matter of course, each residence is provided with a garden and a parking lot (for two cars) necessary for giving a sense of a detached house.

	2	
1	3	4
	5	

1
エントランス側 外観
External view of entrance side.

2
北側外観
External view of north side.

3
エントランス
Entrance

4
共用通路
Common passage.

5
共用通路からの外観
External view from common passage.

1
リビングルーム
Living room

2
ダイニング
Dining room

Data

Title
　Navire Court Hourakucho

Architect
　Teruyuki Morisaki

Location
　Nishinomiya city, Hyogo

Site area
　2,184.11m²

Building area
　859.72m²

Total floor area
　2,546.76m²

Structure
　RC (wall construction)

Completion
　July, 2004

Materials
　Exterior Wall :
　　seepage waterproof material on
　　architectural concrete
　　heat insulation sand spray painting
　　on architectural concrete
　Public Wall :
　　architectural concrete
　Public Floor :
　　ceramic tile
　Interior Wall :
　　eco-cloth, architectural concrete in
　　part, Japanese style wall paper
　Interior Floor :
　　oak flooring, Ryukyu-Tatami

Photo
　Yoshiharu Matsumura

Asuta Shin-nagata Towers Court ALIVIO
アスタ新長田タワーズコート アリビオ
Teruyuki Morisaki & Morisaki Architecture Design Office & Associates

「海への予感」

敷地は、先の阪神淡路大震災で壊滅的打撃を受けた神戸市長田区にある。神戸市はJR新長田駅南地区（約20ha）を復興させるため第二種市街地再開発事業を実施している。地区の景観コンセプト＝『海への道』は、「海に向かって開かれた神戸の地形。」と、「かつて、信仰の山（高取山）に浜から塩を運搬した『潮汲みの道』と呼ばれていた道が事業地区内である。」ということからきている。再開発地区は、北から南への順に、石・土・砂と移行するモチーフや山から海へのイメージ展開が各地区にデザインコードとして決められている。紹介する建築は、再開発事業地区の中では、最も海に近い第1地区南端にあって、そのデザインコンセプトは、「ハーバーマリーナ」である。潮の香りのする雰囲気や柔らかい素材感、パステルカラー調の色彩を選定し、素朴でシンプルな意匠もそのルールから来ている。特に、再開発という事業にあって配慮した留意点は、「周辺環境との調和」であった。この事業は、大規模化する。ややもすると違和感のある都市空間が出現する。ために、「圧迫感を回避のスカイライン」、「ヒューマンスケール（低層）な敷き際」、「都市の重層性を意味させている段状の壁面や浮遊感を表現した屋根」は、その調和装置なのである。最後に、この建築は、震災復興で癒されることを知った「ペット」も共に暮らせる集合住宅でもあることを付け加えておく。

Anticipation of the sea

The site is located in Nagata Ward, Kobe City, which experienced devastating damage from the Great Hanshin and Awaji Earthquake. Kobe City is implementing a second category urban renewal project to rebuild the area in the south of the JR Shin-nagata station (about 20 hectares). The landscaping concept of the area, "the Road to the Sea" is originated from the "geography of Kobe open to the sea" and "the fact that the road called "Shiokumi no Michi" (the road to transport salt from the seashore to the sacred mountain of Takatoriyama) was once in the project area." The redevelopment areas have designated design codes such as a motif of north-south transition from stone to soil and sand and conceptual development from mountains to sea. The building introduced herein is located at the southern end of the 1st Zone closest to the sea in the renewal project area. Its design concept is "harbor marina". Based on this rule, the condominium employs simple and naive designs, having an atmosphere reminding one of the smell of the sea, a soft texture of materials, and finishes in pastel colors. In this redevelopment project, we especially paid attention to "harmony with the surrounding environments". As this project was expected to become large-scaled, there was a possibility to create an urban space with a sense of discomfort. For this reason, we prepared such mechanisms for harmony as "skylines avoiding a sense of oppression", "(low-rise) bordering zones on a human scale between the building walls and road", and "terraced walls signifying a stratified city and roofs giving a floating image". Finally, it is worth to add that this condominium allows "pets" that have became known for their healing powers in the process of recovery from the disaster.

1
南側外観全景
Complete view of the southern exterior

1 2 3	6
4	7
5	8

1
南側外観近景
Close-range view of the southern exterior

2
住宅エントランス外観
Outside view of the entrance

3
住宅エントランス内観
Inside view of the entrance

4
2階ロビー
Lobby on the second floor

5
住戸ルーフバルコニーよりの景色
View from the roof balcony of a dwelling unit

6
トップライト付玄関ホール
Entrance hall with top light

7
リビングダイニング
Living-dining space

8
リビングダイニング
Living-dining space

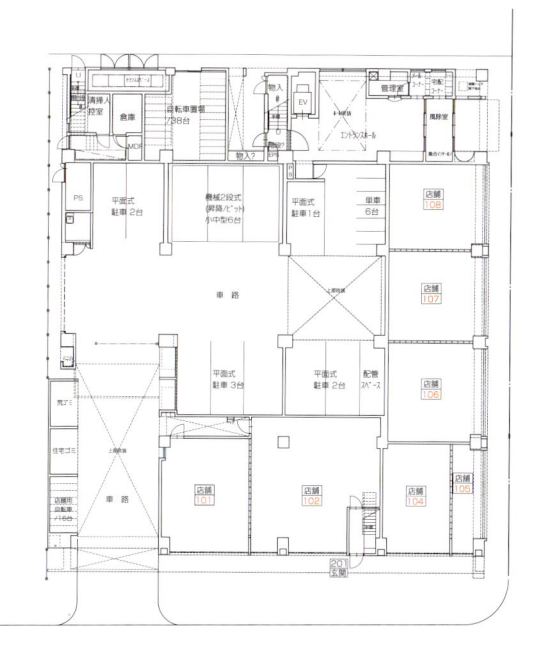

Data

Title
  Asuta Shin-nagata Towers Court ALIVIO
Developer
  KOBE CITY
Architect
  Teruyuki Morisaki & Morisaki
  Architecture Design Office & Associates
Location
  Kobe city, Hyogo
Site area
  1,201.55m²
Building area
  882.45m²
Total floor area
  3,581.22m²
Area
  27.24 - 82.26m²
Structure
  SRC (RC in part)
Completion
  March, 2006
Materials
  Exterior Wall :
    ceramic mosic tile, granite
    sprayed coating in part
  Public Wall :
    JURAKU plastering finish, marble
    exposed concrete bush hammer
    finish in part
  Public Floor :
    granite, marble
  Interior Wall :
    vinyl cloth
  Interior Floor :
    composite natural wood flooring
Photo
  Yoshiharu Matsumura

Brillia Daikanyama Prestige
Brillia代官山プレステージ

Tokyo Tatemono Co.,Ltd. / TOKYU LAND CORPORATION
Chiaki Arai Urban & Architecture Design / Toda Corporation

「代官山の丘の上に、新たな丘を創る」この壮大なコンセプトを表現するのは、個性と自立を表すキューブを積み重ねたアートそのものの姿。建築の歴史を彩ってきたモダニズム思想の、現代にふさわしい結晶体と言える。さらには個々のキューブを微妙にずらすことで、居住空間に広々としたルーフバルコニーが形作られる。アグレッシブな建物の中に、居住者のハイライフに応える提案を盛り込んでいる。代官山の歴史と風景に新たな発展をもたらし、あらゆるHILLSを越える上質の邸宅空間を創り上げる。その思想を実現するために、細部のクオリティにいたるまで一切の妥協を排し、時にはそれまで存在しなかったマテリアルをも開発するなど、飽くなきこだわりをもっている。ジャパニーズモダンを表現したカラーイメージ、タイルをはじめサッシ、手すりガラス、小庇、そして車寄せの床に至る外観周りのマテリアルは、グレー色の微妙な色彩のバリエーションを追求。代官山に息づくモダニズム建築の流れを踏まえつつ、オリジナルの個性を表現している。また、共用部にも、代官山の街にインパクトをもたらす外観設計の思想を踏まえつつ、都心にふさわしいクールなテイストの中に、豊かな安らぎのエッセンスを盛り込んでいる。

"Create a new hill on the hill of Daikanyama." This concept is expressed by the condominium's artistic shape of accumulated cubes representing its uniqueness and independence. It can be regarded as modern crystallization of the modernism philosophy that has colored the history of architecture. By delicately shifting the individual cubes, extensive roof balconies are added to the living spaces. This aggressively designed building is full of proposals to respond to the residents' requirements for high quality life. To materialize the concept of bringing new development to the history and landscape of Daikanyama and creating quality residential spaces exceeding all the residential HILLS, no compromise has been made to quality of every detail, and even some materials were developed from scratch, which illustrates our relentless pursuit. The color image expressing the Japanese modern as well as the materials for the exterior including tiles, sashes, railing glass, small eaves, and porch floors are based on the variations of delicate gray color. Inheriting the modernism architecture alive in the town of Daikanyama, the building reveals its original and unique characteristics. The common use space also takes into account the exterior design concept that cause impact upon the townscape of Daikanyama and has a rich essence of comfort in the cool design befitting the heart of the city.

	2
1	3
	4

1
東側外観：ガラス手摺りは、ガラスの間に和紙を挟み込むなど優しい質感を実現し、さり気なく視界に配慮する遮蔽壁としての役割も果たす
Eastern exterior: Glass railings having Japanese paper in between glass panels have a soft texture and also serve as shielding walls for quiet consideration

2
外観：キューブを積み重ねたアートそのものの姿
Exterior: Artistic outlook by accumulated cubes

3
共用スペース鳥瞰図
Bird's eye view of the common use space

4
夕景外観
Exterior in the evening

1	4
2	5
3	6

1
この街に暮らす喜びを改めて感じさせる、高いデザイン性を備えたエントランス

Entrance with a quality design, letting one feel the joy of living in the town once again

2
地下のエレベーターホールへ至るエントランスアプローチ。光とガラス素材によってアーティスティックに演出

Entrance approach leading to the underground elevator hall, artistically produced by the lighting and glass materials

3
カフェラウンジ／フィットネスゾーン：窓の外にしつらえた「シーベッドテラス」には、海の底を思わせる光の演出

Cafe lounge and fitness zone: "Seabed terrace" installed outside the window is highlighted as if it were at the bottom of the sea.

4
コーチエントランス

Coach entrance

5
エントランスホール：壁面から立ち上がり空間を包む、天然突板による深紅の天井は、紅葉や夕焼け、赤とんぼなど、思い思いのノスタルジーを喚起させる色彩

Entrance hall: The crimson color of the ceiling of natural veneer rising from the wall reminds one of autumn leaves, afterglow, red dragonflies and other nostalgic memories.

6
エントランスホールからさらに奥へと連なる、広々とした空間。自邸と外界との狭間に位置するこのエリアに、多忙な都心生活の基本であるコンシェルジュカウンターを設けている

Wide space extending from the entrance hall to the back. This area in between one's dwelling unit and the outside world has a concierge counter to serve as the basis of busy city life.

Data

Title
 Brillia Daikanyama Prestige

Developer
 Tokyo Tatemono Co.,Ltd.
 TOKYU LAND CORPORATION

Design Supervision
 Chiaki Arai Urban & Architecture Design

Architect
 Toda Corporation

Location
 Shibuya-ku, Tokyo

Site area
 3,089.29m²

Building area
 1,853.56m²

Total floor area
 14,302.81m²

Structure
 RC (SRC in part)

Completion
 March, 2007

Materials
 Exterior Wall :
  Original tile, aluminum panel
 Public Wall :
  wood panel, glass,
  special plasterer finish, tile
 Public Floor :
  clay stone

S-G type
S-G タイプ
Yumiko Kumatani (Mec Design International Corp.)

それぞれの居室に充分な広さをとったのは、開放感や贅沢さの追求だけではなく、家族の間でもお互いの時間を尊重できる、程良い「距離感」を生み出すためである。さらに、個々の感性と自在に融合する懐深い空間づくりのため、プレーンなインテリアカラーを基本としている。

Each room is designed to be sufficiently spacious in pursuit of not only giving a sense of openness and luxury but also creating an appropriate sense of personal "distance" enabling even family members to respect each other's privacy. In addition, the interior is based on a plain color so that an adequate space to embrace individual sensitivities.

	2
1	3
	4

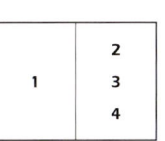

1
リビングルーム：深い色合いのチーク材フローリングなど、自然に材を取ったマテリアルを取り入れ、プレーンな色調の中でくつろぎを演出している
Living room: A sense of comfort and relaxation is produced in a plain texture by using deep textured teak flooring and other natural materials

2
キッチンへのアクセスを意識しながら、毎日の食事を満喫するための華やかな雰囲気づくりを目指したダイニングスペース
Dining space as a result of the design efforts to create a gay atmosphere for enjoying meals everyday while paying due consideration to access to the kitchen

3
インテリアの一部として洗練された空間を形づくる、インテリア性の高いデザインを提案したキッチン
Kitchen as an excellent interior design proposal, serving as sophisticated part of the interior

4
リビングのフローリングと対照的に、ウォームホワイトのカーペットを敷き詰めた寝室
Bedroom whose floor is covered with warm white carpets in contrast with the flooring of the living room

1	2
3	
4	

1
ドアには車と同じウレタン樹脂焼付塗装を採用し、深い色合いと光沢を再現するとともに、長期にわたる耐久性にも配慮している

Doors are finished with urethane resin baking employed for automobiles to give deep colors and luster and in consideration of durability for a long period of time.

2
フロストガラスを効果的に用い、くつろぎと清潔感をデザインした洗面室

Toilet room designed with a sense of comfort and cleanliness by effectively using frosted glass

3
自然石の風合い息づくピエールデコの壁面とライムストーンの床に包まれたエントランス

Entrance with the Pierre Deco walls having a feel of natural stone and limestone floor

4
壁面は大理石のセルベジャンテ、床と浴槽カウンターには御影石のロイヤルベージュを採用したバスルーム

Bathroom employing Serpeggiante marble for the walls and royal beige granite for the floor and bath counter

Data

Title
  S-G type
Coordinate
  Yumiko Kumatani
    (Mec Design International Corp.)
Area
  118.43m²
Materials
  Interior Wall :
    special plasterer finish
  Interior Floor :
    clay stone, flooring, carpet

Scaletta
スカレッタ
Tomoyuki Utsumi / Milligram architectural studio

敷地は発展性のある都心の立地にありながら、戦後の古い木造住宅が今なお残り、区画整理がなかなか進まない下町の密集地です。今回の計画地も前面道路4mの狭小地であり、建て替えられた5層の建築物は、集合住宅とすれば極めて小規模にもかかわらず、軒が重なるほどに小さく立ち並んだ周辺の街並みからすれば突出して高く、相対的に異質なボリュームに見えます。私たちはどんな場所でも既存の街並みの良さを見いだそうとしますが、このケースでは現存への尊重よりも未来の街並みへの足掛かりを考えて、周辺に対してむしろ明確なコントラストを与える事にしました。つまり、依頼主の事業性も考慮して最大限のボリュームを確保する方向です。しかし、それが無作為で乱暴な形態ではなく、小さな敷地でも丁寧に計画すれば、端正かつ容量のある資産が形成できる具体例として成立しなければ、私たちの存在する意味がありません。そんな中で、新たな魅力を派生させることで、現在は高齢者が多いこの街の未来に新たな住民層が加わり、少なからず発展的な住環境が形成されることを期待しています。天空率計算によって前面道路の斜線規制を回避した結果、4層までを同じ基準階とし、型枠をギリギリまで転用しながら厳しいコストの制約をクリアしています。前面道路との緩衝地が設けられないので、賃貸部分を前面道路の視線より高く設定するために、四層の各床は、すべて室内で階段状になっていますが、その床下の有効を配管スペースとし、縦配管はすべて建物の外部に露出させています。各階はシンメトリーに二戸の住戸を配していますが、その中央の間仕切りを乾式として躯体に参入しないかわりに、柱を袖壁としてリブ状に室内に突出させることで構造的に成立させています。この躯体自体が持つ構造的な特徴を、小さな空間の有効性に加担させるために、室内の使用目的が限定される浴室やトイレ等の場所を、すべて躯体が創り出した際の部分に押し込んで、たとえば浴槽は床下、トイレは袖壁の中から引き出して使用するといったように、利用するとき以外は空間に突出しないように工夫されています。

Though the site is at the heart of the city with a potential for development, it is actually in a densely built-up area of the old quarters where old wooden houses built after the war still remain and land readjustment has made slow progress. The lot is a narrow land having a 4-meter-wide frontal road, and though the rebuilt 5-story structure is very small in terms of its scale, it appears extremely high when compared with the low-rise landscape of houses standing side by side and is relatively a presence of different nature. We always try to find out something good about any existing townscape, but, in this case, we looked toward the future of the town rather than preserving the existing one and decided to give a definitive contrast between the new building and its environments. In other words, the building was planned to have a volume as large as possible in consideration of the owner's profitability as well. But our planning would be meaningless unless the plan could serve as a concrete example of creating a beautiful asset with a sufficient volume by carefully planning its design even for such a small site, instead of randomly and roughly doing so. Given the condition, we hope that we built a living environment with a large potential by developing new appeals and attracting new residents in the town currently occupied mainly by the elder citizens. Based on the sky factor calculation, the setback regulation of the frontal road could be avoided, and four floors were planned to have typical floors. Forms were utilized as much as possible to satisfy the severe cost restrictions. No buffer zone with the frontal road could be provided, so in order to set the floors for rent higher than the lines of sight of passers-by, all the floors of the units on these four floors are stepped, and the space below the steps were effectively used for piping while all the vertical piping are installed outside the building. On each floor, two residential units are arranged symmetrically, but instead of inserting a dry partition in between the units as part of the building frame, the rib-like columns are projected in the rooms as side walls to meet structural requirements. To take further advantage of this structural characteristics of the skeleton for effective use of the small volume, indoor spaces whose use are limited such as bathroom and toilet are put to the corners created by the structure; for example, the bathtub is under the floor, and the toilet can be drawn out from the wall. In this way, those spaces do not project themselves into the living space.

1

1
建物正面見上げ
Facade looked up

1	2	4
		5
3		6

1
南側外観
Southern exterior

2
エントランスからの眺め
A view from the entrance

3
エントランスにむかう通路
Passage to the entrance

4
スキップフロアのワンルーム
Studio with skip floors

5
ペントハウス：キッチン
Penthouse: Kitchen

6
ペントハウス：リビング
Penthouse: Living room

125

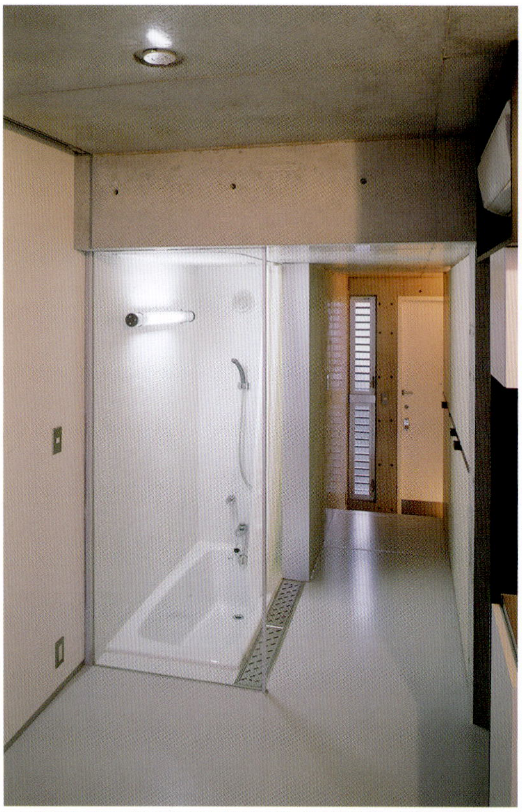
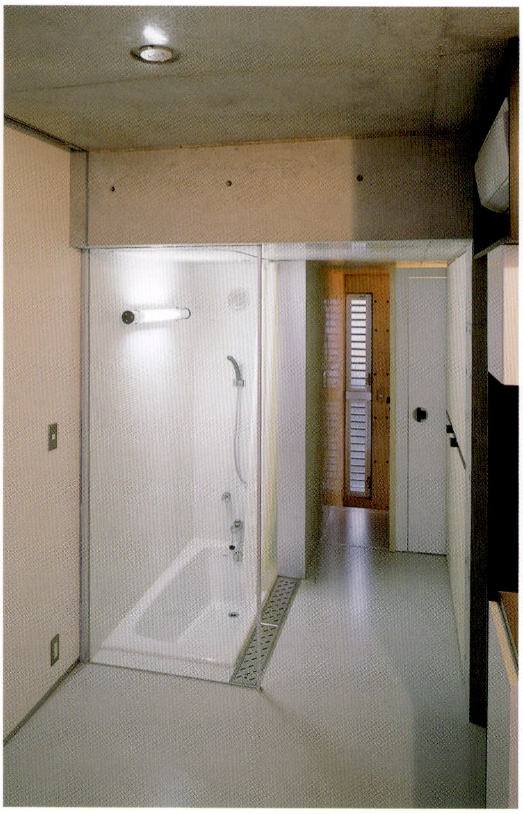
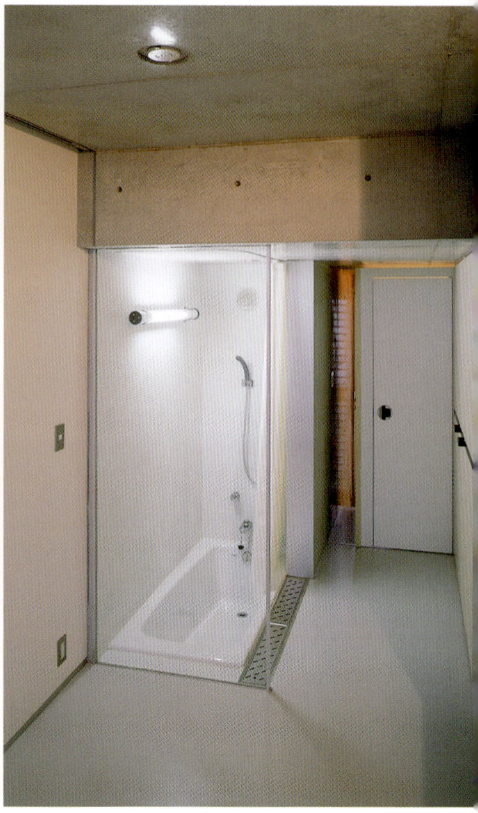
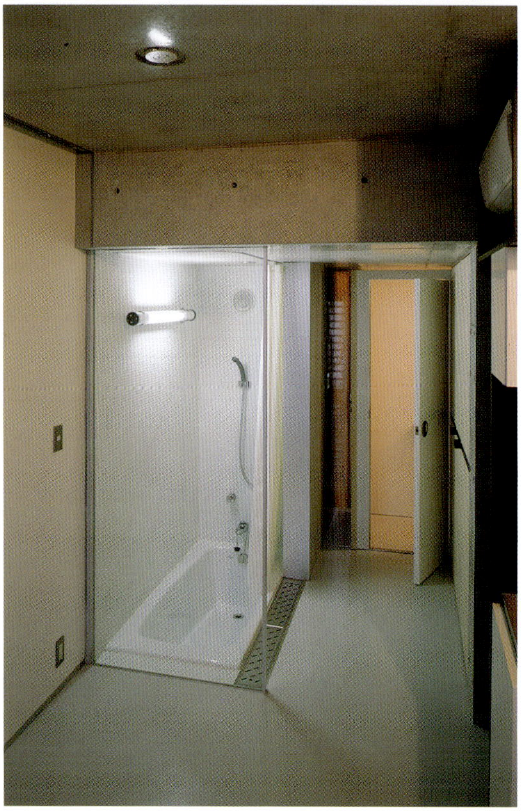
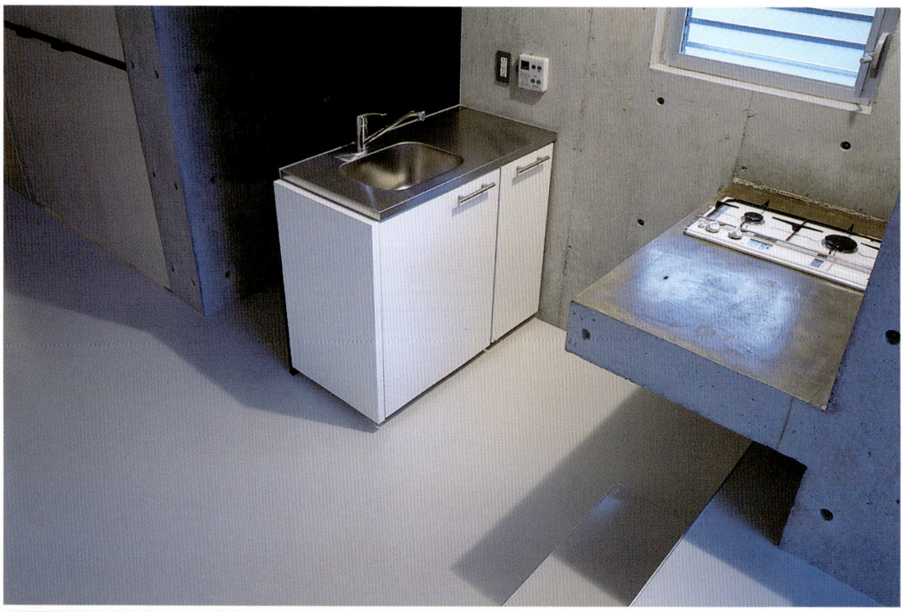
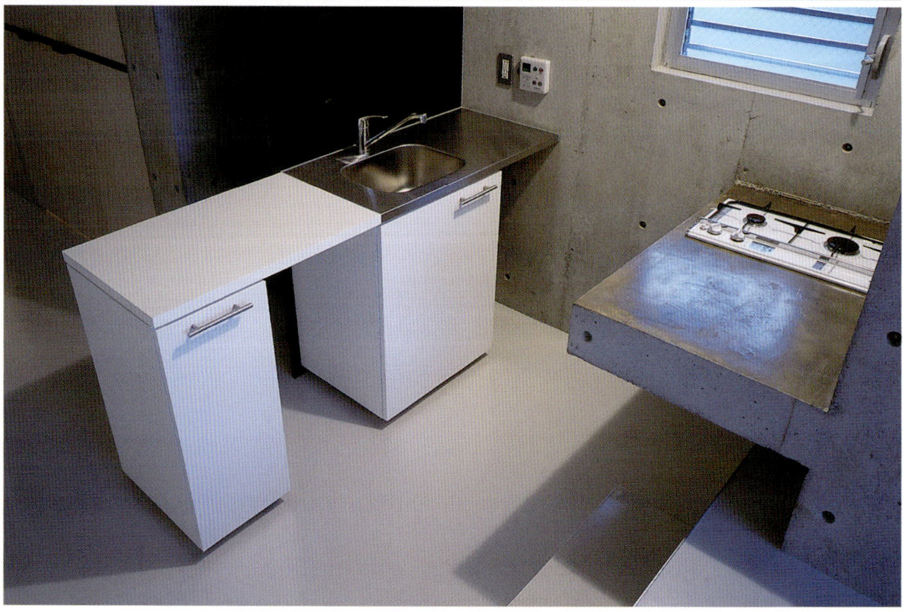

1	2	3	7
4			
	5		8
	6		

1-4
引出せるトイレ：可動部分連続写真
Toilet that can be drawn out (a picture sequence of the mobile part)

5,6
キッチン：可動部分
Kitchen: Mobile part

7
ペントハウス：バスルーム
Penthouse: Bathroom

8
ペントハウス：螺旋階段
Penthouse: Spiral stairs

Data

Title
  Scaletta

Architect
  Tomoyuki Utsumi
  Milligram architectural studio

Location
  Shinagawa-ku, Tokyo

Site area
  105.59m²

Area
  26.5m²-64.3m²

Structure
  RC + S

Completion
  October, 2005

Materials
  Exterior Wall :
    architectural concrete
  Public Wall :
    architectural concrete
  Public Floor :
    dust proofing paint on concrete
    trowel finish
  Interior Wall :
    architectural concrete, cloth
  Interior Floor :
    PVC sheet

Photo
  Takeshi Taira

SORGENTE
ソルジェンテ向丘
Tatsuya Yokawa

オーナー宅の隣地に計画した本物件は、1階店舗（歯科医院）、2、3階賃貸集合住宅8戸から成る。不正形な敷地の各辺から平行移動した変形の四角形を、そのまま立ち上げたボリウムが建築となった。共用部と専有部分を分割する線を引き、その台形を面積4等分にした10坪弱が、各住戸となっている。2つの隣接する住戸は、水廻りを組合せ、可能な限りまとまった広さのワンルーム空間を確保した。配置を少しずらすことにより設備の配管経路を確保し、巾のある部分は、ベッドと収納の配置を考慮した使い勝手の良い空間を生み出している。また、将来2戸をひとつにすることも可能な構造としている。3階床の南面を逆梁とすることにより、2階の住戸は床から天井までの開口部を持つ。3階は逆梁がベンチ状の台となり、斜め天井で高くなった面に十分な開口部が確保される。ボイドスラブにより小梁のない壁・天井は、打ち放し仕上げ。外壁の外断熱とペアガラスの仕様と相まって、10年後にも見劣りしないもの、そして将来的に魅力の薄れないものを目指している。共用部のホールは、3層吹き抜けの打ち放し壁面に片持ちの階段がつき、有孔折板の影が映る、手仕事の緊張感が伝わる造形的な空間になっている。ケヤキの街路樹がある道路に面し、母屋に隣接する建築として、端整かつ清楚な佇まいを心掛けた。

This property planned adjacent to the owner's house has a dentist's office on the first floor and eight apartments for rent on the second and third floors. The site is irregularly shaped, and the footprint of the building equals to its scaled-down shape. For apartment floors, a line is first drawn between the common and private areas, and the trapezoid-shaped private area is divided into four; as a result, each apartment has an area of about 30 square meters. By efficiently arranging plumbing of adjacent studio apartments, the residential space of each room is maximized. The rooms are slightly shifted with each other to secure enough space for piping, and careful consideration is given to a wide section of each room to create a comfortable and convenient layout of a bed and storage. The structure allows future integration of two apartments. As reversed slab is employed for the southern side of the floor on the third floor, each apartment on the second floor has a full opening from the ceiling to the floor. On the third floor, the reversed beam serves as a bench-like base, and the slanted ceiling contributes to secure an opening large enough. Thanks to void slab construction, the walls and ceilings has no binder and are finished with exposed concrete. Outside insulation and double-glazing specifications of the exterior walls add extra features that make the building that will not look ordinary ten years later and maintain its attractiveness in the future. In the hall of the common area, a well is provided from the first floor to the third floor; its exposed concrete wall has cantilever stairs and reflects the shadow of perforated folded plate. It is a plastic-art-like space that conveys a sense of tension accompanying the handiwork. In designing this building facing a street with zelkova roadside trees and standing next to the main house, attention is paid to give a neat and clean appearance.

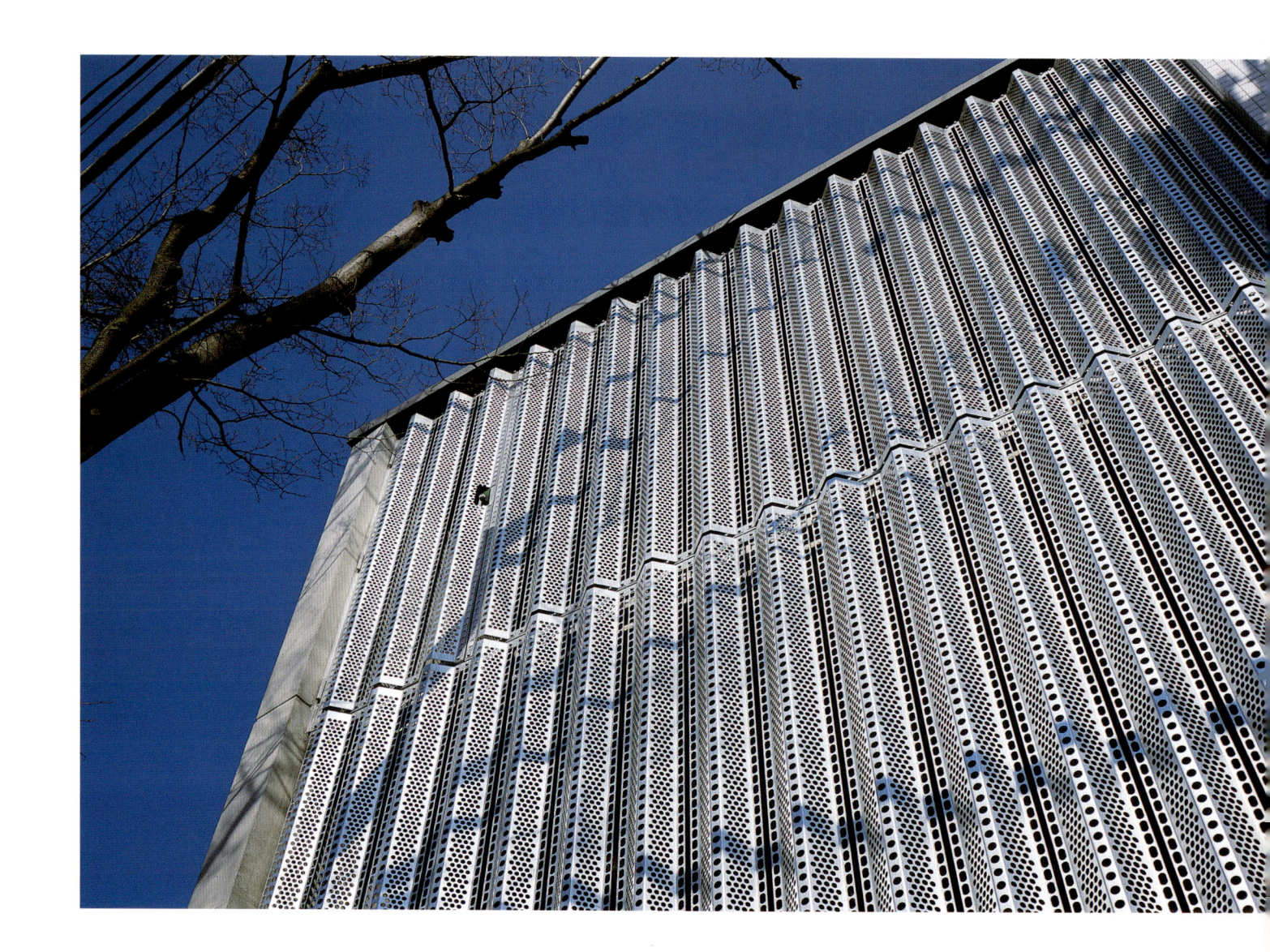

| | 2 | 3 |
|1| 4 | 5 |

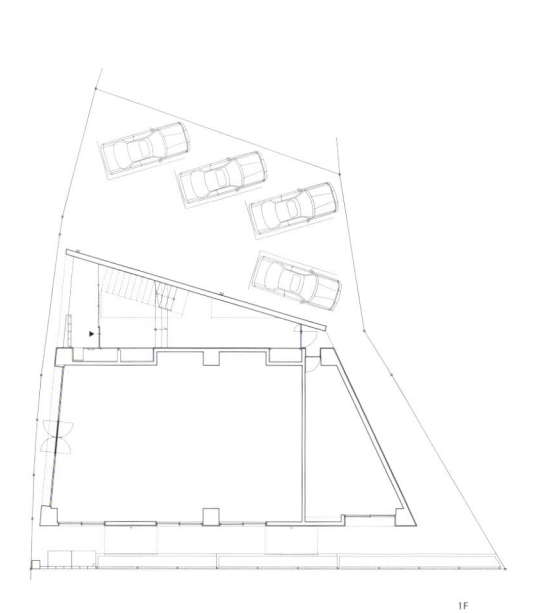

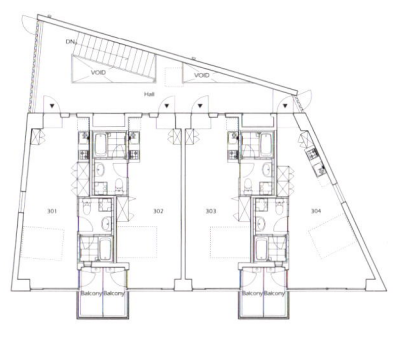

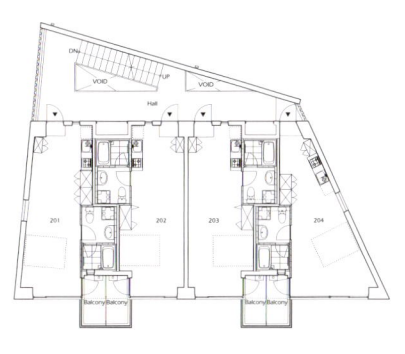

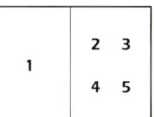

1
有孔折板による外壁ルーバー
Louvers on the external wall using perforated folded plates

2
道路側エレベーション
Elevation on the side of the road

3
エントランス夜景
Entrance at night

4
エントランスホール階段
Stairway in the entrance hall

5
エントランスホール見返り
Entrance hall looked back

|1|
|2|
|3|

1
301 北面
North side of the room 301

2
304 北面
North side of the room 304

3
304 南側開口部と逆梁ベンチ
Opening on the south side and bench taking advantage of reversed beam of the room 304

Data

Title
  SORGENTE

Architect
  Tatsuya Yokawa

Location
  Miyamae-ku, Kawasaki city, Kanagawa

Site area
  367.89m^2

Area
  31.62m^2

Structure
  RC

Completion
  March, 2005

Materials
  Exterior Wall :
    ceramic tile, exposed concrete
  Public Wall :
    ceramic tile, exposed concrete
  Public Floor :
    stoneware tile
  Interior Wall :
    exposed concrete, vinyl cloth
  Interior Floor :
    flooring

Photo
  Takeshi Taira

SILENZIO
シレンツィオ
Tatsuya Yokawa

住宅街の一角に在る敷地はT字路の交点突当たりで、対面する建物がなく、直線の道路に対して真直ぐに見通せる。駐車場の必要から2～4階をオーバーハングさせ、壁式RC造の箱をキール（構造上の背骨）の通りから4m、壁柱から2.5m持ち出している。オーバーハング部の軽量化要求から、その先端は可能な限り開口部とし、その先に鉄骨によるバルコニーが取り付く。手摺面の透明FRPグレージングと相まって、ファサードの浮遊感を強調している。住戸は近くに在る私立大学の学生をターゲットにした賃貸ワンルーム13戸からなる。最上階は乾式の耐火遮音間仕切りで区画し、3戸をひとつに改修することが可能だ。トランクルームがホームエレベーターを設置できるスペースとして確保されている。将来の変化に対応するフレキシビリティと、時の経過にも魅力の失われない建築を目指した。エントランスの扉は、耐候性鋼板とステンレス板による子扉付きの引戸で、入り難さを演出している。大扉脇の盛り塩のオブジェは、「きよめ」や「結界」、そして縁起を担ぐという機能もさることながら、オーナーの姓から連想したものだ。建物名称SILENZIOもその意味はオーナーの名前に由来している。建築は有史以来、オーナーの希望と欲望を具現化する行為であることに変わりはない。

The site in a residential block is located at the end of a T-junction. It has no obstruction to interrupt the line of sight in the direction of the straight road pointing toward it. In order to secure a parking lot, part of the second to fourth floors are all overhanging; in other words, a reinforced concrete wall construction is above the lot 4 meters from the keel (structural backbone of the building) and 2.5 meters from the wall shaped column. To meet the weight reduction requirement of the overhanging section, its edge has as many openings as possible, attached with steel frame balconies. Transparent FRP balustrade glazing emphasizes the floating impression of the facade. The 13 rental studio apartments are targeted for students of a private university in the neighborhood. The top floor is separated by fire- and sound-proof, dry wall partitions and can be modified into one larger room. A storage room is provided as a space to accommodate a home elevator. The primary goal of the design is based on flexibility to meet future changes and attractiveness beyond the passage of time. The entrance door is a sliding door made of atmospheric corrosion-resistant steel and stainless boards accompanied by a smaller door, providing warning against unauthorized entry to the building. The objet of a heap of salt beside the larger door not only has symbolic meanings of purify residents and guests, fixing the bounds of the place, and bringing good luck but also is suggested from the family name of the owner. The source of the name of the building, Silenzio, is also from the owner's name. Throughout the history, construction of a building has always been an act of materializing hopes and desires of an owner.

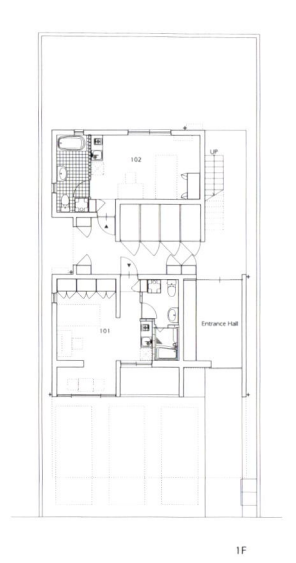

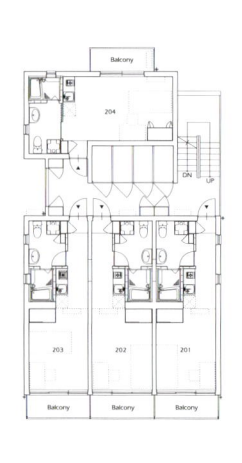

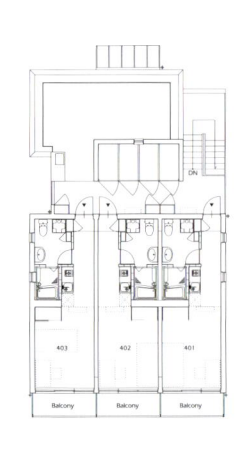

1	2	4
		5
	3	6

1
南側エレベーション夜景
Elevation on the south at night

2
エントランス大扉とオブジェ
Large entrance door and an art object

3
エントランス階段見返り
Entrance and stairway

4
101号室
Room 101

5
102号室
Room 102

6
202号室
Room 202

1F   2,3F   4F

Data

Title
　SILENZIO

Architect
　Tatsuya Yokawa

Location
　Tama-ku, Kawasaki city, Kanagawa

Site area
　231.42m²

Area
　24.00-28.35m²

Structure
　RC

Completion
　February, 2004

Materials
　Exterior Wall :
　　ceramic tile, exposed concrete
　Public Wall:
　　ceramic tile, exposed concrete
　Public Floor :
　　stoneware tile
　Interior Wall :
　　exposed concrete, vinyl cloth
　Interior Floor :
　　tile carpet

Photo
　Takeshi Taira

FLEG Hiroo 2nd Ave.
FLEG広尾2nd Ave.
F.L.E.G. INTERNATIONAL CO., LTD.

高低のある複雑な地形、点在する豊かな水脈‥。意外にも深みのある広尾。大都市をぎゅっと凝縮したような街並みに、エグゼクティブとセレブが求めたハイグレード空間を実現。成熟した空間とくつろぎの空間を叶えることができる。

An undulating, complex landform. Scattered, rich water veins. Hiroo is an area with an unexpected wealth of hidden treasures. Created n this microcosm of the metropolis is a high-grade space required by executives and celebrities, having a sense of maturity and relaxation.

1
外観全景
Exterior

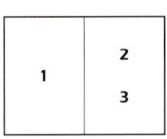

2
Room301：リビング・ダイニングルーム。天井までのハイサッシから陽射しがたっぷりと採り込める
Room301: Living-dining room. Abundant sunlight coming from the ceiling-high windows

3
Room301：ダイニングからキッチンを臨む
Room301: Kitchen seen from the dining

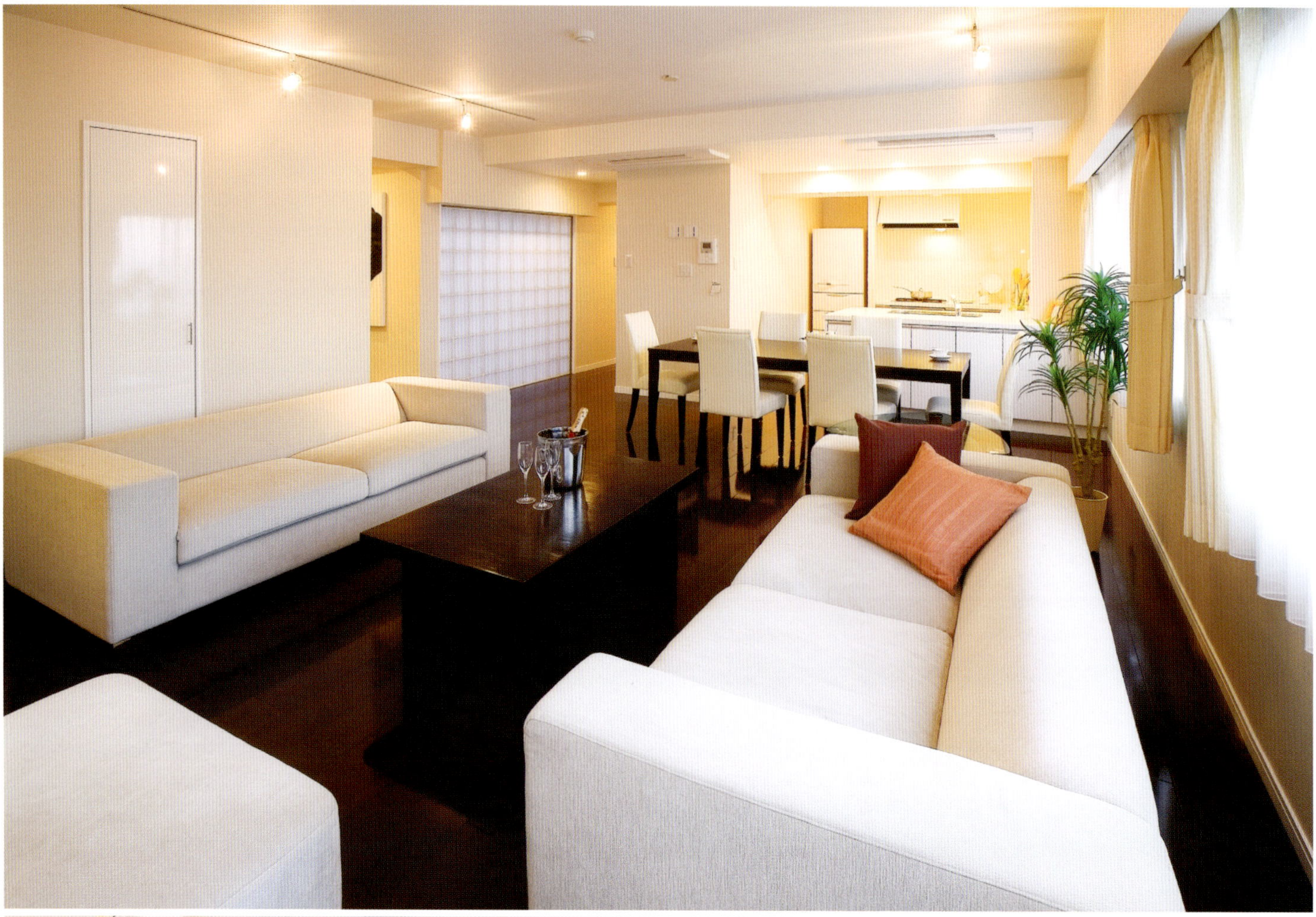

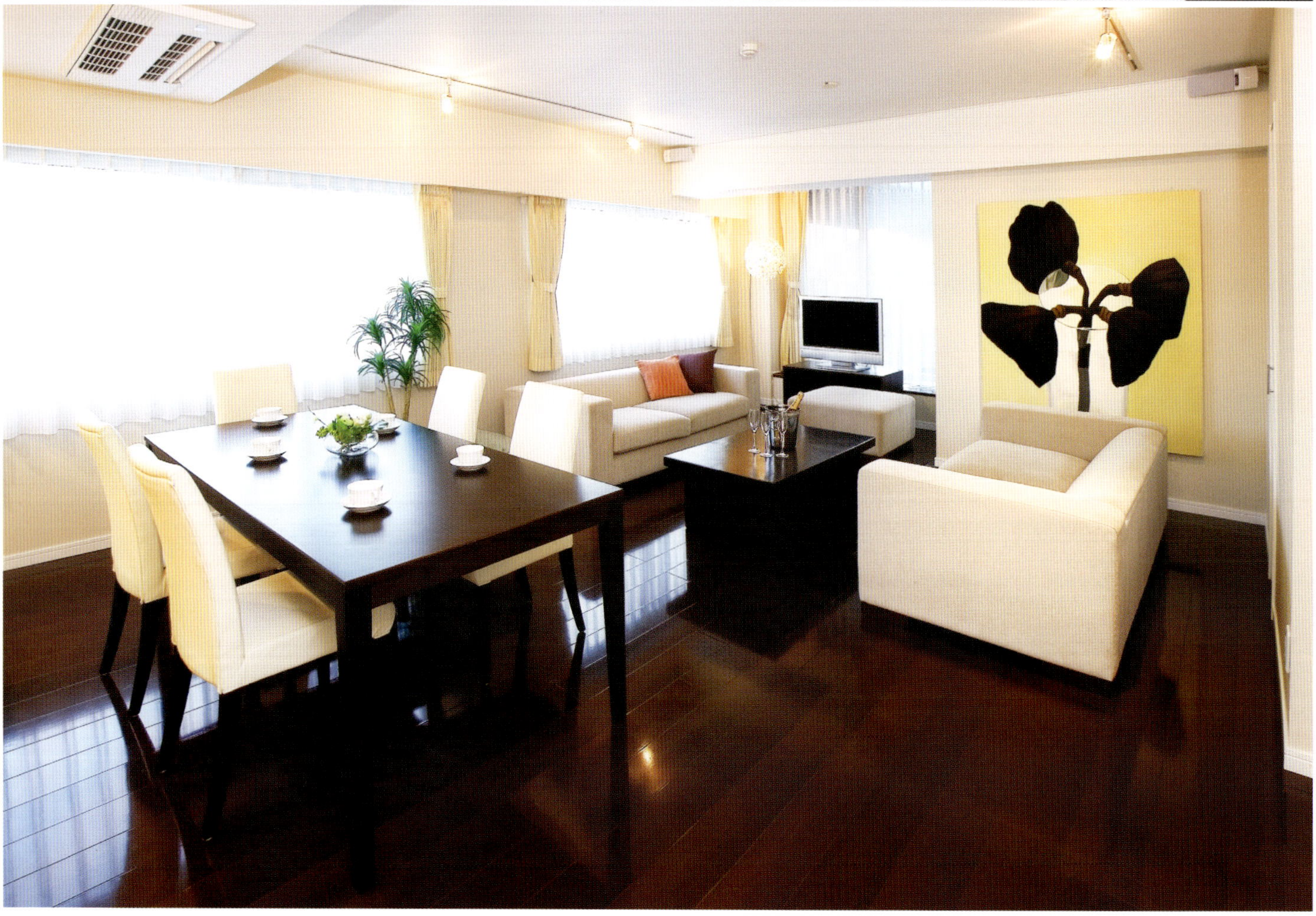

1	3
	4
2	5

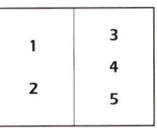

1
Room302：リビングからキッチン・ダイニングを臨む
Room302: Kitchen and dining space seen from the living space

2
Room302：リビング・ダイニング
Room302: Living-dining room

3
Room301：ベッドルーム：奥の曲線を描く窓ガラスは、右手側に配したリビングルームへとつながっている。ベッドルームとリビングとは腰壁とガラスウォールのパーティションで仕切られている
Room301: Bedroom. The curving glass window is leading to the living room behind the wall to the right. The bedroom and the living room are separated by the spandrel walls and glass wall partitions.

4
Room302：キッチン
Room302: Kitchen

5
Room302：ゆったりとした落ち着きのあるベッドルーム
Room302: Comfortable, extensive bedroom

1	4	5
2		
3		

1
Room 401:リビングルームからキッチンを臨む。壁一面の窓からたっぷりと陽射しが入り込んでくる
Room 401: Kitchen seen from the living room. Full-size windows allow natural light to fill the room.

2
Room 401:リビングルーム：奥にベッドルームへ続くらせん階段を臨む
Room 401: Living room: Spiral stairs leading to the bedroom at the back

3
Room 401:広々とした明るいベッドルーム
Room 401: Extensive, well-lit bedroom

4
Room 401:アイランドキッチン
Room 401: Island kitchen

5
Room 401:ルーフバルコニー
Room 401: Roof balcony

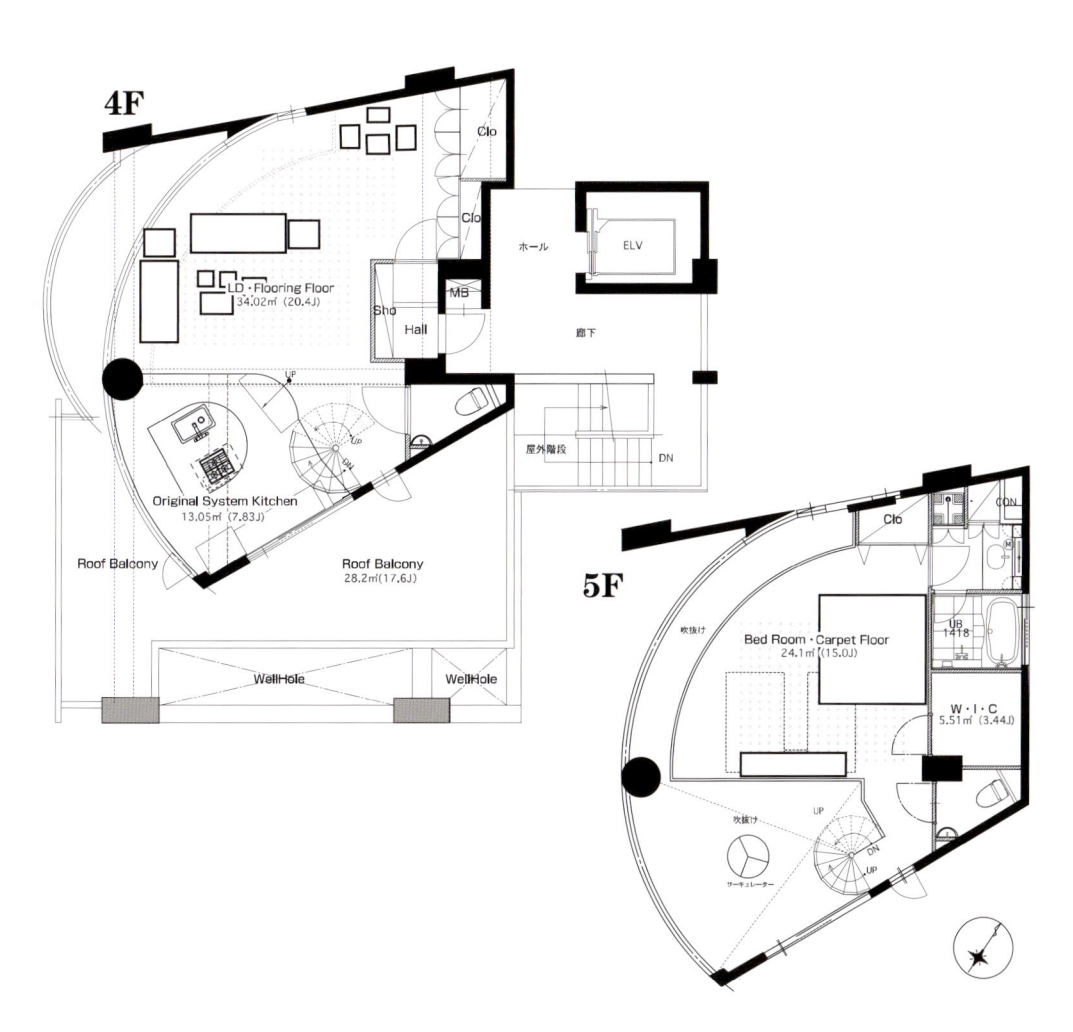

Data

Title
FLEG Hiroo 2nd Ave.

Developer
F.L.E.G. INTERNATIONAL CO., LTD.

Location
Shibuya-ku, Tokyo

Site area
463.58m²

Building area
304.07m²

Total floor area
1,535.87m²

Area
80.70-118.70m²

Structure
RC

Completion
June, 2004

Materials
Exterior Wall :
  45x45 tile, granite
Public Wall :
  plaster finish, marble, sandstone,
  45x45 tile, joly pate
Public Floor :
  self-leveling, marble
Interior Wall :
  cloth
Interior Floor :
  marble, flooring, carpet

I. flat

Love Architecture Inc. / Yukio Asari

立体的にねじれた空間がもたらす豊かさ

幅員22mの幹線道路沿いの3面が開放された敷地に建つ集合住宅である。周囲に小規模の戸建住宅を抱え、表＝反復するバルコニー、裏＝外廊下、そして残された妻側という、広く一般化している集合住宅「らしさ」がもたらす均質やスケール感は避けるべきだと考えた。I.flatは異なる間取りのメゾネットが立体的に絡み合いながら組み上げられている。各住戸は階段の吹抜けを軸に上下階でねじれており、開口部は様々な方向を向いている。結果的に各立面は差別化されることは無く、それが3面開放された敷地への解答となっている。それらの開口部は上下階で異なる風景を切り取り、一日を通して質の異なる自然光を導き、南面採光を重視した集合住宅には無い豊かさをもたらしている。集合住宅「らしさ」を捨て、集合住宅「だからこそ」出来る可能性を追求した結果である。本来、柱、壁の位置を揃えることで構造的強度や施工性を優先するRC造であるが、これにより上下階に不必要な関係性がうまれ各室の自由がせばめられている現実もある。規模の小ささも考慮し柱、壁の位置に適度のずれを許容することで、静かに自由度を提案する構造を採用した。

Richness realized by the three-dimensionally twisted space

This condominium is built on a site open on three sides and is along an arterial road. As there were many small-scale stand-alone houses in the neighborhood, we thought we should avoid giving a sense of uniformity or scale caused by the typical condominium design with a row of the same balconies on the facade, external corridors running at the back, plus the remaining sides. I.flat is configured by three-dimensionally combined maisonnettes with different layouts. Each dwelling unit is twisted with the stair well as its axis, and the openings face various directions. Consequently, no elevation is differentiated, thus being an answer to the site open in three directions. Depending on floors, these openings reveal different views, allow different natural light in, and give richness different from that of a condominium emphasizing natural lighting from the south. The design is a result of pursuit of what a condominium "can" do by giving up what a condominium "should" be. When the RC construction method is employed, columns and walls are aligned to put priority to structural strength and easiness to construct; however, this also leads to unnecessary associations between upper and lower floors, limiting flexibility of individual rooms. In consideration of the small scale of the project, we adopted a structure that informally proposes flexibility by appropriately determining different positions of columns and walls.

	2	
1	3	4
	5	

1
浮遊するボリュームにランダムに穿たれた開口部
Random openings on the walls of the structure that appears to be floating

2
玄関ホールの吹抜け
Open ceiling in the entrance hall

3
大開口を背景にキッチンと一体になったダイニングテーブルとペンダント照明がもたらすパースペクティブ
A unique perspective realized by the dining table integrated with the kitchen and pendant lighting with the large opening as the background

4
街路樹を切り取るように配置された2層分の開口部
Opening rising up two floors as if to frame roadside trees

5
階段の吹抜けを軸に空間がねじれている
Space is twisted with the stair well as its axis

141

1
2

1
各戸の階段は必ずガラスのカーテンウォールを背景とする。同時にファサードの一部となる
The stairway of each floor always has a glass curtain wall as its background and at the same time, serves as part of the facade.

2
バスルームは原則バルコニーとセットになっている
Bathroom essentially associated with a balcony

Data

Title
  I.flat

Designer / Architect
  Love Architecture Inc. / Yukio Asari

Structural Design
  Kenji Nawa

Location
  Kawasaki city, Kanagawa

Site area
  179.29m²

Building area
  122.86m²

Total floor area
  536.08m²

Area
  34.21-42.84m²

Structure
  RC

Completion
  May, 2005

Materials
  Exterior Wall :
    flouride resin spraying (clear frosting) on architectural concrete
  Public Wall :
    flouride resin spraying (clear frosting) on architectural concrete
  Public Floor :
    concrete monolithic surface finish
    natural green slate
    concrete polishing plate
  Interior Wall :
    architectural concrete, painting on PB
  Interior Floor :
    Amazon cherry flooring, ash flooring
    mortal trowel finish
    concrete polishing plate

Photo
  Hiroyasu Sakaguchi

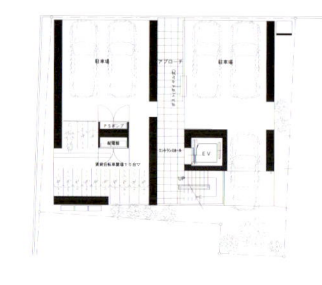

平面図 1 F

平面図 2 F

平面図 3 F

平面図 4 F

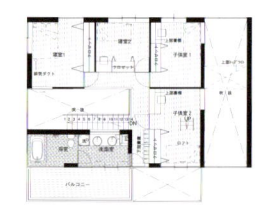

平面図 5 F

Minami-Gyotoku Quartetto
南行徳の4奏住宅

Love Architecture Inc. / Yukio Asari + Nakae Architects
Yuji Nakae + Ohno JAPAN / Hirofumi Ohno

ハーフRCストラクチュアによる4棟相乗デザイン

東京近郊の住宅地、旗竿敷地を含む4区画に分割された80坪ほどの土地に建つ、4棟の「建て売り住宅」の計画である。設計当初より望まれた「コンクリートを部分的に用いる」という条件を拡張し、部分的なコンクリートの扱いが各棟及び全体のデザインを同時に決定していくような構成ルールを考えた。長方形平面の四周を囲む1.5層分の高さの鉄筋コンクリート（RC）壁を各面の半分程度地上から2階床レベルまで持ち上げる。この構成による構造体は、3階床を支持する高さを持ちながら、一度のコンクリート打設でつくることが可能な構造体である。ここに屋根及び床を木軸で架け、必要に応じて外壁や間仕切壁を設けていく。ガレージやエントランスといった外部空間と連続する1階はコンクリート主体の公共性の高い空間、木造となる3階は構造用ラーチ合板をそのまま仕上げとしたあたたかみのある個室空間、中間の2階は1階と3階の雰囲気が互いに浸透するように上下に噛み合った文字通り中心的なリビング空間となり、構成が直接的に各階の性格を決定づけている。従来の「建て売り住宅」がうわべを飾ることによって商品化を図るのとは逆に、建築の素の姿、「すっぴん」の状態に強度を与えることこそが、われわれの提案する「建て売り住宅」である。1棟1棟が特異なものでありながら、共通のルールによってつくられた4棟を並べることで、特徴的とも普遍的ともつかないような、そういう風景をここに生み出したいと考えた。

Synergistic design of four houses by partially reinforced concrete structure

In this project planned in the suburb of Tokyo, four "built-for-sale houses" were to be constructed on the site of about 260 square meters divided into four lots, one of which consisted of a narrow part and a wide part at the rear. From the designing stage, the client requested to partially use concrete in the buildings, and we extended this approach to establish a rule so that meeting this request should determine the individual as well as total designs at the same time. The reinforced concrete (RC) walls was designed to have a height of one and half floors to surround all four sides of each rectangular house in a way that about the half height of each wall should reach the second floor level. The structure with this configuration had a height enough to support the third floor but could be built by pouring concrete only once. The roofs and floors were laid using the wooden frames, and external walls and partition walls were erected as appropriate. The different structure of each floor directly determines the nature of each floor: concrete dominates the first floor connected to the garage, entrance and other external spaces with a public nature; the finish of the third floor uses the structural larch plywood "as-is"; the second floor in between them serves as the central living space where different atmospheres of the upper and lower floors meet as if they penetrated each other. While the conventional "built-for-sale houses" are commercialized by superficial decorations, the shape of those we propose is to give strength to their "naked" state. We wanted to create ambiguous scenery that appears both unique and universal by combining four houses individually unique yet based on a common rule.

1	4 5
2	6
3	7

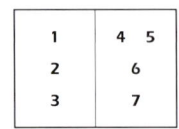

1
同じ構成ルールによる統一性と多様性
Integrity and diversity based on the same configuration rule

2
A棟 構造の特性を生かし、2方向に開放されたオープンガレージ
House A: Open garage open for two directions taking advantage of the characteristics of the structure

3
境界塀を設けないことで4棟の敷地全体を横断するおおらかな外部空間を生み出す
Spacious external space is created across the four lots by erecting no border fence.

4
D棟 階段越しにバスルームとバルコニーを見る
House D: Bathroom and balcony beyond the stairway

5
2階より3階の木造空間を見上げる
Wooden space of the third floor looked up from the second floor

6
D棟 コンクリートとラーチ合板が上下に噛み合ったリビング空間、テラスが組み込まれている
House D: Living space where concrete of the lower floor and larch plywood of the upper floor meet. A terrace is also provided.

7
A棟 コンクリートとラーチ合板が噛み合ったリビング空間、階段越しに見る
House A: Living space where concrete and larch plywood are combined, seen beyond the stairway

1 駐車スペース
2 エントランスホール
3 個室
4 浴室・洗面室
5 LDK
6 吹抜
7 テラス

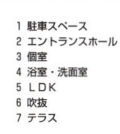

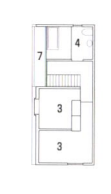

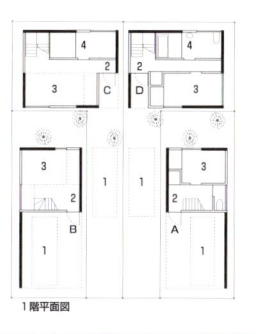

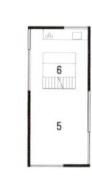

3階平面図

1階平面図　2階平面図

Data

Title
　Minami-Gyotoku Quartetto

Developer
　early-Age co., ltd.

Designer / Architect
　Love Architecture Inc.
　Yukio Asari + Nakae Architects
　Yuji Nakae + Ohno JAPAN
　Hirofumi Ohno

Location
　Ichikawa city, Chiba

Site area
　No.A : 62.15m²
　No.B : 62.22m²
　No.C : 75.07m²
　No.D : 74.97m²

Building area
　No.A : 37.27m²
　No.B : 37.27m²
　No.C : 31.89m²
　No.D : 31.89m²

Total floor area
　No.A : 85.51m²
　No.B : 85.51m²
　No.C : 82.83m²
　No.D : 82.83m²

Structure
　RC (wooden structure in part)

Completion
　December, 2005

Materials
　Exterior Wall :
　　water- repellent coating on
　　architetural concrete
　　color garubarium (seam joint)
　Interior Wall :
　　architetural concrete, painting on PB
　Interior Floor :
　　concrete monolithic surface finish
　　Japanese cedar flooring

Photo
　Hiroyasu Sakaguchi

Sanctus Court Ashiya

サンクタスコート芦屋

ORIX Real Estate Corporation
Tadasu Ohe / Plantec Architects / Kanon Associates

空間デザインの基本テーマは「外へ閉じ、内へ開く」、またイメージとしては、リゾートホテルの空間性能を採り入れている。外部に対してセキュリティー対策を設計の段階から徹底し、マンションの敷地内に於いてはできる限りの開放感と自由度を意識している。植栽や周辺の環境と調和する景観と建造物の圧迫感をなるべく感じさせないデザインを重視しながら、白を基調にモダンなリゾート感を意識している。またガラスブロックを効果的に活用し、建物の独創性を引き出している。基調色の白とガラスやアルミパネル素材の活用によりシンプリティーの美観を醸し出すことに努めている。通常、薄暗く雑然とした感じになりがちな玄関側（共用廊下側）のファサードも洗練されたサンクタスコート芦屋を象徴するような佇まい。また、バーティカル・ヴィラはガラスブロックウォールの効果で昼夜の景観も一変する表情豊かなファサードが実現した。

The basic theme of the spatial design is "closed to the outside, open to the inside". Further, spatial performances of resort hotels are adapted to the concept. A thorough security plan against unauthorized access from the outside has been implemented from the designing stage, but once inside the site of the condominium, one finds that a sense of openness and freedom is provided as much as possible. The exterior of the building based on the color of white gives a sense of modern resorts while close attention is paid to landscaping that matches planting and surrounding environments as well as designing that minimizes a sense of oppression from the structure. Glass blocks are abundantly used to demonstrate the uniqueness of the building. The wide utilization of the while as the basic color and aluminum panels leads to a beauty of simplicity. Even the facade of the entrance (common corridor) side that conventionally tends to be darkish and crowded has an appearance representing the sophistication of Sanctus Court Ashiya. The Vertical Villa has a facade that changes at day and at night, thanks to the effects of the glass block walls.

	2
1	3
	4

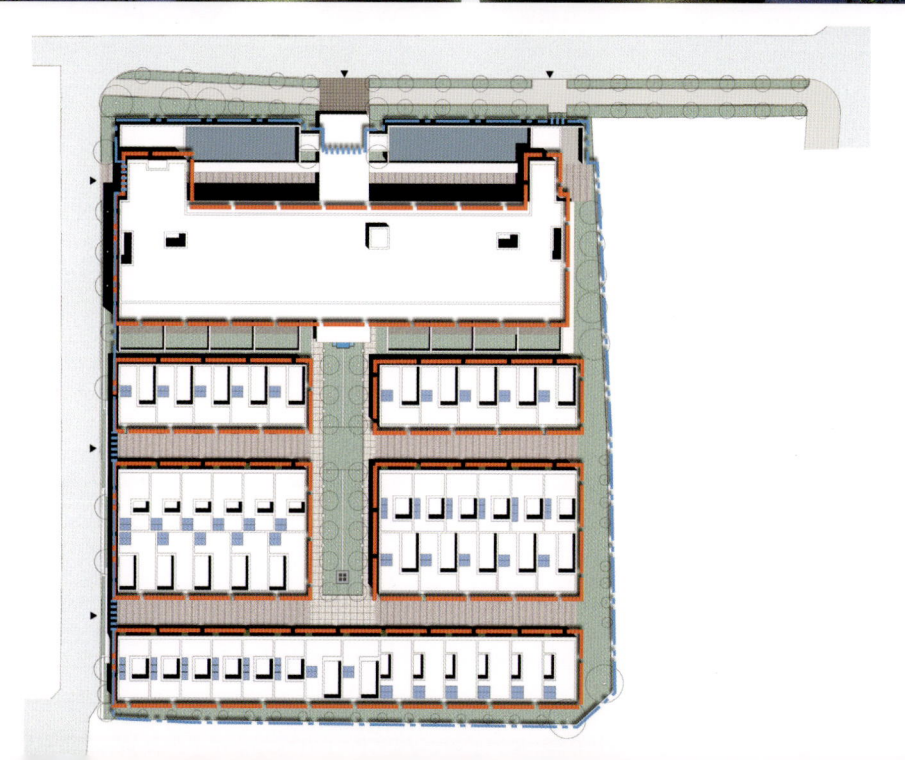

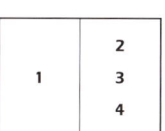

1
外観：北西からエントランス側を臨む
Exterior: Entrance side seen from the northwest

2
アプローチから臨むエントランス
Entrance seen from the approach

3
ラウンジ側（北側）に水のオブジェ、南側に石のオブジェを配置し、その間をライティングラインで結び、昼夜共にサンクタスコート芦屋のシンボリックな景観となるセンターコート
Center court serving as the symbolic landscape of Sanctus Court Ashiya both at day and at night. A line of light connects in between the water object placed on the lounge side (north) and the stone object in the south.

4
敷地配置図
Site Plan

147

Lateral House LE-type
レイトラル・ハウス
Tadasu Ohe / Plantec Architects

横の発想（レイトラル・ハウス）
横に貫く空間のエネルギーを住空間に活かすことが、このプランのコンセプト。このコンセプトと通常のマンションの違いは、「田の字型プラン」の打破から始まる。顕著な違いを導く二つの疑問。ひとつは部屋数（個室）確保のために生じる壁と廊下への疑問。もうひとつは南面を重視し、極端に北面を塞ぐマンションの「南面崇拝」への疑問。本計画は発想を転換し、新たな価値を提案。光や風の通り道を極力妨げない基本ルール。さらに、相対する二つの開口部を同等に開放すること。特に閉塞感のあった玄関スペース（北面であることが多い）は、従来の玄関発想を捨て、もっとも自分らしく、もっとも自由にデザイン出来るパブリックリビングを設置することを計画。

Lateral House: Concept of horizontality
The concept of this plan is to take advantage of the power a space has in the horizontal direction. The difference between this concept and that of ordinary condominiums begins with a move from the grid-shaped layout plan. This is based on two questions about the validity of the architectural "common sense". One is about the walls and corridors required for securing the number of (individual) rooms. The other is about "the southern face worshipping" in condominium design. In this plan, we shifted the paradigm and proposed new values. The basic rule was not to disturb paths of light and wind wherever possible. The other rule was to equally open each pair of two openings. Especially, when we designed the entrance space (often in the north) giving a sense of closeness, we discarded the conventional concept of entrance and planned to provide a public living space that can be originally and flexibly designed.

	2
1	3
	4

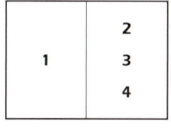

1
パブリックリビングからリビング・ダイニングを臨む：玄関ドアを開けると広がる大空間。住み手の感性やライフスタイルが如実にデザインされるであろうスペースを住空間のファーストアプローチに設計

Living-dining space seen from the public living room: This extensive space appears before one's eyes when one opens the entrance door. The space most likely to reflect the sensitivity and lifestyle of its residents is designed as the first approach to the living space.

2
リビング・ダイニングルーム：右手にガラスで仕切られたベッドルームを配している

Living-dining room: Glass partitioned bed room to the right

3
リビングルーム

Living room

4
キッチンからリビング・ダイニングを臨む

Living-dining space seen from the kitchen

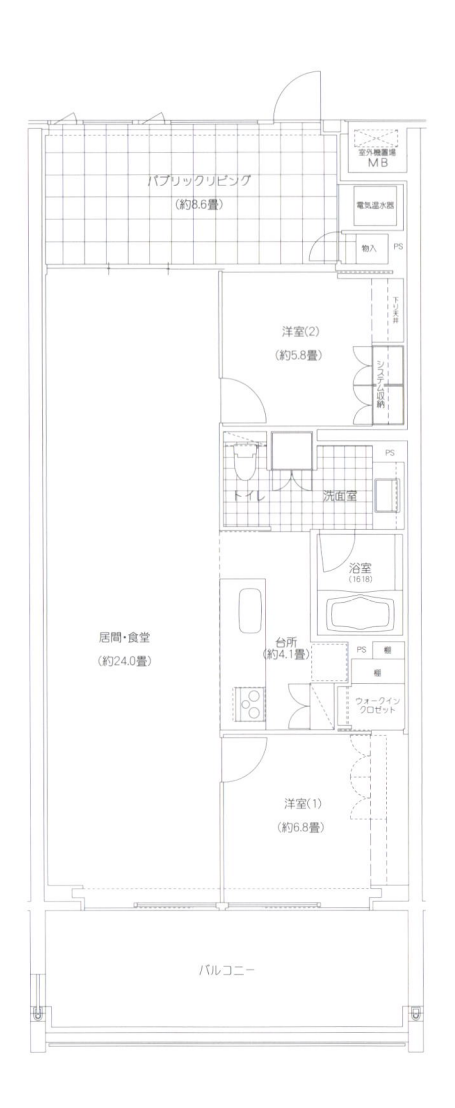

1
ホビールーム
Hobby room

2
キッチンを臨む
View of the kitchen

3
ベッドルームからバルコニーを臨む
Balcony seen from the bedroom

Data

Title
  Lateral House LE-type
Designer / Architect
  Tadasu Ohe / Plantec Architects
Area
  96.48m²
Materials
  Interior Wall :
    vinyl cloth
  Interior Floor :
    400x400 tile, flooring

Vertical Villa

バーティカル・ヴィラ
Tadasu Ohe / Plantec Architects

縦の発想（バーティカル・ヴィラ）

垂直に広がる空間のエネルギーを住空間に活かすことが、このプランのコンセプト。集合住宅で気になる上下住戸に対する気兼ねを軽減し、集合住宅領域の中で限りなく独立性を意識した住空間が誕生。基本3フロアーから構成されるこのプランは、ビルトインガレージを含めた「還るフロアー」・自分を解放する「癒すフロアー」・日常を楽しむ「弾むフロアー」の三構成を、垂直に流れ込む光や風の自然要素で繋いでゆくプラン。1階の「還るフロアー」は、ハードとしての玄関やガレージスペースと共に「自分に還る」ための趣味や研究など時間を忘れて何かに没頭できるパブリックリビングを設置することを計画。

Vertical Villa: Concept of verticality

The concept of this plan is to take advantage of the power a space has in the vertical direction. This living space reduces fear of disturbing the apartments above and below and emphasizes privacy and independence in the condominium. The plan basically configured by three floors connected by natural factors such as vertical light and wind: "floor to return" including the built-in garage; "floor to heal" to make oneself free; "floor to be inspired" to enjoy daily life. The "floor to return" on the first floor has not only the entrance and garage space as hardware but also the public living room where one can be immersed in hobbies or studies to "return to oneself", forgetting the passage of time.

1
3Fリビング・ダイニングルーム
Living-dining room on the third floor

2
1F パブリックリビングからビルトインガレージを臨む
Built-in garage seen from the public living space on the first floor

3
エントランスからパブリックリビングを臨む
Public living space seen from the entrance

4
2F テラスからの見上げ
Upper floor seen from the terrace on the second floor

5
パウダールーム
Powder room

6
キッチン
Kitchen

7
テラスに付随したベッドルーム
Bedroom next to the terrace

1F 2F 3F

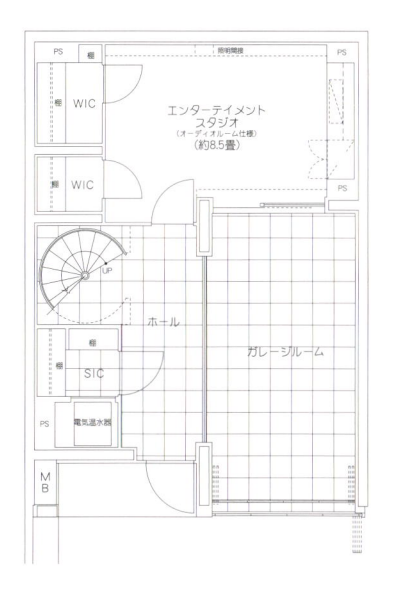

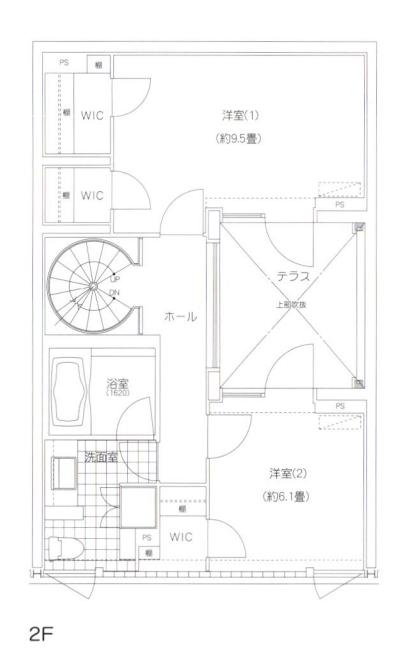

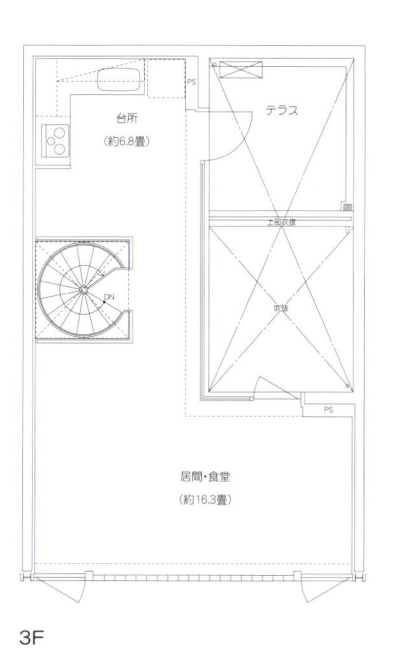

Data

Title
 Vertical Villa VF-type

Designer / Architect
 Tadasu Ohe / Plantec Architects

Area
 125.05m²

Materials
 Interior Wall :
  vinyl cloth
 Interior Floor :
  400x400 tile, flooring

PH-2

Tadashi Suga

JR兵庫から、歩いて8分。平家物語にも出てくるくらい古い町中に位置する。現状は工場地帯でもあるが、よく見ると小さな寺院がたくさん点在している。そのような環境の中で工場の跡地に計画された。建物や敷地のスケール感を考え、ルーバーで覆い、庇でエントランスを強調しこの建物のアイデンティティとした。そのモダンで力強い形体であることが住む人のステイタス感にも繋がる。

Eight minutes on foot from Hyogo Station of the West Japan Railway, the building is located at the heart of an old town as if it were taken from the Tale of Heike (a Japanese war chronicle). Currently, the area is zoned industrial district, but at a closer glance, one finds many scattered small temples. The building is planned on the site where once a factory was built. To convey a sense of scale of the building and site and give it an identity, the exterior walls are covered with louvers, and the presence of the entrance is emphasized with eaves. The modern and strong form of the building leads to a sense of status for its residents.

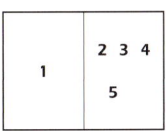

1
北側道路からのファサード夜景
Facade at night seen from the road in the north

2
北側ファサード：アルミルーバーで覆われている
Northern facade: Covered by aluminum louvers

3
エントランス内部
Inside the entrance

4
内部吹け抜見下ろし
The indoor well seen from the above

5
外観夜景：ルーバーは道路より一定の空きに見えるように、上部ほどピッチが大きくなっている
Exterior at night: The higher the positions of the louvers are, the greater the spacing between them so that the spacing should appear to be constant when seen from the road.

1
2

1
北側住戸入口、及びルーバー方向を見る
Entrance of a dwelling unit on the north and louvers

2
6F 南側住戸：アイランドキッチンとロフトを見る
Unit facing south on the 6th floor: Island kitchen and loft can be seen.

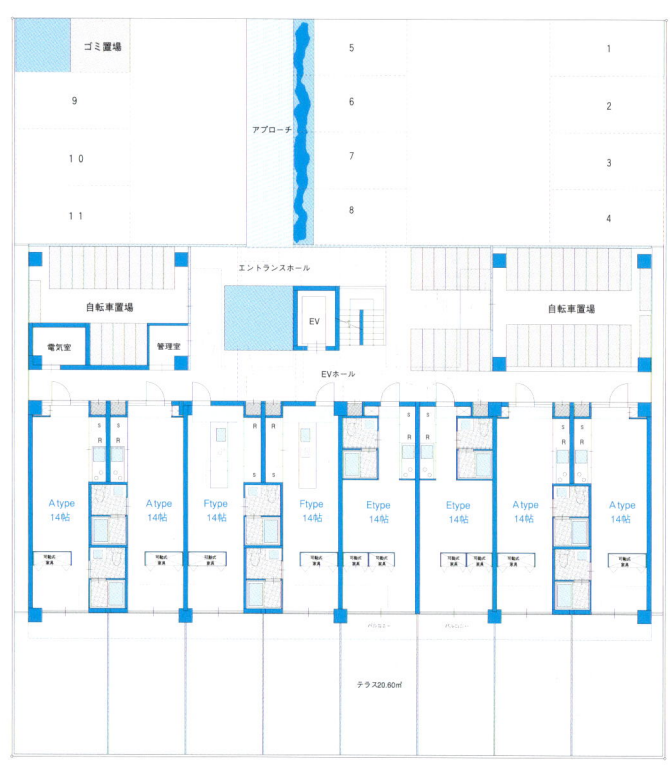

Data

Title
　PH-2
Architect
　Tadashi Suga
Location
　Hyogo-ku, Kobe city, Hyogo
Site area
　899.7m²
Area
　29.92m²
Structure
　rigid frame
Completion
　February, 2005

Materials
　Exterior Wall :
　　aluminium louver, tile
　Public Wall :
　　architectural concrete
　Public Floor :
　　tile
　Interior Wall :
　　architectural concrete, AEP roller
　Interior Floor :
　　flooring tile
Photo
　Yoshiharu Matsumura

curva
Tadashi Suga

まず、重層長屋とは通常の長屋の玄関が道（通路）に直接出入りでき、道、玄関、住戸が並列に並んでいるのに対して、道、玄関は同じであるが、住戸は上下に重なる形態をいう。それは一見共同住宅の様であるが、決定的に違うのは、共同住宅の玄関は共用廊下に面し、共用のエントランスを通って出入りするのに対し、長屋は専用玄関から直接出入りする。実は長屋の方が同規模の共同住宅より、ハイグレードなのである。良い点は、長屋の欠点であるプライバシーの低さ、逆に共同住宅の欠点である閉鎖性、コミュニティの形成の難しさ、そして両方に共通する、生活形式の画一性をシンプルに解決しようとしている。長屋のプライベート空間と半パブリック空間を分けることにより、共同住宅では不可能な外部に直接接続された多目的自由空間がその入居者の必要に応じてスタイルを形成できる。

To begin with, ordinary row houses have entrances with direct access to a road (or a passageway), and the road, entrances and residences all run in parallel; on the other hand, with multistory tenement houses, the road and entrances are again in parallel, but houses are multistoried. Such tenement houses may look like condominiums at a glance, but the greatest difference lies in the fact that their residents have their own entrances to directly access to the road. In the case of the condominiums, the entrance of each residence faces a public corridor, and people use a common entrance hall. Contrary to our common sense, the tenement houses are superior to the condominiums of the same scale. In a simple approach, this design attempted to solve the disadvantages of the two types of the buildings: low privacy of the tenement houses; closed nature and difficulty in community building of the condominiums; and uniform lifestyles commonly found in both architectural types. Separating the private spaces and semi-public spaces of the tenement house and offering a multi-purpose space directly connected to the outside not available with the condominiums helps its residents to establish their own lifestyles as needed.

1
南側共用スペースからの夜景。一階にはエントランスが並ぶ
Condominium at night seen from the common use space on the south. The entrances are on the first floor.

158

1	3
2	4
	5

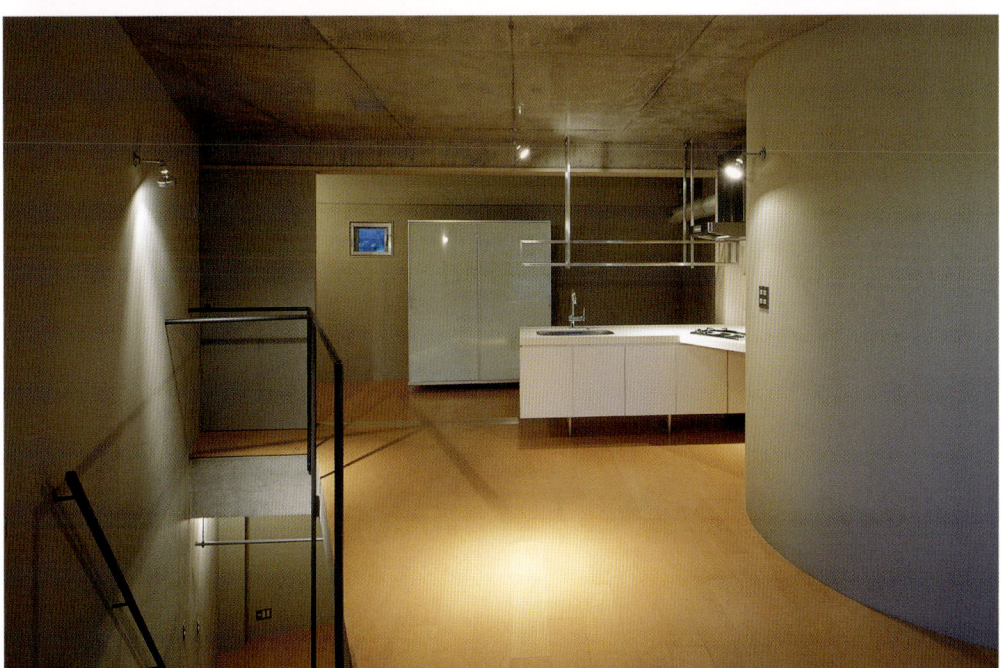

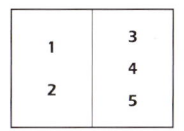

1
北側外観を見る
Exterior facing the north

2
住戸内部から外部共用スペース方向を見る
External common use space seen from the inside of a dwelling unit

3
2階LDK
Living room and dining kitchen on the second floor

4
2階LDK
Living room and dining kitchen on the second floor

5
1階から3階住戸への螺旋階段
Spiral stairs leading to the dwelling unit on the third floor from the first floor

Data

Title
  curva

Architect
  Tadashi Suga

Location
  Ibaraki city, Osaka

Site area
  1,171.53m²

Area
  59.36-85.95m²

Structure
  wall-frame

Completion
  February, 2005

Materials
  Exterior Wall :
    urethane painting on architectural concrete
  Interior Wall :
    AEP, architectural concrete
  Interior Floor :
    500x500 terracotta, flooring

Photo
  Yoshiharu Matsumura

Park Hills Oyake I
パークヒルズ大宅 I
Tatsuro Hagihara / Kenshi Kawai

京都市の東方、御所山の裾野にある敷地から丘にかけてにはまだ農地が点在する。この地に賃貸住宅計画を始めるにあたり、敷地中央に存在する計画道路や建物のボリューム、入居者ニーズなどの問題を如何に対応するかが基本課題であった。また事業用住宅はそれが分譲・賃貸に関らず収益性と入居者の快適性は相反する要素であり常に最大の問題である。都市部でタワーマンションが多数建築されていく現状で、郊外に位置する今回の計画では低層である事をあえて選択した。郊外に高層住宅である理由が見付からない。かつてGLC(大ロンドン庁)が行った高層住宅を低層に移行させたハウジングの理念を理想と考えるからだ。英国人は日本人と同じく接地型住居志向が伝統的に根強いと言われている。低層住宅では子供の心身を健やかに発達させ、人々の安定した生活には屋内空間と屋外空間を一体的に構成した集合住宅が望ましいとの考えに基づいて設計した。計画道路部は郊外型マンションに不可欠な駐車スペースとし、東側を1期工事、西側を2期工事として周囲の環境になじむエクステリアデザイン、プールを持つエントランスホール、花伝舎・松島紫乃氏による造園計画などで「ペットと暮らす幸せな生活」のコンセプトを表現した。

To the east of Kyoto City, farms are sparsely scattered from the site of this project in the outskirts of Mt. Goshoyama toward the hills. In planning a condominium in the lot, the fundamental issues to be considered include the planned load to run through the site, volume requirements of the building, and needs of residents. Further, regardless of units for sales or rent, profitability for owners and comfortability of residents are always contradictory regarding condominiums to be built for business purposes, which is always the largest challenge for architects. Though the trend in the cities is to build tower condominiums, in this project to build a condominium in suburbs, a low-rise design is intentionally selected because we cannot find a reason to build a high-rise building in suburbia and think that ideal is the concept of shifting from high-rise to low rise buildings once presented by the Greater London Council. Like the Japanese, the English are considered to traditionally have a ground-orientation. The condominium is designed on the basis of the philosophy that low-rise buildings enable healthy physical and mental development of children while condominiums where indoor and outdoor spaces are integrally configured are desirable for leading a stable life. The section with the planned road is allocated for the parking space indispensable for a life in suburbs, and its eastern side is developed in the first phase of construction, and its western side is developed in the second phase. The concept of "a happy life with a pet" is realized by taking advantage of such elements as the exterior design to fit with the surroundings, the entrance hall with a pool and landscaping by Shino Matsushima of Kadensha.

	2	3
1		4
		5

1
エントランスからの南・西面ファサード
Northern and western facades seen from the entrance

2
中央パーキングからの西面ファサード
Western facade seen from the central parking lot

3
エントランス内庭からの見返し
Entrance looked back from the inner garden

4
エントランスホール内
Inside the entrance hall

5
メゾメットタイプ室内
Inside the maisonette type

161

1
2

1
メゾネットタイプ上部ロフト見上げ
View of the loft of the maisonette type unit looked up from the floor

2
ロフト付きタイプ室内
Interior of the unit with a loft

Data

Title
  Park Hills Oyake I

Architect
  Tatsuro Hagihara / Kenshi Kawai

Location
  Yamashina-ku, Kyoto city

Site area
  600.89m²

Area
  45.8-69.7m²

Structure
  reinforced concrete wall construction

Completion
  September, 2003

Materials
  Exterior Wall :
    granite, tile, plasterer finish
  Public Wall :
    plasterer finish
  Public Floor :
    black granite, tile
  Interior Wall :
    AEP, cloth
  Interior Floor :
    flooring, vinyl tile

Photo
  Kei Sugino

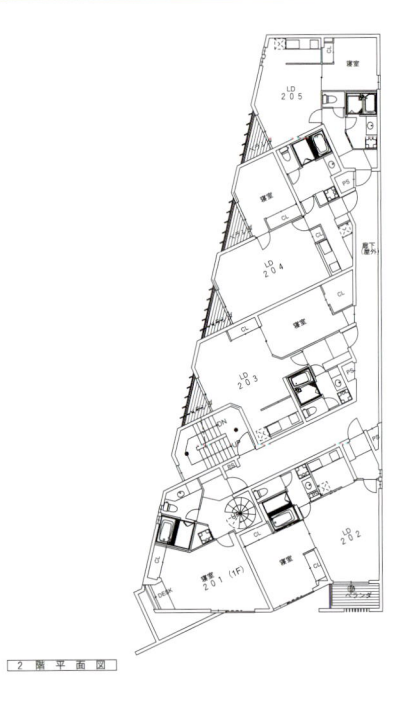

Park Hills Oyake II

パークヒルズ大宅 II

Tatsuro Hagihara / Kenshi Kawai

京都市の東方、御所山の裾野にある敷地から丘にかけてはまだ農地が点在する。この地に賃貸住宅計画を始めるにあたり、敷地中央に存在する計画道路や建物のボリューム、入居者ニーズなどの問題を如何に対応するかが基本課題であった。また事業用住宅はそれが分譲・賃貸に関らず収益性と入居者の快適性は相反する要素であり常に最大の問題である。都市部でタワーマンションが多数建築されていく現状で、郊外に位置する今回の計画では低層である事をあえて選択した。郊外に高層住宅である理由が見付らない。かつてGLC（大ロンドン庁）が行った高層住宅を低層に移行させたハウジングの理念を理想と考えるからだ。英国人は日本人と同じく接地型住居志向が伝統的に根強いと言われている。低層住宅では子供の心身を健やかに発達させ、人々の安定した生活には屋内空間と屋外空間を一体的に構成した集合住宅が望ましいとの考えに基づいて設計した。計画道路部は郊外型マンションに不可欠な駐車スペースとし、東側を1期工事、西側を2期工事として周囲の環境になじむエクステリアデザイン、プールを持つエントランスホール、花伝舎・松島紫乃氏による造園計画などで「ペットと暮らす幸せな生活」のコンセプトを表現した。

To the east of Kyoto City, farms are sparsely scattered from the site of this project in the outskirts of Mt. Goshoyama toward the hills. In planning a condominium in the lot, the fundamental issues to be considered include the planned load to run through the site, volume requirements of the building, and needs of residents. Further, regardless of units for sales or rent, profitability for owners and comfortability of residents are always contradictory regarding condominiums to be built for business purposes, which is always the largest challenge for architects. Though the trend in the cities is to build tower condominiums, in this project to build a condominium in suburbs, a low-rise design is intentionally selected because we cannot find a reason to build a high-rise building in suburbia and think that ideal is the concept of shifting from high-rise to low rise buildings once presented by the Greater London Council. Like the Japanese, the English are considered to traditionally have a ground-orientation. The condominium is designed on the basis of the philosophy that low-rise buildings enable healthy physical and mental development of children while condominiums where indoor and outdoor spaces are integrally configured are desirable for leading a stable life. The section with the planned road is allocated for the parking space indispensable for a life in suburbs, and its eastern side is developed in the first phase of construction, and its western side is developed in the second phase. The concept of "a happy life with a pet" is realized by taking advantage of such elements as the exterior design to fit with the surroundings, the entrance hall with a pool and landscaping by Shino Matsushima of Kadensha.

1	2	5	
3			
4		6	7

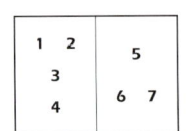

1
中央パーキングからの東面ファサード
Eastern facade seen from the central parking lot

2
エントランス側面
Side of the entrance

3
エントランスホールからの見返し
Entrance looked back from the entrance hall

4
メゾネットタイプ室内
Inside the maisonette type

5
メゾネットタイプ室内
Inside the maisonette type

6
勾配天井タイプ室内
Inside the sloped ceiling type

7
洗面スペース
Lavatory space

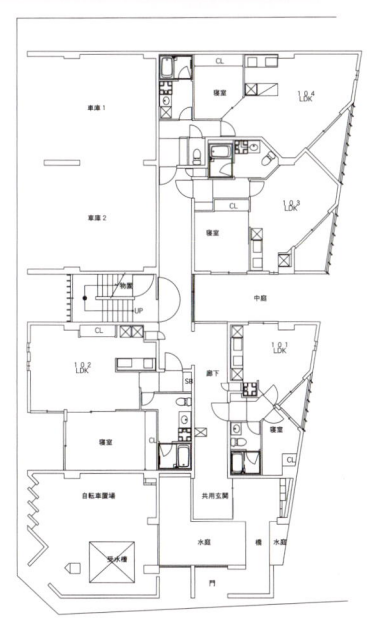

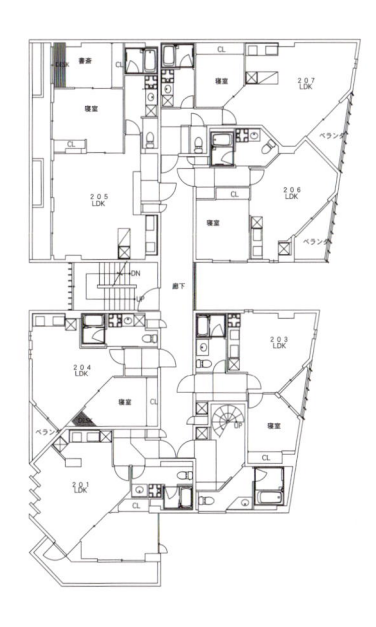

Data

Title
 Park Hills Oyake II

Architect
 Tatsuro Hagihara / Kenshi Kawai

Location
 Yamashina-ku, Kyoto city

Site area
 832.39m²

Area
 35.2 - 72.1m²

Structure
 reinforced concrete frame

Completion
 March, 2005

Materials
 Exterior Wall :
  tile, exposed concrete, plasterer finish
 Public Wall :
  plasterer finish
 Public Floor :
  black granite
 Interior Wall :
  AEP, cloth
 Interior Floor :
  flooring, vinyl tile

Photo
 Yoshiharu Matsumura

FLEG roppongi secondo

FLEG六本木secondo

F.L.E.G. INTERNATIONAL CO., LTD.
Yasumichi Morita / Rowland Kirishima

「Executive Suite」とは、東京都内有数の好立地な場所（広尾・渋谷区東・六本木）にホテルとは一線を期す"高級ホテルのスイートルーム以上のこだわりとプライベートで上質な空間"を提供するサービスアパートメント。Executive Suite「roppongi secondo」は、世界的なデザイナー森田恭通氏が全部屋をプロデュースしている。家具やインテリア小物に至るまで、洗練されたセンスが感じられる空間になっている。業界初となる全部屋完全防音を設備し、通信カラオケ搭載の部屋や、ラグジュアリーリゾートスタイルを存分に感じられるJAXSONのバスタブを使用するなど、六本木の喧噪の中でも落ち着いた時間を過ごせる設えになっている。全部で4部屋しかないこのサービスアパートメントには、その部屋数と広さから、ただ泊まるだけではない、「ゆったり、なごめる」時間を提供できる空間に仕上がっている。その空間は、室内各所に起用したフォトグラファー桐島ローランド氏の自然の写真と、それにうまく調和するシンプルでモダンなインテリアでまとめられている。大都会六本木にある「隠れ家」的なサービスアパートメントでありながら、長期滞在を考え、隠れ家独特の閉塞感を感じさせない様な造りになっている。間取りも「住む」ことを一番に考え、使う側に配慮されたものに。自分の家に居るような「リラックス感」、その一方で普段の生活とは明らかに違う「特別感」の両方を感じられる空間になっている。

Clearly different from city hotels, "The Executive Suite" is a serviced apartment that offers "services with more care than high grade hotels and a quality space with a strong sense of privacy" in one of the most convenient city center locations (Hiroo, Eastern Shibuya-ku, and Roppongi). The Executive Suite "roppongi secondo" is produced by Yasumichi Morita, an internationally renowned designer. From furniture to small interior articles, each space gives a sense of sophistication. Careful consideration is given to details of the design including completely soundproof rooms which is the first in the industry, rooms equipped with on-line karaoke facilities and Jaxson baths whose style reminds one of luxurious resorts so that one can enjoy time of relaxation and comfort in the hustles and bustles of Roppongi. This service apartment has just four dwelling units, but having a small number of spacious rooms, they are finished as spaces where one can feel "easy and at peace." Each space is decorated with nature pictures taken by Rowland Kirishima, a photographer, in various places and completed with a simple and modern interior design matching them. Though it is a "hideaway-like" service apartment at the city center of Roppongi, the individual rooms are designed to avoid a sense of entrapment in consideration of a guest's long stay. The arrangement of the rooms also put priority to "living", and convenience is especially paid attention to. The apartment offers a "sense of relaxation" as if one were at one's own home. At the same time, in this space, one can feel "something special", different from one's daily life.

	2	3
1		4
	5	6

1
外観全景
Exterior

2
外部階段見下ろし
External stairway seen from the above

3
桐島ローランド氏の自然の写真パネルが配された2階ホール
Hall on the 2nd floor where Rowland Kirishima's nature photos are displayed

4
家具や木調のオブジェなど、こだわりのあるリビングルーム
Living room with furniture and wooden objects carefully selected

5
リビングルーム
Living room

6
入口が回転ドアになっているベッドルーム。天井には桐島ローランド氏の写真が配されている
Bedroom with a revolving door. A Rowland Kirishima's photo decorates the ceiling.

167

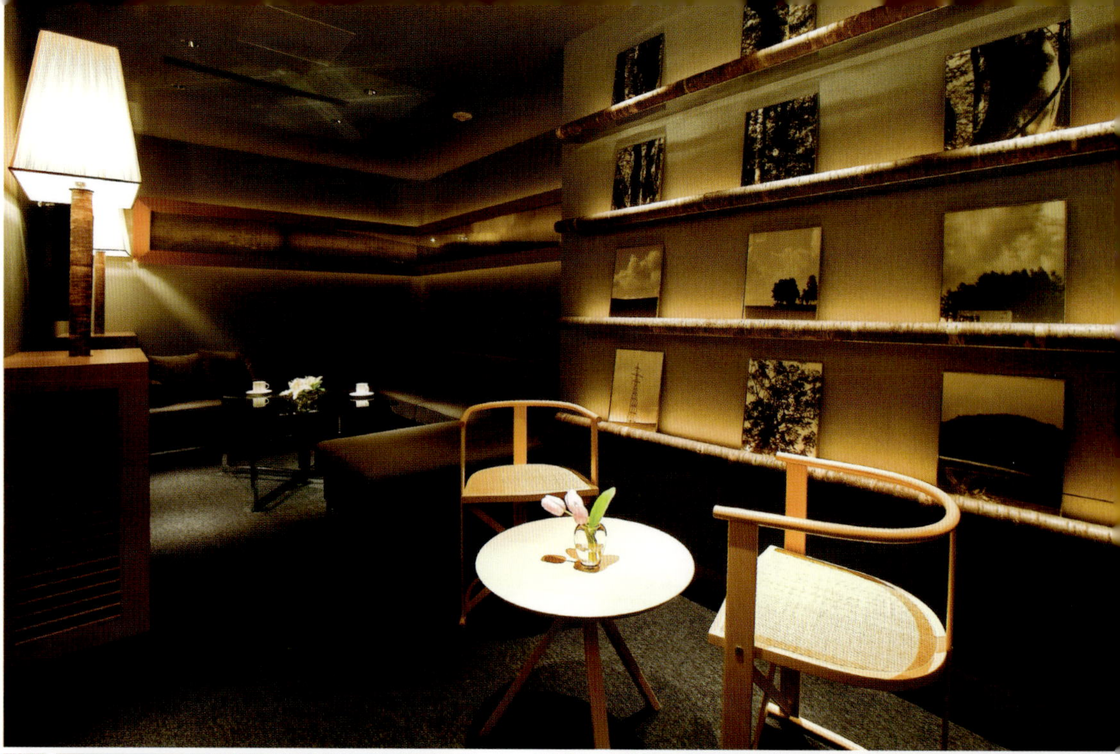

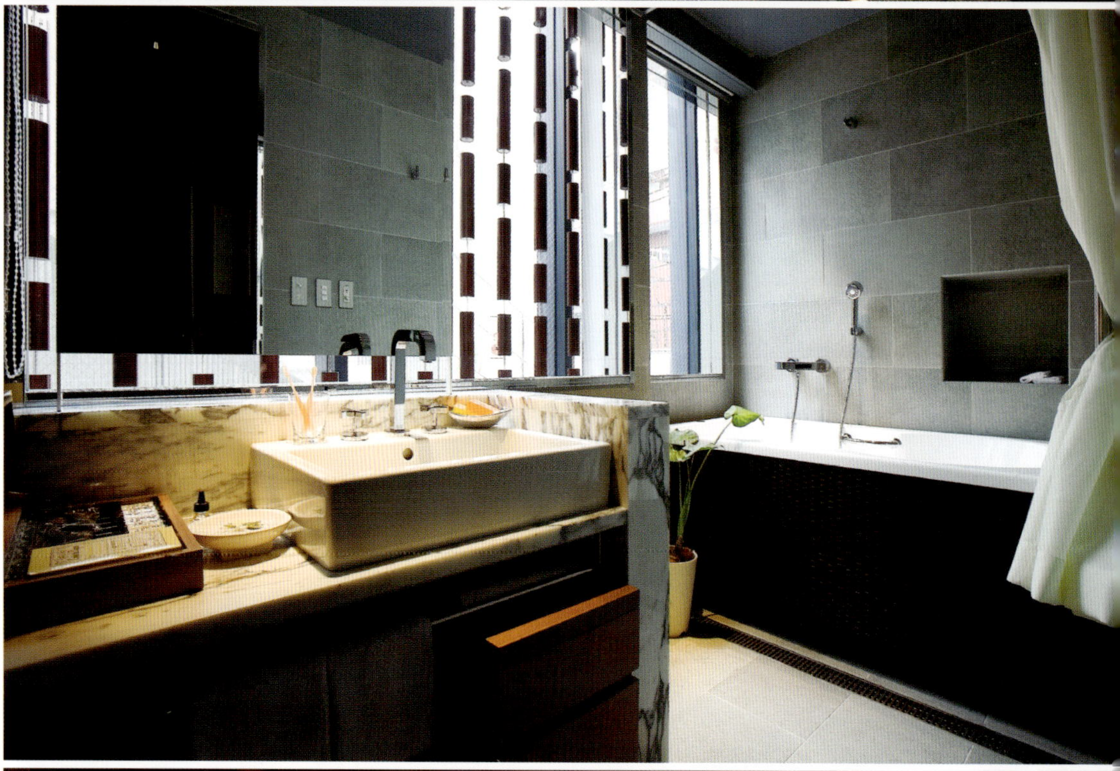

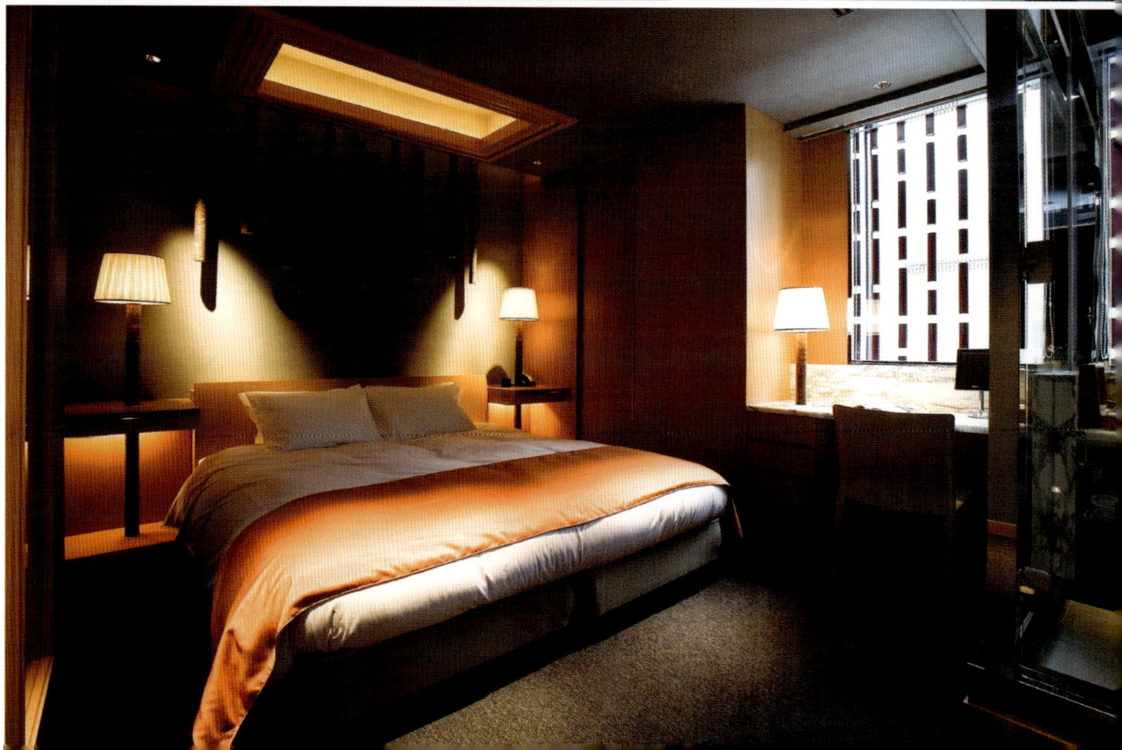

1

リビングルーム：家具やインテリア小物に至るまで、洗練されたセンスが感じられる

Living room: A sense of sophistication to every detail from furniture to small interior items

2

JAXSON・BARCA SERISEのバスタブを採用したバスルーム。ラグジュアリーなリゾートスタイルを楽しめる

Bathroom employing the Barca Series bathtub from Jaxson, offering time in a luxurious resort style

3

書斎スペースが付随した落ち着いた雰囲気のベッドルーム

Bedroom with a comfortable atmosphere, having a study space

4

フリースタンディングバスをインテリアとして楽しめるJAXSONのバスタブを採用したバスルーム

Bathroom employing a Jaxson freestanding bathtub that can be enjoyed as part of the interior

5

ベッドルーム
Bedroom

6

ベッドルームに付随した書斎スペース
Study space accompanying the bedroom

7

リビングルーム
Living room

169

1	4	
2		
3	5	6

1
通信カラオケ搭載のリビングルーム
Living room with on-line karaoke facilities

2
リビングルーム．ゆったりなごめる空間に仕上がっている
Living room: Finished as a space to laid back

3
落ち着いた雰囲気のベッドルーム
Bedroom with a comfortable atmosphere

4
広々とした屋上テラス
Extensive roof terrace

5
サニタリールーム
Sanitary room

6
屋上テラスへ続く階段
Stairway to the roof terrace

Data

Title
 FLEG roppongi secondo

Developer
 F.L.E.G. INTERNATIONAL CO., LTD.

Design Supervision
 Yasumichi Morita

Location
 Minato-ku, Tokyo

Site area
 224.82m²

Building area
 133.12m²

Total floor area
 489.52m²

Area
 41.5-47m²

Completion
 February, 2006

Materials
 Public Floor :
  stone, carpet, granite
 Interior Wall :
  cloth, gray boder tile
 Interior Floor :
  carpet, gray boder tile

Wakohre Suma Passo
ワコーレ須磨パッソ
Jun Setomoto

この敷地がもっている特異な性格、環境としてあげられるのは、誕生したばかりの10,000㎡の広さをもつ千歳公園内で、まるで公園の一部のような場所に、この建物が建っていることである。地域のコミュニティプレイスとしてのこの公園は、多彩な広場をもっているが、元は歴史ある千歳小学校であった。新長田に近いこの東須磨地区は、教育・ショッピング・文化・スポーツ等の生活施設に恵まれた、下町情趣あふれる成熟した住環境であるが、区画整理事業内のこの敷地は街の視線をひとり占めするような面白いロケーションにある。海と山を身近に感じるこの街の中では、個性的な風格をもちつつも、明るいビビッドな親しめるスタイリングが似合うと考えた。小さなかわいいアールのバルコニーの連続、塔状のアール、曲線の屋根など、小さな魅力で街を活性化させると共に、さらに上質な暮らしをめざして発展していく期待を込めて計画した。景色の良い角部屋が80％あり、独立性の高い開放的なプランニングが可能となった。公園に囲まれたくつろぎを楽しむオープンテラスは、ギャラリーエントランスホールからの景観を重視すると共に、パブリックスペースの充実による生活像の転換を試みている。

The unique character and condition of this site is the fact that the building is located as if it were part of the 10,000-square-meter Chitose Park that was just opened. As community place of the area, this park now has a variety of plazas on the site on which Chitose Elementary School that had a long history had once been built. The Higashi-suma area close to Shinnagata offers a mature living environment with educational, shopping, cultural, sport and other community facilities and has the friendly atmosphere of the old quarters. The site, however, is within the area of interest subject to land readjustment project, which attracts all the attention of the town. We thought that a style of design that is gay, vivid and familiar seemed to fit while maintaining the unique dignity in the town where one can familiarize oneself with both mountains and sea. This collection of small devices of attraction including a series of small, cute balconies, and curved towers and roofs contributes to vitalize the townscape and is expected to develop into realization of a better life. 80% of the units are corner rooms with an excellent view, giving opportunities for planning units with a sense of both privacy and openness. The open terrace to enjoy life surrounded by the park is designed with an emphasis on the view from the gallery and entrance hall and represents an attempt to change the pattern of lifestyle by improving public spaces.

1	2	3
		4

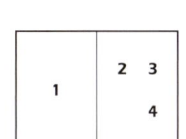

1
小さなかわいいバルコニーが特徴的な外観
Exterior featuring small, charming balconies

2
昼も夜も楽しいオープンテラス
Open terrace enjoyable day and night

3
公園から見た外観
Exterior seen from the park

4
オープンテラスにつながるエントランスホール
Entrance hall leading to the open terrace

173

Data

Title
  Wakohre Suma Passo

Developer
  Wadakohsan Corporation

Architect
  Jun Setomoto

Location
  Suma-ku, Kobe city, Hyogo

Site area
  688.58m²

Building area
  424.70m²

Total floor area
  2,543.54m²

Structure
  RC

Completion
  August, 2005

Materials
  Exterior Wall :
    50x50 tile, sprayed coating, 45x90tile
    architectural concrete
  Public Wall :
    architectural concrete
  Public Floor :
    300x300tile, 150x150tile
  Interior Wall :
    cloth
  Interior Floor :
    300x300tile, flooring

Photo
  Takashi Ehara (Ehara Photo Office)

1	2	
3	4	5

1
玄関ホール
Entrance hall

2
リビング・ダイニング
Living-dining

3
和室
Japanese-style room

4
リビング・ダイニング
Living-dining

5
寝室
Bedroom

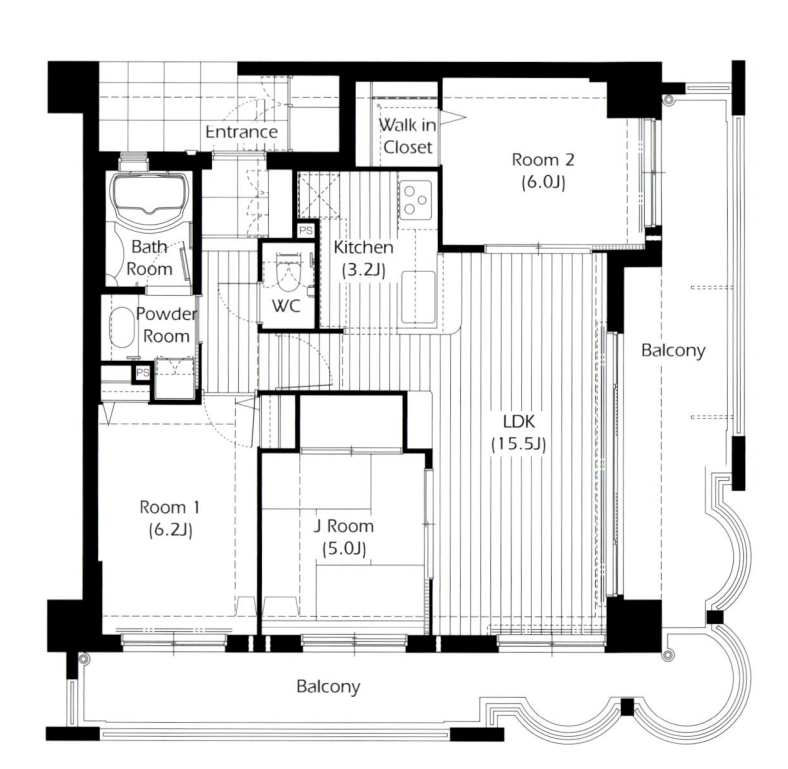

Phoenix Building

フェニックス・ビルディング

Misawa Homeing Tokyo Co., Ltd. / Roble Jun Veara Kanna+Ryuji Fujimura ISSHO Architects, Hirofumi Ohno / Ohno JAPAN

東京郊外の住宅地に計画された、9室からなる集合住宅である。賃室は約30㎡の独身者向けワンルームが中心である。ここでは、容積率いっぱいに床面積を確保するため大井高を2200mmに抑え、最大建築面積を高さ制限の範囲内で最大数（6層）積層し、容積率をオーバーした分だけインナーバルコニー（約4㎡）として容積率対象床面積から除外する計画としている。したがって、ここではまず、吹き抜け等を用いた垂直方向の広がりよりも、インナーバルコニーを用いた水平方向の広がりを獲得することを目指すことにした。また、ワンルームの空間を抽象的に眺めると、キッチンカウンターのレベル（FL+850mm）を基準に、キッチンやベッドの配置など、機能的な根拠が大きく関わる下の空間と、視覚的な体験が大きく関わる上の空間に大きく整理する事が出来るのではないかと考えた。そこでここでは、窓や収納をキッチンカウンターレベルの上下に分散して配置することで、囲まれた感覚と、圧迫感なく水平に広がりを同時に感じられるような、居心地のよいインテリアを作ろうとした。外観は、コンクリート打放しの上に薄く青紫色に着色することによって柔らかな表情のものとし、空調室外機、ガス給湯器、キッチン、水回りの排気口、雨樋等を外壁面に現れないようインナーバルコニーにまとめ、窓をランダムに配置することによって、抽象的なものとなっている。

This is a condominium planned in a suburban residential area in the outskirts of Tokyo, having nine dwelling units. Each studio for rent intended mainly for a single person is about 30 square meters in size. In order to take maximum advantage of the given floor area ratio, the ceiling height is kept as low as 2,200mm while the building has the maximum number of floors with maximum building area as far as the applicable building height restriction allows (6 stories). The amount of volume exceeding the maximum allowable floor area ratio is made into inner balconies (about 4 square meters) to be excluded from the floor area subject to the floor area ratio. For this reason, the primary target is set to allow a horizontal expansion rather than vertical one by, for example, providing open ceilings. Further, if we abstractly looked at the studio space, we thought that, by taking the height of the kitchen countertop (850mm from the floor) as reference, we can roughly categorize it into the lower space highly associated with functional objectives such as kitchen and bed layout and the higher space strongly related to visual experience. So in designing the apartment, we scattered windows and storages in the lower and upper parts seen the kitchen counter level and attempted to create a comfortable interior offering a sense of expansion in the horizontal direction without a sense of oppression. The exterior has a soft expression by painting the surface of the exposed concrete in light violet, and the outdoor unit, water heater, water pipes, and rain gutters are installed in the inner balcony and made invisible, giving the building an abstract image.

1	4
2	5
3	6

1
玄関から見た室内風景
Interior seen from the entrance

2
浴室とバルコニー越しに外部を見る
Exterior seen through the bathroom and balcony

3
浴室内部から見た室内風景
Interior of the room seen from the bathroom

4
収納と浴室によって緩やかに区切られている
Softly partitioned by storages and bathroom

5
収納や開口が上下に分散することで生まれる広がり
A sense of spaciousness given by scattering storages and openings in the lower and upper sections.

6
眺望のよいオーナー住居
Owner's residence with an excellent command of view

Data

Title
 Phoenix Building

Developer
 Misawa Homeing Tokyo Co., Ltd.

Architect
 Roble Jun Veara Kanna+Ryuji Fujimura
 ISSHO Architects, Hirofumi Ohno
 Ohno JAPAN

Location
 Edogawa-ku, Tokyo

Site area
 213.87m²

Building area
 119.29m²

Total floor area
 523.53m²

Structure
 RC

Completion
 October, 2005

Materials
 Exterior Wall :
  exposed concrete + waterproofing
  coating (color)
 Public Wall :
  exposed concrete
 Public Floor :
  exposed concrete + coating
 Interior Wall :
  vinyl cloth
 Interior Floor :
  flooring

Photo
 DAICI ANO / FWD INC.

K court
Kコート
Seiichi Kubo

社会性、歴史性、文化性から見た環境デザイン

計画地は、大阪市街地の南部、閑静な住宅地として知られる帝塚山から西に広がる良好な環境をもつ住宅地である。かつて多くの小説家たちが生活を営み、文豪・開高健が住んだ高質の戦前長屋もこのKコートのすぐ裏手にある。ここ北田辺のメインストリートには、銀杏並木が配され、歴史的かつ文化的な景観を抱えつつも、現代をクリエイトするハイセンスな環境を示唆している。周辺地域に対する環境促進のためのデザインの重要性をアピールし、自分たちが暮らす街のポテンシャルを上げる工夫を示す。銀杏並木を写し出すガラスのスクリーンや歩道に面した水面（池）の効果や夜間のライトアップ、開放的なエントランスギャラリーなど町並み景観形成の向上を目指している。敷地形状は、間口4間弱・奥行き12.5間の南北に細長い50坪の土地で、典型的な大阪町屋より少し奥行きの長いタイプの2軒分に相当する。プランは採光を得るための中庭を中心に南北2棟構成であり、共用廊下でそれを連結している。薄肉ラーメン構造の採用により、南北両面の壁を完全開放させることが可能となり、外・内部の空間の連続性が高められた。2つの職住棟そしてEV棟と階段棟、それら4つの棟の廻りには常に外部が成立している。1階エントランスのセキュリティを通過するとまた外部に出るという構成は、戦前長屋のプラン特徴をベースにバーティカルにその可能性を拡張させたものであり、積層型の大阪長屋を想起させる。

Environmental design from social, historical and cultural viewpoints

The site is located in a residential area with a pleasant environment in the outskirts of Teizukayama in the south of Osaka city. A quality pre-war tenement house where Takeshi Kaiko and other renowned novelists once lived stands behind this K court. The main streets of Kitatanabe are lined with ginkgo trees and suggest surroundings for creating modern lifestyles with a good taste while embracing historical and cultural townscape. The building appeals the importance of design in promoting environment improvement in the neighborhood and represents devices to enhance potential of the town to live in. Elements of the design contributing to better townscape include glass screens reflecting the rows of trees, the surface of the water (pond) facing the sidewalk, illuminations at night, and an inviting atmosphere of the entrance gallery. The lot of 50 tsubo (about 160m3) is elongated in north-south direction and is nearly 4 ken (about 7 meters) and 12.5 ken (22.5 meters) deep. The area is equivalent to two typical Osaka tenement houses with a slightly longer depth. The plan offers two buildings in north and south with a patio for natural lighting in between and connected by the common corridor. Employment of the thin frame construction enabled us to design fully open walls in north and south, strengthening continuity between the interior and exterior spaces. The outside is always present around the two commercial/residential buildings, the elevator tower and the staircase tower. When one passes through the security at the ground level entrance, one finds oneself outside of the building again. This configuration is a vertical extension of the features of the pre-ware tenement houses, reminding one of a laminated structure of the Osaka tenement houses.

	2	3	4
1		5	
		6	

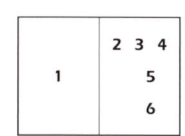

1
北側（エントランス側）外観
Northern exterior (entrance side)

2
エントランス夜景
Entrance at night

3
中庭側から住戸を見る。各戸南北両面にプライベートテラスをもつ
Unit seen from the inner garden. Each unit has private terraces on the north and south.

4
5階屋上庭園
Roof garden for the unit on the 5th floor

5
エントランスから中庭を見た夜景。奥にはスタジオが見える
Inner garden seen from the entrance at night. The studio can be seen at the back.

6
東側外観。中庭・共用棟をはさむツインタワー型の構成
Eastern exterior. This condominium has an inner garden and a common building in between its two towers.

1	2	4
3		5

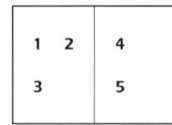

1
5階住戸のリビング・ダイニング吹抜見下ろし。右側の建具を介して上階の主寝室とつながる
Open ceiling of the living-dining room of the 5th floor unit. The room leads to the main bedroom behind the furnishings on the right.

2
リビング・ダイニングの吹抜より北側を見る
Northern side seen from the open ceiling area of the living dining room

3
外部専用廊下と連続するリビング・ダイニング
Living-dining room continues to the private corridor outside

4
杉板型枠によるコンクリート打放し仕上壁におちる光と影
Light and shade over the walls of exposed concrete finish using cedar board formwork

5
5階和室から外部の町並みを見通す
Townscape seen from the Japanese-style room on the 5th floor

RF Plan

5F Plan

2F - 4F Plan

1F Plan

B1F Plan

1. Entrance gallery
2. Light court
3. Design studio
4. Rent room
5. Living dining room
6. Tatami room
7. Child room
8. Bed room
9. EV

N

Data

Title
  K court

Architect
  Seiichi Kubo

Location
  HigashiSumiyoshi-ku, Osaka City

Site area
  170.05m²

Area
  20.4m²

Structure
  RC (thin rigid frame)

Completion
  April, 2003

Materials
  Exterior Wall :
    exposed concrete
    (Japanese cedar form in part)
  Public Wall :
    exposed concrete
    (Japanese cedar form in part)
    white lauan venneer
  Public Floor :
    concrete trowel finish
  Interior Wall :
    exposed concrete
    (Japanese cedar form in part)
  Interior Floor :
    PVC sheet

Photo
  Yoshiharu Matsumura

Proud Minami-Aoyama

プラウド南青山

Nomura Real Estate Development Co., Ltd.
Takenaka Corporation

明治神宮の森の息づかいを伝える、表参道のケヤキ並木。青山の中心エリアとなる表参道交差点。表通りは国内外のブランドショップが建ち並ぶ華やかな街並み。そのストリートから一歩奥へ入ると、いままでの賑わいを忘れる落ち着いた空気が漂っている。大人の表情を湛えて、「動」の街の中に味わい深い「静」の世界を醸し出している場所。その南青山の魅力を使いこなす拠点として存在し、都心の中にあって孤立したものではなく、街の個性と響き合う佇まいへ。そして都心だからこそ、より光と風と同化した空間へ。メタルとガラスを多用したシャープな印象のフォルム。それと美しい対比を見せる外壁の素材。窓やバルコニーの配置を凝らして変化を持たせたファサード。ワイドに広がるガラス窓から日差しを採り込み、開放的で風を感じさせつつ、建物それ自体が光を受けて輝き、街並みの中の顔として視線を注がれるものに。周囲に光彩を放ち続ける都心の集邸を創り上げる。都市のただ中にあってプライバシーを確保。その一方、街の雰囲気とひとつになる"見せる"エントランスを演出。車寄せの車路に沿ってカーブを描く壁面は「光の壁」をイメージし、人々を温かく出迎える。エントランスまわりにはワイドなガラスを巡らし、明るく開放感にあふれて都会的な個性を放つ、ショップを思わせる設えとしている。その一方で漆を塗った和紙の壁紙をエントランスに使用するなど和の趣も醸成。

The row of zelkova trees along the Omotesando street lets one feel the breath of the woods in the Meiji Shrine. The Omotesando intersection is the heart of the Aoyama area. The splendid main street is lined with domestic and foreign brand shops, but just one step away is an atmosphere quiet and comfortable, isolated from the hustles and bustles of the main street. Minami-Aoyama is a place of fascinating tranquility in the dynamism of the town. The condominium is present as the base to fully enjoy the town, having an appearance not isolated from but befitting the townscape. The design focuses on the creation of a space that is one with light and wind at the heart of the city. The building makes a great use of metal and glass in contrast with the materials of the outer walls. The facade is accentuated by careful arrangements of the windows and balconies. Wide glass windows abundantly let sunshine in the units, and while it gives a sense of openness bathed in a refreshing wind, the building reflects the sunshine as if it shone in itself, attracting people's attention as a landmark of the town. It is an urban condominium shedding lights on surroundings. Privacy at the heart of the city is secured; on the other hand, the "attractive" entrance is designed in a way to be one with the atmosphere of the town. The curving wall along the marquee welcomes people with an image of "light wall". Around the entrance are wide-span glass walls, suggesting a shop-like appearance with a sense of openness and urban characteristics. At the same time, a Japanesque taste is given by using lacquered Japanese wallpaper.

	2
1	3
	4

1
ガラスとメタルを多用したシャープな外観：周囲に光彩を放ち続ける都心の集邸
Well-defined appearance using much glass and metal: Condominium at the heart of the city shedding light and colors in the neighborhood

2
ラウンジ：都心に居ながら自然の光を享受できるように、吹き抜けを設け、トップライトから日差しを誘う。さらに壁面いっぱいに広がる窓からも外光を採り込み、格調のあるフロア、外壁と同素材の壁面が美しく映えて上質な空間を創り上げる
Lounge: An open ceiling is provided to guide sunlight from top light so that one can enjoy natural light in the city. The full-length window also brings in natural light, reflected by the decent floor and the surfaces of the walls using materials same as that of the exterior walls to create a quality space.

3
エントランスホール：壁面の一部に和紙に漆を塗った素材を採用し、和の趣も醸成している
Entrance hall: Part of the wall surface is covered with the material made of the Japanese paper painted with lacquer for a Japanesque atmosphere.

4
ガラス張りによる光と開放感が心地よい内廊下
Inner corridor full of light through glass walls, giving a sense of openness

煌めく都市の世界は窓の外側にとどめて、ここは自分の世界に浸れるとっておきの場所。天井まで窓が広がり、柱型や梁型の張り出しを抑えたすっきりとした室内。個性あふれる住空間に自分のスタイルを映し出し、都市のただなかに居ながらにして、やすらぎにあふれた日々を愉しめる。美しく洗練されたデザインと優れた機能も味わえるキッチン。クオリティが高く、心地の良い感触のパウダールームやバスルームなど。日常の空間に、美しさを味わい、機能を愉しむゆとりを加える。

The world of brilliant city is kept outside the windows, and the room is a much-valued place where one can be on one's own. The window runs up to the ceiling and protruding columns and beams are reduced for a more spacious impression. The one-of-a-kind living space reflects one's style and lets one enjoy days of comfort at the heart of the city. The kitchen is provided with beautiful, sophisticated designs and excellent functional features. The quality powder room and bathroom with a sense of comfort. The daily spaces are added with a joy of beauty and a feeling of ease.

1	3
2	4

1
開放感あふれるリビングルーム。自分の世界に浸れるとっておきの場所
Living room with a sense of spaciousness. The place where one can be on one's own.

2
落ち着いた雰囲気のエントランスホール
Comfortable entrance hall

3
天井まで窓が広がり、柱型や梁型の張り出しを抑えたすっきりとした室内
Window reaching to the ceiling. Spacious room with minimum protrusion of columns and beams

4
リビングからダイニングを臨む
Dining area seen from the living space

Data

Title
Proud Minami-Aoyama

Developer
Nomura Real Estate Development Co.,Ltd.

Architect
Takenaka Corporation

Location
Minato-ku, Tokyo

Site area
1,343.33m²

Building area
762.38m²

Total floor area
3,365.02m²

Structure
RC

Completion
March, 2006

Materials
Exterior Wall :
  tile, waterproofing coating on exposed concrete, painting
Public Wall :
  tile, glass
Public Floor :
  stone-finish tile, tile carpet
Interior Wall :
  painting on cloth
Interior Floor :
  stone-finish tile, flooring, carpet

1	2
	3

1
機能の美と先端の仕様に、空間全体が上質さを湛えたパウダールーム
Powder room with a sense of quality space, having functional beauty and cutting-edge specifications

2
美しく洗練されたデザインと優れた機能性も味わえるキッチン
Kitchen provided with beautiful, sophisticated designs and excellent functionality

3
バスルーム
Bathroom

Maison de parc
パークメゾン
Kenichi Hirai / Kenichi Hirai Architect & Associates

大阪谷町4丁目に建つこのパークメゾンは、約30年前に建てられた本社ビルの北隣に、2～5階を事務所、6階～12階をワンルームに、最上階をファミリー向け住宅として計画。古くなった南側本社ファサードも改修する為、新築棟と一体化したデザインとして考え、ファサードは事務所ビルとしてのイメージを強く意識したデザインとした。1・2階は石貼とし、その上部カーテンウォールは疎と密に割付、熱線反射ガラスもランダムに4色張分けとして、水平・垂直な単純な構成で複雑かつ、シンプルで密度の高いファサードになるようにした。内部床は石とブナの無垢材、壁は珪藻土を使用して柔らかい色調でコーディネートした。

Maison de parc in Tanimachi in Osaka is planned on the lot adjacent to the north of the headquarters building constructed about 30 years ago and has offices on the 2nd to 5th floors, residential studios on the 6th to 12th floors, and apartments for families on the top floor. In the design, the southern facade of the old headquarters building to be modified is considered as part of the new building whose facade emphasizes its presence as an office building. The external walls of the 1st and the 2nd floors are finished with stone panels, and "sparse" and "dense" curtain walls are arranged up above them. Four different colored heat-reflecting glass panels are attached at random. Thanks to this approach, the facade's simple configuration in vertical and horizontal directions can reveal a complicated in appearance yet simple and compact in structure. Colors of the interior floors employing stone and solid natural beech wood and the walls made from diatomite are coordinated in soft tones.

1	2
3	4

1
アールのついたガラスモザイク壁のある１Ｆホール
Hall on the first floor decorated with a curved glass mosaic wall

2
玄関ホール：左側に下駄箱・クローゼットを設けている
Entrance hall: A shoe cabinet and a closet are on the left

3
天井がアールになったリビング・ダイニング
Living-dining room with a curved ceiling

4
キッチンからリビング・ダイニングを見る
Living-dining space seen from the kitchen

Data

Title
　Maison de parc

Architect
　Kenichi Hirai
　Kenichi Hirai Architect & Associates

Location
　Chuo-ku, Osaka

Site area
　156.24m²

Area
　32.34-94.21m²

Structure
　steel structure

Completion
　May, 2005

Materials
　Exterior Wall :
　　curtain wall + heat reflecting ALC panel
　Public Wall :
　　stone + EP
　Public Floor :
　　stone
　Interior Wall :
　　diatomaceous earth
　Interior Floor :
　　Japanese beech flooring

Photo
　Yoshiharu Matsumura

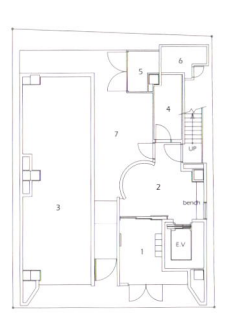

1F PLAN S=1:100 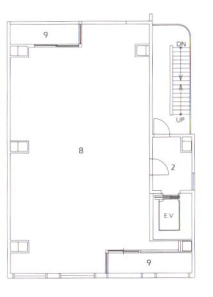　　2F PLAN S=1:100 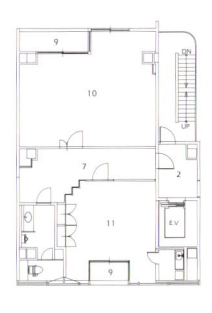　　3F PLAN S=1:100 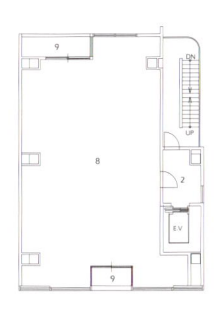　　4 - 5F PLAN S=1:100

6 - 11F PLAN S=1:100 　　12F PLAN S=1:100 　　13F PLAN S=1:100

#		
1	入口	entrance
2	ホール	hall
3	駐車場	parking
4	防災管理室	Disaster prevention management room
5	ダストルーム	dust room
6	機械室	machine room
7	廊下	corridor
8	事務所	office
9	バルコニー	balcony
10	社長室	president's room
11	会議室	meeting room
12	住戸	individual room
13	納戸	closet
14	食堂	dining room
15	主寝室	master's bed room
16	居間	living room

BARONG

バロン

Tadashi Suga

この建物はかつての新興住宅地にある。道路と川の間に位置し、敷地は川にむかって傾斜し、三角形の建築条件的には理想ではない敷地である。川の向こう側には50〜70Mくらいの距離に電車がたまに走る。つまり都市部でありながら、将来にわたり近隣には大きな建物が建ちにくい好環境でもある。ここで、単身者用共同住宅を計画するにあたり、敷地形状を利用し、間口と開放性を取ることにより地域環境を住戸内に取り入れることをコンセプトと考えた。川側に突き出たバルコニーは、ステンレス鏡面、スチール、アートメタル、フロストガラスをランダムに配置し、透過もしくは反射して、多彩な表情を見せる。道路側の鉄骨直階段は、敷地境界に沿うように建物から斜めに切り離されて行きながら、拡幅しつつ地面にすり付いていく。それは、エントランスで平面的にも断面的にも弧を描き、幅を狭めながら川へと連続する。同じく川へ導かれるように傾斜している駐輪場と共に、1階の店舗は4方全て、ガラスに覆われており、川への透過性を期待している。室内は、コンクリート打放しと白色を基調とし、折戸などによって、キッチンや洗濯機等の生活空間を、必要に応じて閉じることが出来る。また、バーチカルブラインドで外部を調節して取り入れることや、可動家具によってそのワンルーム空間を自由に分けることも容易である。そこは、日常と少しの努力を伴うが非日常空間も楽しめる空間となっている。

This building is located in an area where once a new housing development was carried out. The site between a road and a river is inclined toward the river and is triangle-shaped, which is not ideal as construction conditions. On the other side of the river, about 50 or 70 meters away from the site run trains from time to time. In other words, if we take into the consideration the fact that the site is in the city, at least, this is a good condition because possibilities of future constructions of high buildings nearby are not so high. In planning a condominium for singles, we conceptualized an idea to take advantage of the local environments as part of the units by utilizing the shape of the site and securing a wide frontage and sufficient openness. The balconies protruding on the side of the river have stainless mirror finishes, steel, art metals, and frosted glass installed at random, and lights passing through or reflected upon them contribute to give different expressions on the facade. The straight steel-frame stairway on the roadside gradually runs away from the building in parallel with the boundary, widening its width toward the ground. It makes an arc at the entrance both horizontally and vertically and continues on toward the river, narrowing its width. The shops on the first floor as well as the bicycle parking lot similarly inclined toward the river are covered by glass in all four directions, expected to offer a sense of transparency to reveal the river. The dominant color of the interior is that of exposed concrete and white, and by using the folding doors, the kitchen, the washing machine, and other elements of daily life can be hidden. Also possible are adjusting the vertical blind to enable the residents to integrate the outside view as part of the room and flexibly separating the studio space by repositioning mobile furniture. The unit is a space to enjoy both ordinary life and non-daily space with a little effort required.

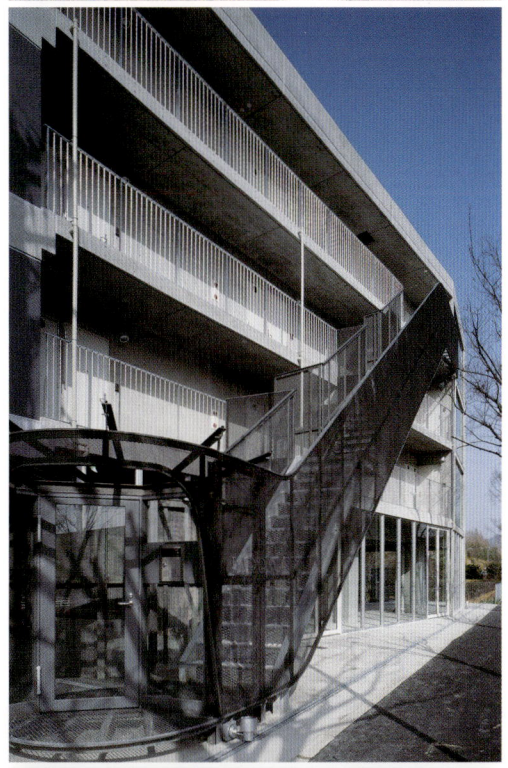

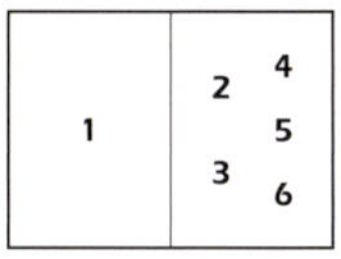

		4
1	2	5
	3	6

1
川側外観
Exterior on the side of the river

2
道路側外観
Exterior on the side of the road

3
道路側外観正面
Front of the exterior on the side of the road

4
川側外観見上げ
Looked up view of the exterior on the side of the river

5
エントランス前より外部階段見上げ
External stairway looked up from the position in front of the entrance

6
エントランス内部
Inside the entrance

1
リビングより折戸内キッチンをみる
Kitchen with the folding doors opened seen from the living space

2
アイランドキッチン、可動収納
Island kitchen and mobile storage unit

3
狭い室においては、このアイランドキッチンはダイニング兼デスクでもある
In the small room, this island kitchen also serves as a dining table and desk.

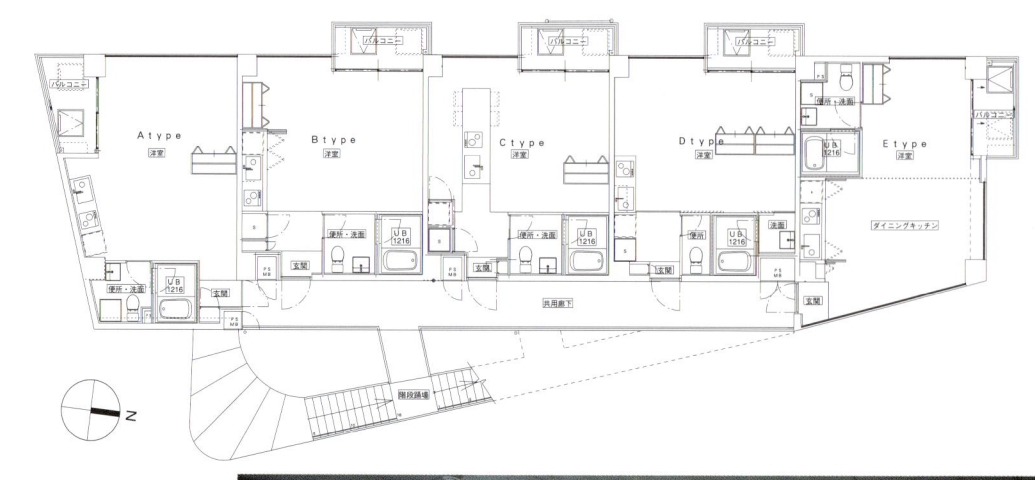

Data

Title
　BARONG

Developer
　TAKUTO CO., LTD.

Architect
　Tadashi Suga

Location
　Suita city, Osaka

Site area
　330.15m²

Building area
　198.01m²

Total floor area
　703.92m²

Area
　32.53-68.81m²

Structure
　RC

Completion
　March, 2006

Materials
　Exterior Wall :
　　exposed concrete
　Public Wall :
　　exposed concrete
　Public Floor :
　　mortal trowel finish
　Interior Wall :
　　exposed concrete, AEP
　Interior Floor :
　　homogeneous vinyl tile

Photo
　Yoshiharu Matsumura

Syukugawa FLAT
夙川FLAT
Masaharu Ogawa

阪急夙川の西方、芦屋との市境に敷地は位置する。このあたり一帯は阪神間有数の成熟した住宅地であり、当建築は従前の住宅の建替えに際し、集合住宅として生れ変ったものである。建物は、自走式で全戸分の地下駐車場、1〜3階に中庭を介してメゾネットタイプとフラットタイプの11戸、4階に3LDKの1戸という構成である。計画は、周辺の閑静な住環境への配慮を慎重に検討することから始まった。コンクリートの持つモノトーンでシンプルな表情を基調に、ボリューム感の軽減のために最上階を金属板で包み込んだのは、モダンさと、適度な軽快さを表現し、しとやかに佇むことを願ったからであり、ややもすると集合住宅が併せ持つ煩雑な印象を避けた結果である。開口部は内部機能を損なうことなく、相互にストレスとならない配置、形状、材質を念頭に選び、道路面については、歩行者からの目線で、心地良い変化という観点からの検討を行っていった。1〜3階の各住戸は10帖と20帖の2つのエリアと水まわりを持つ。内装についても、コンクリート、木、ペンキの素材だけのシンプルな構成にとどめ、こだわりの各パーツが彩りを添える。この空間が住まい手の感性に響くとき、趣くままの多様なライフスタイルを演出しはじめる。

The site is located to the west of the Hankyu Shukugawa station near the city limits with Ashiya. The neighborhood is one of the most mature residential areas between Osaka and Kobe, and this condominium is constructed on the site as the existing building needed to be rebuilt. The building with an inner court has a underground drive-in parking lot enough to cover all the rooms, a total of 11 maisonnette and flat type apartments on the first to third floors, and an apartment with three rooms and a living room with a combined dining room and kitchen. The plan has started with a careful consideration for the living environment in the neighborhood. The building is based on the monotone and simple expression, and in order to reduce a sense of volume, the top floor is covered with steel plates. The objective of this design approach is to give an appropriate modern and light impression to the building so that it should have a graceful appearance and to avoid a mixed impression that collective housing tends to have. When selecting positions, we paid attention to forms and materials of the opening that do not adversely affect the interior functionality and give no stress on one another. The design of the facade facing the street is studied from the viewpoint of pedestrians on the theme of comfortable transition. The residences on the first to third floors have two rooms (ten-mat and twenty-mat rooms) plus a bathroom and a kitchen. The interior is also simply designed by using concrete, wood and paint as materials, and careful attention is paid to individual parts. When this space touches on the sensitivity of the residents, it starts to produce quality lifestyles as they wish.

1	4
2	5
3	6

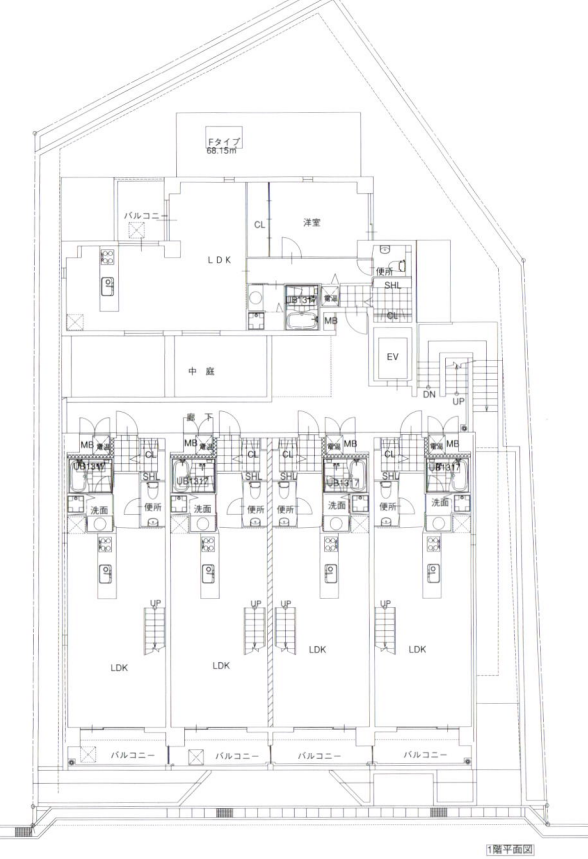

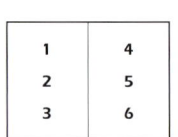

1
差しこむ陽光が、時を演出する中庭
Inner garden where the rays of the sun indicate the passage of time

2
最上階デッキテラス：光庭がテラスに変化を添える
Deck terrace on the top floor: The light court adds a variation to the terrace.

3
テラスと一体の、透明感あふれるリビング
Living space integrated with the terrace, giving a sense of transparency

4
キッチンからダイニング：光の筒の向こうにリビングを臨む
Dining area seen from the kitchen: Living space behind the tube of light

5
フラットタイプのLDK：コンクリート・木・ペンキで仕上げられた、シンプルな空間
Flat-type living-dining room + kitchen: A simply designed space finished with concrete, wood and paint

6
北向きの洋室：切りとられた眺望から、安定した光がそそぐ
Western-style room facing north: Light coming in constantly from the window framing the townscape

Data
Title
  Syukugawa FLAT
Architect
  Masaharu Ogawa
Location
  Nishinomiya city, Hyogo
Site area
  568.07m²
Area
  68.15-160.31m²
Structure
  RC
Completion
  July, 2005
Materials
  Exterior Wall : exposed concrete, tile, metal sheet
  Public Wall : exposed concrete
  Public Floor : granite
  Interior Wall : exposed concrete, water paint in part
  Interior Floor : maple flooring, tile
Photo
  Yoshiharu Matsumura

Forest Plaza Omotesando
フォレストプラザ表参道
Mori Building Co., Ltd.
Tadao Ando Architect & Associates

コンクリート打放しの外壁、豆砂利洗い出しの床・・・ストイックなまでに整理された素材は、硬質でありながら、熟練したアルチザンが丁寧に造りあげたもの。自然の色彩、有機的な曲線を柔軟に受け入れる。周辺環境の豊かな緑はもとより、屋上や屋根など、随所に植えられた緑ととけあい、響きあうことによって、ふくよかな表情を醸しだす。また美しいグリッドを描くコンクリートモデュール、幾何学的に空間を構成しながら、光の表情によって優美さをそなえる計算し尽くされたフォルム。一見無機質に見える外観は、そこに人が暮らし、緑が成熟するにつれ、のびやかな生命力を放ちはじめる。そしてこれこそが、安藤忠雄氏の設計した建物ならではの特徴ともいえるだろう。

Bare concrete outer walls. Floors of fine water-polished gravel. These basic materials are created by skilled artisans in precise, almost austere arrangements, presenting a varying counterpoint to natural colors and organic curves, the materials harmonize and echo with the plants placed on the roof and in other key locations. The fine combination of materials and plants creates a striking atmosphere of luxury. Concrete modules of perfectly calculated shapes are set in beautiful grid patterns, creating a geometrical space that gleams with elegance when lit. The presence of residents and the flourishing plants will combine with the simple materials of this residence to create a fresh and lively complex —— a characteristic shared by all structures designed by Tadao Ando.

	2
1	3
	4

1
エントランス側外観：コンクリート打放しとガラスとのコントラストなど、ストイックなまでに整理されたデザイン
Exterior on the entrance side: Contrast between bare concrete outer walls and glass, and other stoically organized design

2
外観見上げ
Exterior appearance

3
北側外観：手前は駐輪場になっている
Exterior on the north side: Bicycle parking area at the front

4
同じ棟内に建つ商業部外観を臨む
Exterior of the commercial facilities in the same building

1	2
3	5
4	6

1
エントランスアプローチ
Entrance approach

2
サブエントランス
Sub-entrance

3
豆砂利あらいだしの床が採用された玄関ホール
Entrance hall employing washed pea gravel concrete floor

4
廊下からマスターベッドルーム、テラスを臨む
Master bedroom and terrace seen from the corridor

5
マスターベッドルームに付随した広いテラスを臨む。周りには豊かな植栽が配されている
Wide balcony connected to the master bedroom, surrounded by rich planting

6
壁一面の大きな窓からふんだんに自然光が入るマスターベッドルーム
Master bedroom abundant with natural light from a large full-size window

リビング・ダイニングルームを中心とする専有面積48.22㎡〜129.27㎡のゆとりある構成。緑あふれる生活空間は都会生活をやさしく癒し、住まう方に安らぎと潤いを与えるように配慮されている。また、上質なウッドベースの床や自然光をふんだんに取り込める壁一面の大きな窓により、室内全体を穏やかで暖かみのある雰囲気に包み込む。

The floor area of all condominiums is between 48.22~129.27 square meters, with a spacious living-dining room. These large spaces full of greenery sooth urbanites, providing comfort and restoring energy. Floors made of high-quality wood and large floor-to-ceiling windows, designed to provide an abundance of natural light, lend a feeling of peace and warmth to these rooms.

Data

Title
Forest Plaza Omotesando

Developer
Mori Building Co., Ltd.

Architect
Tadao Ando Architect & Associates

Location
Shibuya-ku, Tokyo

Total floor area
2,211.09m²

Area
48.22-129.27m²

Structure
RC

Completion
November, 2001

Materials
 Exterior Wall :
  exposed concrete
 Public Floor :
  scrubbed finishing ballast
 Interior Floor :
  scrubbed finishing ballast, flooring

Photo
 Toshinori Irie

略歴

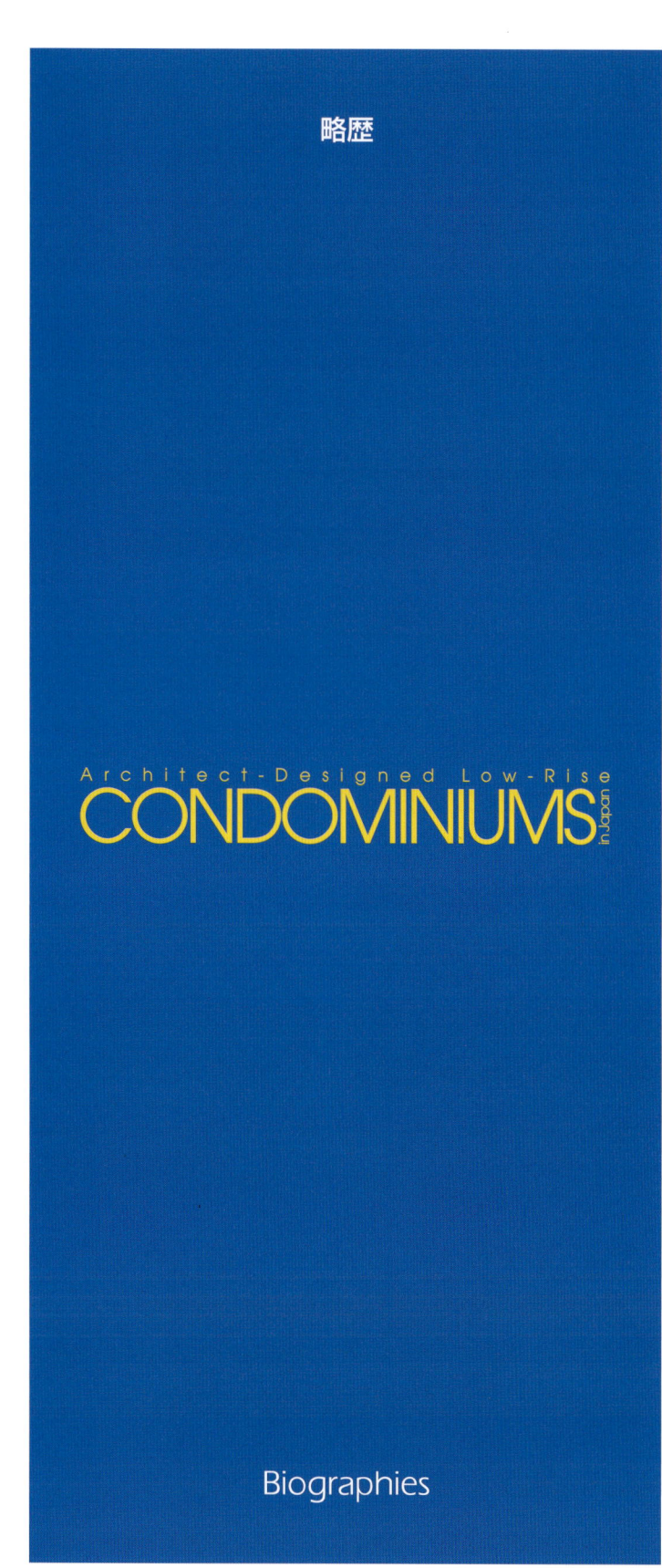

Architect-Designed Low-Rise
CONDOMINIUMS in Japan

Biographies

浅井謙
Ken Asai
P-48

浅井謙建築研究所株式会社代表
建築・都市・人を有機的に結ぶヒューマンアーキテクチャーを基本理念に、多様化・多極化する建築への社会的ニーズに応え、機能的で明快な作品を創り続けている。日本建築士会連合会賞、大阪府建築コンクール大阪府知事賞ほか、多数受賞。

Ken Asai Architectural Research Inc. Representative.
Under the basic concept of "architecture that harmonizes urban development and human needs", he has created functional and clear architectural works, responding to diversified and multipolarized requirements for architecture by the society. Awards: Japan Federation of Architects & Building Engineers Associations Award, Osaka Architecture Contest (Governor Award) and many others

浅利幸男
Yukio Asari
P-140, 143

ラブアーキテクチャー一級建築士事務所
1969年東京都生まれ
1994年武蔵野美術大学造形学部建築学科卒業
1996年芝浦工業大学大学院修士課程修了
1996年〜2001年株式会社相和技術研究所勤務
2001年有限会社ラブアーキテクチャー一級建築士事務所設立

Love Architecture Inc.
1969 Born in Tokyo
1994 Graduated from Department of Architecture, Musashino Art University
1996 Graduated from Graduate School of Shibaura Institute of Technology
1996 Joined Sowa Architects and Engineers (-2001)
2001 Established Love Architecture, Inc.

アトリエ G&B
Atelier G&B Co.
P-100

建築・インテリア設計、家具のデザイン、コーディネート、納入に留まらず、サイン計画、アートコーディネート、グラフィックデザイン、ランドスケープに至る。建築にとりまくさまざまなクライアントのニーズに対応した、総合的な環境デザインへの取り組みを展開している。

The company is engaged in a wide range of activities including design, coordination and supply of architecture, interior, and furniture as well as signage planning, art coordination, graphic designs, and landscaping. Responding to various needs of clients associated with architecture, it offers comprehensive environmental design services.

新居千秋
Chiaki Arai
P-116

ペンシルバニア大学大学院卒業。巨匠ルイス.I.カーンに師事。武蔵工業大学客員教授、ペンシルバニア大学大学院客員教授、東京理科大学非常勤講師
主な受賞：
1973年 シャンク賞受賞
（ペンシルバニア大学修士設計第一位）
1993年 第18回吉田五十八賞受賞
（水戸市立西部図書館）
1996年 日本建築学会賞（作品）
（黒部市国際文化センター／コラーレ）
2004年 日本建築学会賞（業績）
（横浜赤レンガ倉庫）
2004年 BCS賞（横浜赤レンガ倉庫）他、多数

Graduated from Graduate School, University of Pennsylvania. Studied under Louis I. Kahn. Visiting professor at Musashi Institute of Technology and University of Pennsylvania. Lecturer at Tokyo University of Science.
Awards:
1973: Schenk Award (1st prize for master course design competition); 1993 18th Isohachi Yoshida Award (Mito City West Library); 1996: Architectural Institute of Japan Award (Kurobe City Cultural Center Colare); 2004 Architectural Institute of Japan Award (Distinguished Achievement Award for Yokohama Red Brick Warehouse); 2004 BCS Award (Yokohama Red Brick Warehouse), etc.

安藤忠雄
Tadao Ando
P-10, 196

1941年大阪府生まれ。独学で建築を学んだ後、1969年安藤忠雄建築研究所を設立。わが国を代表する建築家として、つねに世界の第一線で活躍。主な作品に、安藤建築の思想と手法を確立した「住吉の長屋」をはじめ、「六甲の集合住宅」「光の教会」などがある。
1993年日本芸術院賞、1995年プリツカー賞など受賞多数。

Born in Osaka Prefecture in 1941, Tadao Ando established Tadao Ando Architect & Associates in 1969 after a period spent studying architecture on his own. Ando has since solidified his position at the forefront of the international architectural community as a major representative of Japanese talent. Major design by Ando includes Row House, Sumiyoshi (Azuma House), Rokko Housings, and Church of the Light. Ando established his design concept and method with the first of these structures. He is the recipient of numerous awards, including the Japan Art Academy Prize in 1993 and the Pritzker Architecture Prize in 1995.

今川憲英
Norihide Imagawa
P-82

構造建築家
1969年：日本大学理工学部建築学科卒業。
1970年：構造設計集団（S.D.G.）入社。
1978年：TIS & PARTNERS 代表。
2000年：東京電気大学 工学部建築学科教授／同大学大学院教授

Structural Architect
Graduated from Department of Architecture, College of Science and Technology, Nihon University in 1969
Joined Structural Design Group SDG in 1970
Appointed representative of TIS & PARTNERS in 1978
professor of Architecture and Building Engineering, Graduate School of Engineering and Department of Architecture, School of Engineering, Tokyo Denki University since 2000.

内海智行
Tomoyuki Utsumi
P-123

1963年 茨城県生まれ
R.C.A.（英国王立芸術大学院）修了後、筑波大学大学院修士課程修了
大成建設設計本部を経て
1998年 milligram studio 設立、同代表
慶應義塾大学非常勤講師

Architect
Representative of milligram studio inc.
1963 : Born in Ibaraki.
After graduation of Royal College of Arts (London)
Complete M.A. of Tsukuba University.
Founded milligram studio inc. in 1998 after working at Taisei Corporation.
Docent of Keio University

衛藤信一
Shinichi Eto
P-48

1988年にウィーンにて衛藤信一建築都市デザイン・アトリエを設立。
1994年に日本オフィスを大阪に設立。
作品：フランクフルト近代美術館／アンビエントホテル堂島（旧インターナショナル堂島ホテル）三基食品本社パビリオン、など他多数。

Established Shinichi Eto Architecture and Urban Design Atelier in Vienna in 1988. Opened its Japan Office in 1994.
His major works include Modern Art Museum, Frankfurt, Ambient Hotel Dojima (formerly International Dojima Hotel), and Miki Foods Headquarters pavilion.

遠藤剛生
Takao Endo
P-76, 80, 106

1941年生まれ。1964年大阪工業大学建築学科卒業。1969年遠藤剛生建築設計事務所設立。「キーエンス」（87年）で第2回建築士会連合会賞優秀賞。「熊本県農業公園」（92年）で商環境デザイン賞優秀賞・特別賞、第8回建築士会連合会優秀賞受賞。西宮名塩ニュータウン（94年）が都市景観大賞の「都市景観100選部門」を受賞、箕面市営桜ケ丘南住宅（96年）が小空間レベルで都市景観大賞受賞。「リーセントヒルズ」がグッドデザイン賞受賞。（03年）その他大阪都市景観建築賞大阪府知事賞など受賞多数。
神戸大学工学部非常勤講師、神戸芸術工科大学客員教授を歴任し、1997年より大阪大学工学部非常勤講師。
代表作に「西宮名塩ニュータウン斜行エレベーター、屋外劇場、回廊、集合住宅」「EXPO '90（国際花と緑の博覧会）西口ゲート」「六甲アイランドCITY イーストコート5番街」「大阪府営東大阪吉田住宅」「長野今井ニュータウンG工区（長野オリンピック選手村）」「C.T.O岡山プロジェクト」ほか多数。

Born in 1941. Graduated from Department of Architecture, Osaka Engineering University. Established Takao Endo Architect Office in 1969.Received the 2nd Annual Architects Association 1st Place Award for "Keyence" in 1987. He is also a recipient of the Commercial Environmental Design 1st Place Award and Honorary Award for "Kumamoto Prefecture Agricultural Park" (1992), and the 8th Annual Architects Association 1st Place Award. His Nishinomiya Najio New Town (1994) was recognized as one of the "Best 100 Metropolitan Scenic Sites" in the Metropolitan Scenic Sites Grand Prize Award and his "Minoh City Sakuragaoka Minami Housing Project" (1996) was awarded the City Scenic Site Award in the Limited Space Level Category. Good Design Award for "Recent Hills" Among many other prizes, he has also won the Osaka City Scenic Architecture Award in the Osaka Governor's Prizes.A part-time instructor at Kobe University Engineering Department, has also been visiting professor at the Kobe Art Engineering University and, since 1997, a part-time instructor at the Osaka University's Department of Engineering.His most prominent designs and projects include "Nishinomiya Najio New town Inclining elevator, amphitheater, corridors, and apartment housing," "EXPO 90 (International Flower and Greenery Exhibition) West Gate," "Rokko Island City East Coast 5th Avenue," "Higashi-Osaka Yoshita Public housing Complex " "Nagano Imai New Town G District (Nagano Olympics Athlete's Village)" and "C.T.O. Okayama Project."

大江匡
Tadasu Ohe
P-146

株式会社プランテック総合計画事務所
東京大学大学院工学建築研究科修了
1977年　菊竹清訓建築設計事務所入所
1985年　株式会社プランテック総合計画事務所設立
受賞
1977年　卒業計画賞（辰野賞）
1993年　日本建築家協会新人賞
　　　　（ファンハウス）
1999年　第40回建築業協会賞
　　　　（細見美術館）
2000年　第13回日経ニューオフィス賞
　　　　（フューチャーシステムコンサルティング）
2001年　第42回建築業協会賞
　　　　（岐阜ドリームコア）
2001年　グッドデザイン賞（横浜の茶室）、その他受賞多数。

Plantec Architects, Inc.
Master of Architecture, University of Tokyo
1977 Joined the office of Kikutake
1985 Established Plantec Architects
Awards:
1977 Tatsuno Prize for Thesis Project
1993 Japan Institute of Architects 'Young Architect of the Year' (Fun House)
1999 The 40th Building Contractors Society (BCS) Award (Hosomi Museum)
2000 The 13th Nikkei New Office Awards (Future System Consulting)
2001 The 42nd Building Contractors Society (BCS) Award (GIFU SOFTOPIA JAPAN)
2001 Good Design Award (Tea house in Yokohama) and many others.

大野博史
Hirofumi Ohno
P-143, 175

オーノJAPAN
1974年大分県生まれ／1997年日本大学理工学部建築学科卒業／1998年～99年ユーゴスラビアENERGOPROJEKTにて海外研修／2000年日本大学大学院修士課程修了
2000年～04年池田昌弘建築研究所勤務
2005年オーノJAPAN設立

Ohno JAPAN
1974 Born in Oita / 1997 Graduated from Department of Architecture, College of Sci

ence and Technology, Nihon University
1998-1999 Received as an international trainee at Energoprojekt, Yugoslavia
2000-2004 Joined Masahiro Ikeda Co., Ltd.
2005 Established Ohno JAPAN

小川正晴
Masaharu Ogawa
P-193

1949年 京都府生まれ
1974年 神戸大学工学部建築学科卒業
1974～77年 柄谷工務店（株）設計部勤務 主に住宅設計に携わる
1978年 １級建築士事務所アーキボックス 共同設立
1981年 上記を（有）アーキボックスに改組
1994年 上記代表取締役として現在にいたる
受賞歴
1986年 尼崎市建築景観賞（まちかどチャーミング賞） 岡本歯科医院
2000年 兵庫県人間サイズのまちづくり賞（建築部門）マリンピア神戸さかなの学校

1949 Born in Kyoto
1974 Graduated from Department of Architecture and Civil Engineering, Faculty of Engineering, Kobe University
1974 Joined Karatani. Assigned to the Design Department, mainly responsible for residential design
1978 Jointly established Archi Box
1981 Reorganized Archi Box to a limited company
1993 Assigned president (-present)
Awards:
1986 Amagasaki Architecture and Landscape Award (Machikado Charming Award): Okamoto Dental Office
2000 "Ningen Size no Machidukuri Award" (Architecture Award), Hyogo Prefecture: Fish School, Marinepia Kobe

河合健之
Kenshi Kawai
P-160, 163

一級建築士
京都府建築士会　会員
1959／京都府生まれ
1978／京都市立伏見工業高校　建築科卒業
1983／大阪デザイナー専門学校　建築、インテリアパース科卒業
建築事務所、デザイン事務所勤務
1993／河合建築デザイン事務所設立
2001／京都国際建築技術専門学校　非常勤講師

First-class registered architect
Member of Kyoto Society of Architects and Building Engineers
1959 Born in Kyoto
1978 Graduated from Engineering Department, Fushimi School of Industry
1983 Graduated from Architecture and Interior Design Department, Osaka Designers' College.
Worked at architectural firms and design firms
1993 Established Kawai Design
2001 Lecturer, KASD

桐島ローランド
Rowland kirishima
P-166

フォトグラファー
1991年ニューヨーク大学芸術学部・写真科卒業。本格的にフリーランス・フォトグラファーとしてのキャリアをNYでスタート。1993年仕事のベースを東京に移し、ファッションやポートレートを中心に、雑誌、広告、CDジャケット（宇多田ヒカル、TOKIOなど）、TV-CM、プロモーションビデオ（クリスタル・ケイのPVで2003年 MTV Award 最優秀R&B VIDEO賞受賞）など幅広く活躍中。一方、PCのデザインや六本木ヒルズのクリスマスツリーのデザインなどを手がけるなど、各界で独自のクリエイティビティーを発揮。

Photographer
Graduated from the Photography Department of New York University in 1991. He started his career as freelance photographer in New York. Tokyo-based since 1993, he has actively produced works in the field of fashion and portraits for magazines, advertisements, CD jackets (Hikaru Utada, TOKYO, etc.), TV commercials, promotion videos (the Best R&B Video Award at the 2003 MTV Awards for his Crystal Kay's PV). His area of activities is extensive including designs of PC's and Christmas trees at Roppongi Hills.

隈研吾
Kengo Kuma
P-15

1954年横浜生まれ。79年東京大学建築学科大学院修了後、コロンビア大学各員研究員を経て99年、隈研吾建築都市設計事務所設立。自然と技術と人間との新しい関係を切り開く建築を提案。2001年から慶應義塾大学理工学部教授を務める。主な作品は「亀老山展望台」や「石の美術館」など。著書には「負ける建築」、「反オブジェクト」など多数。国際木の建築賞（フィンランド）ほか数々の賞を受賞している。

Born in Yokohama in 1954. He graduated from the Graduate School of Engineering at The University Of Tokyo in 1979 and continued his studies at Columbia University. He established Kengo Kuma & Associates in 1999 and explored designing with emphasis on a new relationship among nature, technology and mankind. He was a professor at the Faculty of Science and Technology, Keio University. His major works include Kiro-san Observatory and Stone Plaza. His books include "Failing Architecture", and "Architecture as Anti-object". He won many awards including Spirit of Nature Wood Architecture Award (Finland).

熊谷由美子
Yumiko Kumatani
P-116

株式会社メック・デザインインターナショナル
インテリアコーディネーター
「Brillia 代官山プレステージ」インテリアプランニング。
その他「高輪ザ・レジデンス」「ザ・ハウス南麻布」など数多くの都心高級マンションのインテリアプランニングおよびコーディネートを手掛ける。

Mec Design International Corp.
Interior coordinator.
Responsible for the interior planning of Brillia Daikanyama Prestige.

She has been engaged in interior planning and coordination of Takanawa the Residence, the House Minami-azabu and many other high-grade condominiums.

久保清一
Seiichi Kubo
P-178

1953年 静岡県生まれ。
1977年 大阪芸術大学芸術学部建築学科卒業。
1981年 ミラノ工科大学建築学部AC修了。
V・グレゴッティ・アソシエイツ勤務。
1984年 （株）アルキービ総合計画事務所設立。
2002年 大阪芸術大学教授、日本建築家協会監事。
1999年 「蜜柑花の家」でARCASIA Awards ゴールドメダル受賞。
「MAYUMIYAの工房」で第11回甍賞金賞（経済産業大臣賞）、第16回日本建築士会連合会優秀賞受賞。他多数受賞

1953 Born in Shizuoka
1977 Graduated from Architecture Department, Faculty of Fine Arts, Osaka University of Arts
1981 Graduated from AC, Architecture Department, Milan Polytechnic
Joined Vittorio Gregotti Associates
1984 Established Archivi Architects & Associates
2002 Appointed professor, Osaka University of Arts; auditor, Japan Institute of Architecture
Won Gold Medal of ARCASIA Awards in 1999 for his design of "Mikanbana no Ie" (House of Orange Flowers). Won the 11th Iraka Award, Gold Prize/Prize of the Minister of International Trade and Industry for "MAYUMIYA no Kobo". Other awards he has won include the 16th Japan Federation of Architects and Building Engineers Award/Merit Award, etc.

ジェローム・クリンクマイリー
Jerome Clynckemaillie
P-54

フランス国立美術工芸学校卒業。世界各国のエルメスブティックのデザインを手掛け、その後、アンドレプットマンと共に、主にホテル・個人邸を中心に活動。常にハイクラスな仕事に関わってきただけに、そのデザインは上品さ、落ち着き、エレガントさに満ちている。現在、ジャン・フランソワ・ボダンと共にナント美術館やシャイヨー宮のデザイン、そしてエルワン・ル・ボルドネックと共にデザイン活動を行っている。

Graduated from the National High School

of Arts and Crafts, France. He was once responsible for the designs of Hermes boutiques throughout the world and then mainly involved in designs fro hotels and private mansions with Andre Putman. As he was always at the forefront of high-end works, his designs are fully decent, balanced, and elegant. At present, he is engaged in designs for Nantes Museum and the Chaillot Palace with Jean Francois Bodin as well as other design activities with Erwan Le Bourdonnec.

児玉卓志
Takushi Kodama
P-92

建築家、博士（学術）、東京農業大学，芝浦工業大学 非常勤講師
1953 年　広島県生まれ。
1976 年　芝浦工業大学建築工学科卒業
1979 年　一級建築士取得
1980 年　同大学大学院建設工学専攻修了
1981〜83 年　ベルリン工科大学建築学部留学
1983〜87 年　（株）相田武文設計研究所
1987 年　「卯辰山ガーデンヒルズ」金沢都市美文化賞
1987 年　アーキベルク設立。現在に至る
1996 年　「岩上邸」佐野市建築デザイン賞
2000 年　博士（学術）学位取得

Architect, lecturer at Tokyo University of Agriculture and Shibaura Institute of Technology
1953 Born in Hiroshima
1976 Graduated from Faculty of Architecture and Building Engineering, Shibaura Institute of Technology
1979 Registered as first-class architect
1980 Graduated from Division of Architecture and Civil Engineering Graduate School of Engineering, Shibaura Institute of Technology
1981 Studied at Berlin University of Technology (-1983)
1983 Joined Takefumi Aida Architects and Associates (-1987)
1987 Won the Kanazawa Urban Structure Award for Utatsuyama Garden Hills
1987 Establish Archiwerk (-present)
1996 Won the Sano Architectural Design Award for the Iwagami residence
2000 Earned a Ph. D

白澤廣海
Hiromi Shirasawa
P-66

株式会社白澤建築事務所 代表
建築家
1952 年生まれ。共同住宅を中心に、手がけたプロジェクトは 200 を越える実績を持つ。ヨーロッパ建築に造形が深く、生み出されるデザインは安定感ある、説得力のあるものが多い。近年は社寺建築や旅館など現代和風にも数多くの作品を残す。

Architectural Creator's Group
Architect
Born in 1952. He has been engaged in more than 200 projects mainly focusing on condominiums. Familiar with European architecture, many of his designs are stable and persuasive. His recent works are mainly in the field of the modern Japanesque including temples, shrines, and inns.

菅匡史
Tadashi Suga
P-154, 157, 190

建築家
1966 年兵庫県生まれ
1989 年近畿大学理工学部建築学科卒業
1993 年菅匡史建築研究所を設立
2004 年 American Wood Design Award 受賞
日本建築士会連合会賞受賞
神戸市景観ポイント賞受賞

Born in Hyogo prefecture in 1966.
After graduating the Department of Architecture, School of Science and Engineering, Kinki University, he established Suga Architects Office Co., Ltd in 1993.

Awards:
2004 American Wood Design Award
Japan Federation of Architects & Building Engineers Associations Award
Kobe City Landscape Point Award

ステュディオ・ペル
Studio P.E.R
P-26

ミラノを拠点に、イタリア国内はもちろん国際的な舞台において建築設計、インダストリアルデザインなど様々なプロジェクトを手がける。特にレジデンスデザイン、商空間デザインに多彩な実績をもち、これまでグッチ・イタリア、イヴサンローラン パリ、ゼニアのショップデザインで高い評価を集めている

This Milan-based studio has been engaged in architectural design, industrial design and many other projects in the international forum as well as in Italy. The studio has ample experience in residential and commercial space design and enjoys a high reputation for shop designs including Gucci Italia, Yves Saint Laurent Paris and Zegna.

瀬戸本淳
Jun Setomoto
P-96, 172

建築家（APEC ARCHITECT）
1947 年神戸に生まれる。
1969 年神戸大学で建築の学位取得。
鹿島建設、安井建築設計事務所を経て
1977 年、神戸に瀬戸本淳建築研究室を開設。
公的福祉施設、商業ビル、集合住宅、個人住宅など、様々な建築を手掛けている。神戸市建築文化賞、兵庫県さわやか街づくり賞、神戸市景観ポイント賞など、多くの賞を受賞。兵庫県建築設計監理協会会長などの建築家職能団体の役員を務める。

APEC ARCHITECT
Born in Kobe in 1947.
Graduated the Architecture and Civil Engineering Department, Faculty of Engineering, Kobe University in 1969.
After working for Kajima Corporation and Yasui Architect and Engineers, he established Jun Setomoto & Architects in Kobe in 1977.
He has designed various types of architecture including public welfare facilities, commercial buildings, condominiums, and private houses.
Awarded many prizes including Kobe City Architectural Culture Award, Hyogo Sawayaka Machizukuri Award, and Kobe City Landscape Point Award.

He also serves for Hyogo Prefecture Construction Design and Supervision Association (president) and other architect shopcraft unions.

竹下英南
Einan Takeshita
P-66, 84

三井デザインテック株式会社
三井デザインテックは、住宅からオフィス、商業施設まで幅広い分野で空間を創造するインテリアデザインのリーディングカンパニー。商空間としてはホテル、レストラン、ホスピタル、オフィスなど幅広い分野をプロデュースし、住空間では年間 100 を超えるプロジェクトのインテリアデザイン、5000 戸以上のコーディネート実績を誇る。

MITSUI Designtec Co., Ltd.
This is a leading company in the field of the interior design for a wide range of structures from residences, offices to commercial facilities. It has designed many hotels, restaurants, hospitals, and offices and, for residential space design, has a track record of more than 100 interior design works per year as well as coordination services for more than 5,000 housing units.

中永勇司
Yuji Nakae
P-143

ナカエ・アーキテクツ
1975 年　石川県生まれ
1998 年　横浜国立大学工学部建築学科卒業
2000 年　同大学大学院修士課程修了
2000 年〜04 年　EDH 遠藤設計室勤務
2004 年　ナカエ・アーキテクツ設立

Nakae Architects
1975 Born in Ishikawa
1998 Graduated from Division of Architecture and Building Science, Faculty of Engineering, Yokohama National University
2000 Graduated from Graduate School of Engineering
2000 Joined Endoh Design House (-2004)
2004 Established Nakae Architects

中根昌樹
Masaki Nakane
P-84
メディアフォースペース
建築家 1952年生まれ
国内、パシフィックエリア（ハワイ、パラオ等）、アジアなどのホテル&リゾートプロジェクトで活躍。海外デザイナーとの親交を通じ、グローバルな視点で、斬新ながらも快適な空間創造をめざす。
Media For Space Inc.
Architect; born in 1952
Active in designing hotel & resort projects in Japan, Pacific (Hawaii, Palau, etc.) and Asia. Through friendship and exchange with foreign designers, he attempts to create cutting-edge yet comfortable spaces from a global viewpoint.

南條洋雄
Hiroo Nanjo
P-71, 82
1971年　東京大学工学部都市工学科卒業。
1975～85年　ブラジル・サンパウロにて arquiteto Joaquim Guedes e associados 他に勤務。1985年帰国、株式会社 南條設計室を設立、現在に至る。
東京都立短期大学非常勤講師、日本建築家協会会員。
1971 Graduated from Department of Urban Engineering, University of Tokyo
1975-85 Worked for Arquiteto Joaquim Guedes e Associado, etc. in Sao Paulo, Brazil. Returned to Japan and established atelier Nanjo, Inc. in 1985.
Lecturer, Tokyo Metropolitan College, member of the Japan Institute of Architects

萩原達郎
Tatsuro Hagihara
P-160, 163
1957/　京都市生まれ
1980/　青野建築設計事務所勤務
1983/　カネサキデザイン事務所勤務
1986/　萩原工務店勤務
2004/　株式会社 PRESENCE. CO 設立
1957 Born in Kyoto
1980 Joined Aono and Architects
1983 Joined Kanesaki Design
1986 Joined Hagiwara Engineering
2004 Established

平井憲一
Kenichi Hirai
P-187
1951年 大阪生まれ
1978年 アトリエ・サム設立
1987年 平井憲一建築事務所に改名
1985～98年 商環境デザイン賞 8作品入選
1997年 大阪まちなみ賞（大阪都市景観建築賞）奨励賞
1997年 奈良市建築文化賞 奨励賞
1998年 奈良県景観調和デザイン賞 奨励賞
2003年 古民家再生ネットワークへの活動開始
2005年 リフォーム&リニューアル設計アイデアコンテスト 佳作
2005年 住まいのリフォームコンクール 国土交通大臣賞及び優秀賞
2005年 関西電力 住まいの設計コンテスト（リフォーム部） 最優秀賞
1951 Born in Osaka
1978 Established Atelier Sam
1987 Changed firm name to Kenich Hirai Architect & Associates
1985-1998 8 JCD Design Awards
1997 Award of Encouragement, Osaka Machinami Award (Osaka Urban Landscape Construction Award)
1997 Award of Encouragement, Nara Architecture/Culture Award
1998 Award of Encouragement, Nara Prefectural Landscape Harmony Design Prize
2003 Started activities for Japan Minka Reuse and Recycle Association
2005 Honorable mention, Reform & Renewal Design Idea Contest
2005 Award of the Minister of Land, Infrastructure and Transport and Merit Award, Sumai no Reform Contest
2005 Grand Award, KEPCO Housing Design Contest (Reform category)

フォワード・スタイル株式会社
Forward Style
P-26, 42
レジデンシャルあるいはエグゼクティブオフィスを中心に、時代を読み解く鋭敏な感性をもとに、様々なスタイルの設計・デザイン、施工監修までをトータルにプロデュースする。
Mainly focusing on residential and executive office design, the company has been involved in many aspects of construction projects from planning/design to supervision with keen sensitivity to the spirit of the age.

藤村龍至
Ryuji Fujimura
P-175
1976年東京都生まれ
2000年 東京工業大学工学部社会工学科卒業
2002年東京工業大学大学院理工学研究科建築学専攻修士課程修了
2002～03年ベルラーヘ・インスティテュート（オランダ）在籍
2002～05年ISSHO建築設計事務所共同主宰
2005年藤村龍至建築設計事務所設立
現在、藤村龍至建築設計事務所主宰、東京工業大学大学院理工学研究科建築学専攻修士課程在籍
Born in Tokyo in 1976.
Graduated from Department of Social Engineering, School of Engineering, Tokyo Institute of Technology in 2000.
Graduated from Department of Architecture and Building Engineering, Graduate School of Engineering, Tokyo Institute of Technology. Studied at the Berlage Institute (Holland) between 2002 and 2003.
Jointly established ISSHO Architects and co-partner of the same company between 2002 and 2005.
Established Ryuji Fujimura Architects in 2005.
Currently representative of the same and studying at doctoral course, Department of Architecture and Building Engineering, Graduate School of Engineering, Tokyo Institute of Technology.

ロブレ・ジュン・ベラ・カンナ
Roble Jun Veara Kanna
P-175
ISSHO建築設計事務所
1976年カラカス（ベネズエラ）生まれ
2001年神奈川大学工学部建築学科卒業
2002年ISSHO建築設計事務所共同設立
現在、ISSHO建築設計事務所共同主宰
ISSHO Architects
Born in Caracas, Venezuela in 1976
Graduated from Department of Architecture, Faculty of Engineering, Kanagawa University in 2001
Jointly established ISSHO Architects/Currently co-partner of the same company

エルワン・ル・ボルドネック
Erwan Le Bourdonnec
P-54
フランス国立装飾美術学校卒業。アンドレプットマンの元で、プロジェクトマネージャーとして活躍。グッゲンハイムミュージアム（ニューヨーク）、装飾美術館（パリ）、国際写真センター（ニューヨーク）で展示会やデザインや、ロダンミュージアム、プッチコレクションなどの家具のデザインも手掛けた。2002年からは、パリの個人マンションのインテリアデザイン、家具デザインを中心に居住空間のデザインを積極的に行っている。
Graduated from the National High School of Decorative Arts. Actively worked as project manager under Andre Putman. He designed for exhibitions, etc. at Guggenheim Museum (New York), Decorative Art Museum (Paris) and International Center of Photography (New York) as well as furniture at Rodin Museum and Petit Collection. He has actively engaged in interior, furniture and other residential-space designs for condominiums in Paris.

三沢亮一
Ryoichi Misawa
P-33. 54
株式会社　ミサワアソシエイツ
一級建築士事務所代表
1998年、株式会社ミサワアソシエイツ代表取締役
2000年株式会社エム・エイ・アイ代表取締役に就任。数多くの大規模マンションの建築設計や、ランドスケープデザインを手がけ、高い信頼と評価を得ている。目黒区景観賞や、グッドデザイン賞を受賞した作品など、高いクオリティーを持つデザインに定評がある。
Representative, Misawa Associates
Appointed representative director of Misawa Associates in 1998 and MAI Corporation in 2000.
Involved in designs of many large-scale

condominium and landscapes, winning implicit trust and high evaluation. He enjoys an established reputation for his quality design including those awarded with Meguro Ward Landscape Award and Good Design Award.

蓑昌弘
Masahiro Mino
P-84

五洋建設株式会社
1965 年生まれ。
個人住宅をはじめ、中、高層マンション、商業ビル、企業の保養所など幅広い実績を持つ。時の流れとともに愛着が深まり、いつまでも愛され続ける建築物の設計をテーマとしている。
Penta-Ocean Construction Co., Ltd.
Born in 1965. Has a wide range of accomplishments including private houses, mid- and high-rise condominiums, commercial buildings, and company-owned resort facilities. His theme is to design buildings that strengthen their owners' attachment and love with a passage of time.

森崎輝行
Teruyuki Morisaki
P-110, 113

1948 年佐賀県生・一級建築士
神戸大学工学部建築学科卒（1972）
双星社竹腰建築事務所、安藤忠雄建築研究所を経て、森崎建築設計事務所設立（1976）
神戸市景観審議会委員等の公職や神戸新開地デザイン委員会等の各委員を勤める傍ら神戸市民のコンサルタント及びアドバイザーとして日本初の街並誘導型の地区計画の成立、鷹取東第一地区の区画整理、新長田駅南久二塚6地区の2種再開発事業等のまちづくり、都市計画も手掛けている。
代表作
グランドメゾン箕面クレアコート
（第14回大阪都市景観建築賞）所属団体
（社）日本建築家協会他 受賞作
日本都市計画学会賞
計画設計奨励賞（都通4丁目街区再建事業）他
著書・共著
「光と風」【1991】
「21 世紀の家族と住まい」【1997】他

Born in Saga in1948,
first grade architect. Graduate of Department of Architecture and Civil Engineering, Faculty of Engineering, Kobe University in 1972.
After working at Soseisha Takegoshi Architects and Tadao Ando Architects, established Morisaki Architects in 1976.
While filling such posts as members of Kobe City Landscaping Council and Kobe City Shinkaichi Design Committee, he is also active as consultants for first-in-Japan establishment of the District Plan for the Guidance of the Appearance of the Townscape, land readjustment of the 1st Takatorihigashi Area, and 2nd-class redevelopment at 6 Udezuka in the Shinnagata Station South Area, North Noda.
*Representative work:
Grand Maison Minoo Clare Court
(14th Osaka Urban Landscape Architecture Award)
*Organizations:
Japan Institute of Architect, etc.
*Awards:
The City Planning Institute of Japan Award, Planning and Design Encouragement Award
(4 Miyakodori block redevelopment project)
*Books: Light and Wind (1991); Families and Houses in the 21st Century (1997), etc.

森田恭通
Yasumichi Morita
P-166

1967 年大阪生まれ。
現場で積み重ねた経験を活かし、フリーランスとして活動ののち、（株）イマジンにてチーフデザイナーを勤める。
1996 年、森田恭通デザインオフィスを設立。
2000 年 6 月には GLAMOROUS CO., LTD として再スタートを切り、2001 年には香港に Y.MORITA DESIGN（HK）LTD. を設立した。
2001 年、香港での自身初の海外プロジェクトを皮切りに、現在では、NY、マレーシア、香港、上海、等、世界にその活動の場所を広げている。
さらにクリエイティブディレクターとして、デザイナー集団『ERO ERO』を率い、インテリアに限らず、グラフィックやプロダクトといった幅広い創作活動を行っている。
Born in Osaka in 1967.
Based on his experience working in the field, he became the chief designer at Imagine after working as a freelance designer. Established Yoshimichi Morita Design Office in 1996 and renamed it GLAMOROUS, LTD in June 2000.
Established Y. MORITA DESIGN (HK) LTD in Hong Kong in 2001.
With the project in Hong Kong in 2001 as the start, he has expanded his areas of work including New York, Malaysia, Hong Kong and Shanghai. As the creative director, he also leads a group of designers, ERO ERO, and is engaged in various fields including graphic and product designs, not limited in the field of interior design.

余川辰哉
Tatsuya Yokawa
P-128, 131

1959 年 東京生まれ。
1983 年 芝浦工業大学建築学科卒業。
1983 ～ 1986 年
神谷五男＋都市環境建築設計所在籍。
1987 ～ 1992 年ワークショップ在籍。
1993 年アルボス設立、現在に至る。
2003 年「登戸地区商業ビジョン基本計画検討委員会」に係わったのをきっかけに、市民活動グループ「のぼりとゆうえん隊」結成。
37ha におよぶ大きな区画整理が進行中の地元登戸。「楽しい我がまちと誇れるようなまちにしたい」との思いを共有する仲間を集めて、市民自らの手による「まちづくり」を模索している。
現在、岡本太郎美術館を背景とした、まちなかアートプロジェクト〈noborito-map〉を企画推進中。
Born in Tokyo in 1959.
Graduated from Faculty of Architecture and Building Engineering, Shibaura Institute of Technology in 1983.
Joined Itsuo Kamiya + Urban Environment Architecture Design in 1983 (-1986).
Joined Workshop in 1987 (-1992).
Established Arbos in 1993 (-present).
Involved in the Noborito Area Commercial Vision Basic Plan Study Committee in 2003 and established NPO "Noborito Yuen Tai". He is trying to establish a way of town planning by citizens with partners who share the idea of "making Noborito as a town we can be proud of".
At present, he is planning and promoting Machinaka Art Project <noborito-map> with the Taro Okamoto Museum of Art as background.

横堀健一
Kenichi Yokobori
P-61

1960 年石川県生まれ。
国立石川工業専門学校建築学科、
86 ～ 88 年マイアミ大学建築学科にて建築を学ぶ。
帰国後、（株）Studio 80 にてホテル・住宅等を設計する。
1989 年、SDA（アルド・ロッシ建築設計事務所）へ移り、アルド・ロッシの日本における一連の建築作品の設計を手掛ける。
1995 年、横堀建築設計事務所を設立。
1991 年より ICS カレッジ・オブ・アーツ、
2002 年より桑沢デザイン研究所講師。
Born in Ishikawa in 1960.
Graduated from Architecture Course, Ishikawa National College of Technology. Studied architecture at College of Engineering, University of Miami between 1986 and 1988.
After returning to Japan,
he joined Studio 80 and designed for hotels, houses, etc.
In 1989, he started to work in SDA Aldo Rossi Architectural Design Office and was involved in a series of architectural works by Aldo Rossi. Established Yokobori Associates in 1995.
He has also been a lecturer at ICS College of Arts since 1991 and Kuwasawa Design School since 2002.

あとがき
清水文夫

Architect-Designed Low-Rise CONDOMINIUMS in Japan

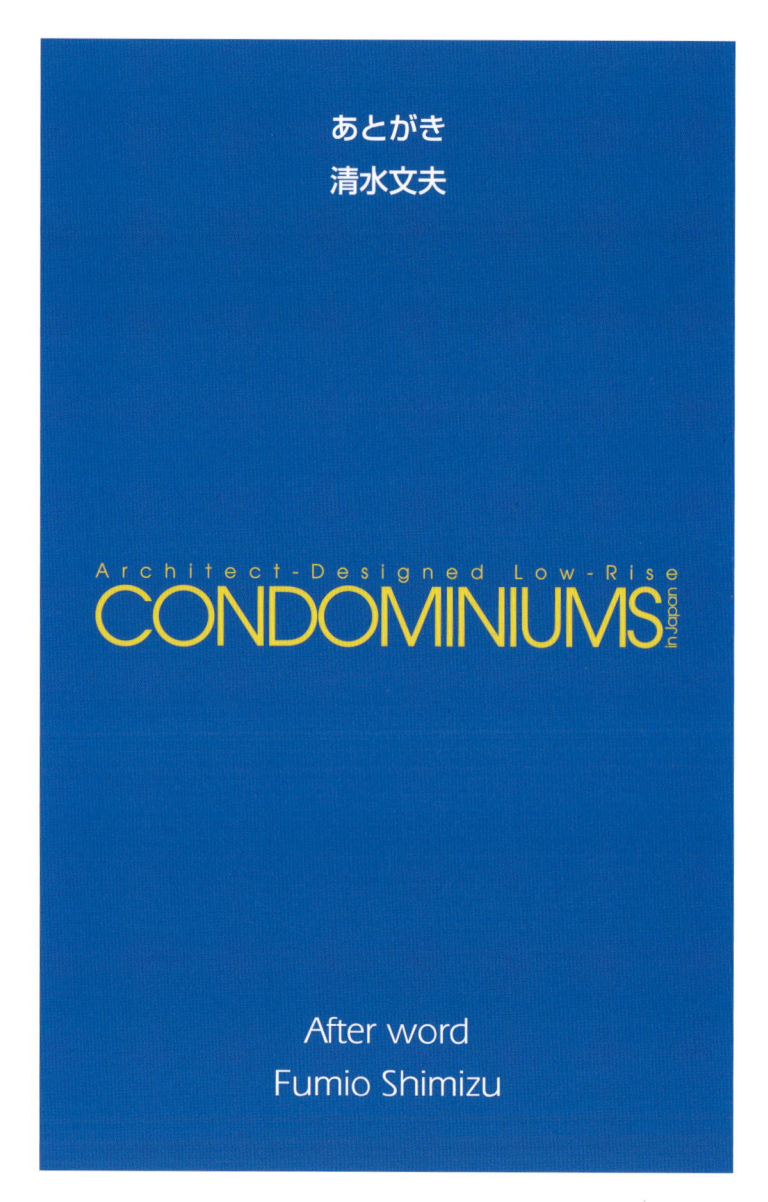

After word
Fumio Shimizu

近年、集合住宅はデベロッパー、建築家、デザイナーによって確実に進化をとげている。当初、革命的であった同潤会や住宅公団のアパートから建築家不在の形式化したnLDKのデベロッパー物件に至るマンネリズムの軸線上で、パブリックスペースや新しい間取りの形式、人と自然を近づける設計など新しい住居空間を再編成しようという試みが地道に、かつ確実に続いてきました。ここでは、住み手の生活意識、生活文化を基軸において、生活そのものの価値や精神性の充足を求めて、日常生活の中にある良い部分を見つめ、それに形を与え生活の場面の中に喜びや心地良さを与えられる一般解を探求しています。そこには、生活スタイルの変革を無理に進めるような実験的な特別に異形の形態を求める姿もなければ、中途半端な住み手の意識に迎合するような形式もありません。現実の目の前にある生活の場面を深く読み、その中から生活の自然な力、人々の安心や心地良さのあり方を見出そうとい

Condominiums have undergone steady evolution, thanks to developers, architects and designers. In their history from initially revolutionary apartments of Dojunkai and Japan Housing Corporation to the n-LDK mannerism of developer projects where architects seem to be absent, sure and steady attempts to define new residential spaces have been made through redefining public spaces, new layouts, and designs to bring man and nature closer. In the process, attention has been paid to residents' views toward life as well as life culture in order to enhance physical and spiritual values of living, and general solutions have been pursued by focusing on merits found in daily life, materialize them in architecture, and provide pleasure and comfort in different life scenes. You find neither any attitude to seek for abnormal, experimental structures to forcefully change life styles nor any style to carry favor with incomplete requirements from residents. The attitude taken has been to critically analyze real life scenes at hand and to try to find out natural principles underlying out daily lives

う姿があります。

本書では、このような住み手の成熟した生活意識、生活文化に対して意欲的に取り組んだ例を数多く収録しています。例えば、エントランスの土間とリビングが一体化して、プライベートな空間とパブリックな空間のしかるべき関係に新しい秩序を与えている例。小さな空間に、住み手の生活と様々な空間要素が響き合う、三層の長屋。周辺環境の緑、屋上やテラスなど、随所に植え込まれた緑によって、人と自然を近づけ、都市生活の中に安らぎと潤いを与えるように配慮した例。住み手の思いを満たす絶対的な条件である場所の設定。丘の上に眺望絶景の土地で自然と借景を活かした雅趣に富んだ庭と一体化したマンションなど。

人と人との微妙な心の触れ合い、日常生活の中で住み手自身が組み立て、独自のライフスタイルを織りあげ、生活と住居の形式やデザインとの素敵な関係が生まれています。北大路魯山人が求めた器と料理の関係のように。人それぞれの状況に即して、人が住むことによって活きる生活の器こそ、今求められていると思えるのですが・・。

出版にあたり今回も多くの方々にお世話になりました。本書のために素晴らしいテキストをお寄せ下さった恩師の相田武文先生に深く感謝致します。根気よく最後まで担当して下さったグラフィック社の大田悟さん、翻訳者の宮坂聖一さんには本当にお世話になりました。また、美しい写真を提供して下さった著名な写真家の皆様、奥村浩司氏、松村芳治氏にも心より感謝申し上げます。最後になりましたが、素晴らしい装丁デザインと、膨大な資料を美しくレイアウトして下さった丹治竜一さん、有り難うございました。

and the way people's sense of safety, security and comfort should be.

This book amply exemplifies condominiums as results of architects' positive efforts toward such mature ideas toward living and life culture of residents: the dirt floor integrated with living room so that a new relationship between private and public spaces should be established; a three-story tenement house where lives of residents and various spatial elements interact with each other; consideration to provide a sense of comfort and richness in the city life and to make man and nature closer by bringing planting on the roof and terrace and surrounding green setting together; careful selection of the site to satisfy residents' hopes and resulting units integrated with picturesque gardens borrowing nature and landscape at the top of the hill with a good view.

Through delicate human interactions and the context of daily life, residents customize their dwelling units, create their own life styles, and consequently, build new relationship with their life and living styles and architectural designs. Like a relation between vessels and cuisines pursued by Rosanjin Kitaoji.

What is sought for now seems to be a vessel to lead one's life to which meanings are given by residents who lives in them in accordance with their own contexts.

I would like to thank all the people who helped me writing and publishing this book. My appreciation is extended to my beloved teacher, Takefumi Aida, who also contributed a wonderful text. I would also like to thank Satoru Ohta at Graphic-sha Publishing Co., Ltd who shepherded all of the writing and production efforts, Seiichi Miyasaka for his translation, all the celebrated photographers for their photograph preparations. I appreciate the support of Mr. Koji Okumura and Mr. Yoshiharu Matsumura. Last, surely not least, I would like to acknowledge the wonderful cover design as well as content design by Ryuichi Tanji.

清水文夫

1950年島根県生まれ

芝浦工大、A.Aスクール（英国）、ミラノ工科大学（伊国）にて建築を学ぶ。

相田武文設計研究所、マッテオ・トゥン・アーキテクツを経て、1988年（株）清水文夫アーキテクツを設立、現在に至る。

建築、プロダクトデザイン、インテリアデザインの分野で日本、イタリア、ベトナムにて活動している。編著書に「イタリアン・デザイン」、「ブリティッシュ・アーキテクチャー＆インテイア」、「ブリティッシュ・ドローイング」など多数。1989年より「FP」「Kukan」「Japan Avenue」「First Class」「casa nuova」の編集長を歴任。1999年よりUNESCO, UNIDO, JICA, JETROによるベトナム・タイ・ラオスにおける伝統工芸振興のプロジェクト、及びハノイ市の都市計画に参画。現在もタイ・ベトナムにおいて活動を続けている。

Born in Shimane in 1950. Educated at Shibaura Institute of Technology in Tokyo, Architectural Association School of Architecture in London. and Politecnico di Milano. Worked for Takefumi Aida Architects and Associates and Matteo Thun Architetto in Milano.
In1988, Established Shimizu Fumio Architects, working in the separate fields of Architecture, Industrial and Interior design. Published "Italian Design" "British Architecture & Interior" "British drawing" etc. From 1989 editorial director of magazine of "FP" "Kukan" "Japan Avenue" "First Class" "casa nuova" .
From 1999, development of traditional crafts in the project of UNESCO, UNIDO, JICA, JETRO and Urban Development in Hanoi in JICA.

Architect-Designed Low-Rise CONDOMINIUMS in Japan

デザイナーズ・アパートメンツ

発行
2006年7月25日　初版第1刷発行

編纂
清水文夫 ©

発行者
久世利郎

発行所
株式会社グラフィック社
〒102-0073
東京都千代田区九段北1-14-17　三創九段ビル4F
Tel.03-3263-4318／Fax.03-3263-5297
郵便振替：00130-6-114345
http://www.graphicsha.co.jp

印刷・製本
錦明印刷株式会社

© 2006　本書の内容は、著作権上の保護を受けています。著作権者及び出版社の文書による事前の同意を得ずに、本書の内容の一部、あるいは全部を無断で複写複製、転載することは禁じられています。

本書の内容における電話での質問はお受けできませんので、返信葉書同封の上、弊社編集部宛にお送り下さい。

乱丁・落丁はお取り替えいたします。

ISBN4-7661-1712-3 C3052